HABIT AND IN

BY

C. LLOYD MORGAN, F.G.S

AUTHOR OF

" ANIMAL LIFE AND INTELLIGENCE," " PSYCHOLOGY FOR TEACHERS," ETC.

EDWARD ARNOLD,

Publisher to the India Office.

LONDON :   NEW YORK :

37, BEDFORD STREET.   70, FIFTH AVENUE.

1896.

Spaniel   Tame Ducks   Wild Duck   Canvas Foot   Red Legged Partridge   Waterhen

Chicken   Hare   Partridge

Group of Young Birds

Printed in Oil

HABIT AND INSTINCT

PREFACE.

———◆◇◆———

I wish that dedications were still in vogue, so that these pages could be inscribed to all those many friends whose unfailing kindness and courtesy made my visit to the United States so pleasant, when the substance of this volume was delivered as a Lowell Course at Boston, and as lectures in New York, Chicago, and other university centres, during the early part of this year.

The reader will doubtless be glad to learn that further observations—and they are much needed—on habit and instinct will probably form part of Prof. Whitman's work at an experimental station in connection with the Biological Department of Chicago University. Similar observations might also be prosecuted with advantage in some of our own zoological gardens, as was the earnest wish of George Romanes, to whose influence and encouragement I am, like many others, so deeply indebted.

A few passages from the *Fortnightly Review*, *Nature*, *Natural Science*, the *Monist*, and the *Humanitarian*, may perhaps be recognized. Much of the chapter on Modification has appeared by request in *Science*.

My best thanks are due to Mr. F. Howard Collins for many valuable suggestions.

C. Ll. M.

Bristol, *October*, 1896

CONTENTS.

———◆◇◆———

———————

FRONTISPIECE: GROUP OF YOUNG BIRDS, FROM A DRAWING BY
    G. E. LODGE.

HABIT AND INSTINCT.

CHAPTER I.

THE naturalist commonly uses the word " habits " in describing the activities and behaviour of animals, each after his kind. Having given some account, for example, of the external form and internal structure of beast or bird or insect, he proceeds to deal with its habits, its general mode of life—how it seeks its food, how it rears or makes provision for its young, and so forth. The habits of animals thus constitute a wide and interesting field for observation and study. The word is, however, often used in a more restricted sense. In speaking of human beings, we generally use the word " habit " to describe some action or mode of behaviour which results from repetition in the course of individual experience. We should not speak of an act that is only occasionally performed under special circumstances as a habit. In employing the word " habit " as a technical term for purposes of scientific description, it is expedient to adopt this restriction. In this sense a habit is a more or less definite mode of procedure or kind of behaviour which has been acquired by the individual, and has become, so to speak, stereotyped through repetition. There can be little objection, however, to the concurrent use of the word in its broader and more general acceptation;

B

and when it is so employed in this work, the context will, it is hoped, serve to make the meaning clear and to prevent misapprehension. Still, wherever it is so used there will be implied, at least, some element of that individual acquisition and repetition which gives to habit, in the narrower and more restricted sense, its salient characteristic.

The word " instinct," too, is used in daily conversation and in popular speech with a signification somewhat wider and less restricted than that which attaches to it as a technical term. In the first place, it is commonly employed to distinguish broadly the doings of animals from the ways of man. The former are said to be due to instinct, while the latter are described as rational. But not all the ways, not even all the thoughts, of man are rational. And thus, in the second place, the word " instinct " is used in describing that part of human character and conduct which is not the outcome of a consciously rational process. The man who acts without deliberation is said to do so instinctively ; the girl who shrinks, she knows not why, from the companionship of some of her schoolfellows, is guided, it is said, by her natural instincts. These two uses are closely connected. There is in both a common antithesis to rational ; in both a reference to something deeply ingrained in the nature. And each is serviceable, seldom giving rise to mis-apprehension, since the meaning is sufficiently defined by the context.

But for use as a technical term, we need further precision. The difference between a word as employed for the daily purposes of familiar conversation or in general literature, and the same word in its usage as a technical term, is this : that in the former case it is in itself freer and more mobile, being, in its usage, moulded to definiteness by the context of the passage in which it occurs ; while in the latter case, as a technical term, it has to a large extent lost its freedom and mobility, being bound in the chains of a more or less precise, but at the same time more or less arbitrary, definition. For the purposes of exact science such bondage is necessary; and there are many words, such as "force," "energy," "impression," "sensation," which we continually use in daily conversation or in general literature with a freedom which would be inadmissible in technical descriptions. Such a word is "instinct." But it unfortunately happens that, whereas physicists are generally agreed among themselves as to the exact meaning which the words "force" and "energy" shall carry as technical terms, naturalists and psychologists are by no means fully agreed * as to the precise sense in which the term "instinct" shall be used.

There is, moreover, in the case of "instinct," a source of difficulty which is absent in that of the technical terms which are employed in the science of physics. Let us suppose that we are watching a silkworm spinning its cocoon. A set of activities, for the carrying out of which the structure of the caterpillar is admirably adapted, are performed before our eyes, and may be watched in all their stages; such activities, if they fulfil certain conditions, we term instinctive. But if now we are asked what prompts the silkworm at a certain stage of its existence to spin its cocoon, the reply is that this is due to "instinct." How far such a reply is justifiable we shall have to consider. But it is clear that, in the case of the activities themselves, we are dealing with matters of actual observation; but if we say that the activities are due to instinct, we are dealing with something which cannot be directly observed, but which we infer to be present. And that which we thus

---

* Cf. "Some Definitions of Instinct" in *Natural Science* for May, 1895, vol. vii. p. 321.

infer to be present is commonly ascribed to the sphere of mental phenomena, and regarded as a special mode of the workings of consciousness. If, then, we are putting the matter fairly and correctly; if observation of the activities provides us with the facts from which to infer the existence of a special mode of the workings of consciousness, termed "instinct;" it is clearly our duty, as scientific inquirers, to deal first with the observable facts, and then with the psychological inferences which may be drawn from them. Thus only can we hope to overcome the difficulties which arise from the circumstance that the term "instinctive" is applied on the one hand to certain observable activities, and on the other hand to certain inferred mental faculties.

Let us, then, proceed to consider some of the leading characteristics of instinctive activities as they present themselves to our observation and study in the animal world. In popular speech, as was noted at the outset, all the activities of animals are comprehensively instinctive. What we have to do, therefore, is to show in what respects the use of the word as a technical term has undergone limitation; and to indicate the more restricted group of activities to which it is specifically applicable.

In the first place, instinctive activities are severally common to, and similarly performed by, all the like members of the same more or less restricted group of animals. They are essentially lacking in individuality. The spinning of a cocoon by the silkworm, the migration of the swallow, the fieldfare, or the golden plover, the hibernation of the frog or the bear, the behaviour of an irritated bee, an irritated skunk, an irritated cuttle-fish,— these and a thousand other peculiar activities are characteristic of particular individuals, not in virtue of their individuality, but as representatives of their kind. I once heard instinctive activities defined as those on which you could safely bet; but, if the element of chance is that which gives zest to the wager, one must add that such betting would be dull work. You might almost as well lay a wager that the sun will rise to-morrow morning, as bet, for example, that the larva of the great water-beetle (*Hydrophilus piceus*) will, as the period of pupation draws nigh when the insect is soon to pass into the chrysalis stage, leave the pool and bury itself in the damp earth, so constant, under the appropriate circumstances, is the performance of an instinctive activity.

It need hardly be said that there is the closest possible connection between the structure and organization of any given animal and its instinctive activities. The spinnerets of the spider are associated with its web-making instinct; the activities of flight are rendered possible by the possession of wings; the burrowing habits of the mole are correlated with many peculiarities and adaptations of structure. The specific way in which any essential life-function—say, for example, that of respiration—is performed, and the activities which are rendered necessary for its performance, have been developed in direct association with the organic mechanism which is subservient to the process and the activities in question. In insects respiration is effected by means of a delicate system of ramifying tubes (the tracheal system) which open to the outer air by orifices or spiracles on either side both of the middle or thoracic and of the posterior or abdominal region. Of the two large aquatic beetles that are found in our English ponds, each must come from time to time to the surface to renew its supply of air; * but the manner in which they take in and store the air is quite different. *Dytiscus* floats slowly to the surface with its hinder end

---

* See Professor Miall's " Natural History of Aquatic Insects " (1895).

at a slightly higher level than its head, and this end
breaks the surface film and rises into the air. The last
pair of spiracles, or breathing orifices, near the hinder
end of the body, are large and take in a direct supply,
while air is also stored in the space between the wing-
cases and the body, and is thus supplied to the smaller
abdominal spiracles. In the great water-beetle, *Hydrophilus*, however, the front pair of abdominal spiracles are
the largest, and the air is stored not only beneath the wing-
cases, but along the hairy ventral surface of the beetle.
When the insect comes up to breathe, it is the head
and not the hinder end that reaches the surface; the
feeler, or antenna, is specially modified so as to effect
a communication between the whole storage area and the
atmosphere; and the air is taken in at the junction of
head and thorax. Thus the activities which minister to
the process of respiration are seen in each case to have
a close dependence on the general structural organization
of the insect. And throughout the whole animal kingdom
we have abundant illustration, not only of the intimate
connection between the structure of a given organ and
its particular function, but also between such specific
performance and the activities which lead up to it. In
other words, not only does an organ respond functionally
under the appropriate conditions, but the whole organism
co-operates by carrying out a sometimes complicated set
of activities subservient to what we see to be the end
in view.

This leads us on to consider the relation which an
instinctive activity bears to what is termed a reflex action.
If the foot of a sleeping child be lightly tickled, the foot
and limb will be withdrawn from the source of irritation.
This is a case of reflex action. The effects of the stimulus
(tickling) are carried inwards by nerves to the spinal cord;

there certain nervous centres are called into activity, as the result of which an orderly (co-ordinated) set of out-going nerve-currents are distributed to the muscles which are concerned in moving the leg. If a frog be killed by the rapid extirpation of the brain, and then its flank be sharply pinched, the hind leg of the same side will be raised, and the foot will scratch at the irritated spot. This again is a reflex action; and the fact that the brain has been extirpated shows that spinal centres alone are sufficient for its due and accurate performance. Now, it is by no means easy, if indeed it be possible, to draw any sharp and decisive line of demarcation between instinctive activities and reflex acts. Instinct has been well described by Mr. Herbert Spencer as compound reflex action; hence the distinction between them turns in large degree on their relative complexity. It would seem, therefore, that, whereas a reflex act—such, for example, as the winking of the eye when an object is seen to approach it rapidly—is a restricted and localized response, involving a particular organ or a definite group of muscles, and is initiated by a more or less specialized external stimulus; an instinctive activity is a response of the organism as a whole, and involves the co-operation of several organs and many groups of muscles. Initiated by an external stimulus or group of stimuli, it is, at any rate in many cases, determined also in greater degree than reflex action by an internal factor which causes uneasiness or distress, more or less marked, if it do not find its normal instinctive satisfaction. Take, for example, the before-mentioned instinct of the great water-beetle to leave the pond and burrow in its bank when the time for pupation is at hand. There is something more here than a local response to an external stimulus; something more, it would seem, than mere reflex action. There are activities

affecting the whole behaviour of the organism, and there
seem to be internal promptings of some kind due to organic
conditions whose seat is within the body of the developing
larva. Or take the migration of birds, their nest-building
instincts, the activities involved in incubation and in
the rearing of their young; there is surely, it may be
said, something in all this which may be distinguished,
even if the line of demarcation be hard to draw, from reflex
action. We cannot say more, however, than that the one
is a more fully corporate act than the other.

Reflex action is involved in the carrying out of many
instinctive activities. When the great water-beetle weaves
with her spinnerets the delicate silken cocoon in which
she deposits her eggs, there are reflex acts connected with
the extrusion of the fluid which hardens to form the silk;
reflex acts accompany the moulding of the cocoon and its
being supplied with air; reflex acts are concerned in the
laying of her eggs, "not at hazard, but in regular order,
side by side;" but during the hours of maternal labour
there is an organization of all the activities into a definite
line of behaviour, directed to what *we* see to be a final and
adaptive end, and prompted, we feel sure, by some internal
impulse; and all this tends to raise series of activities, as
a whole, above the level of mere reflex action. If we say
that reflex acts are local responses due to specialized stimuli,
while instinctive activities are matters of general behaviour,
usually involving a larger measure of central (as opposed
to merely local or ganglionic) co-ordination, and due to
the more widely spread effects of stimuli in which both
external and internal factors co-operate, we shall probably
get as near as possible to the distinction of which we are in
search. But it must be remembered that there are border-
land cases in which the distinction can hardly be maintained.

Reverting now to the close connection we have seen to

exist between structure and habit, it must be noted that there are many instinctive activities that no examination of structure, with our present means and appliances, would enable us to foretell. In the tributaries of the Severn there is a spring migration of little eels, or elvers. Thousands may be seen swimming up stream, and even surmounting such obstacles as small waterfalls and mill-sluices by wriggling up the conferva-clad surface. But there is nothing in their structure to give a hint of this migratory instinct. If an ant-lion larva were given to a naturalist ignorant of its habits, he would no doubt be able to say that it led a predatory life. He would not infer from its structure that it made a conical pit in the sand to entrap unwary ants and other insects, and, as it lay almost concealed at the apex of the cone, scattered a shower of sand-grains, by which its victim was brought down into its very jaws. No examination of the structure of a limpet would enable us to foretell that it would wander in search of food within a radius of about a yard from its scar, performing its peregrination when the rocks were wetted by the tide, but returning home to its own particular scar on the rock ere the sun and air had baked and dried the surface, and ere the returning tide had deeply submerged its home.* Very many such cases might be given of activities to which the study of structure alone would afford no clue.

The fact that the same organ often subserves more than one purpose may sometimes lead one astray in attempting to infer habit from structure. In Trinidad there occurs a climbing picarian bird, the red-tailed jacamar (*Galbula ruficauda*). It has a long, sharp, pointed bill, and no one from a study of its structure would be likely to foretell that it subsists on flies, which it catches

* See *Nature*, vol. xxxi. p. 200; and vol. li. pp. 127 and 511.

on the wing.   And Mr. F. M. Chapman says * that these
birds "are the most expert fly-catchers he has ever
seen.   Their watchfulness permits no insect to pass in
safety.   They maintain a constant look-out, turning the
head quickly from side to side.   The dart into the air is
made with wonderful celerity.   Sometimes it is straight
up, again at various angles, and they go as far as thirty or
thirty-five feet from their perch, to which they return after
each sally."   Fly-catchers, as a rule, have short bills and
a broad gape.   Why, then, is the long pointed bill preserved
in these jacamars?   Mr. Chapman tells me that they scoop
holes in the sand, in which they build their nest, and that
they use their bills for this purpose.   Hence, perhaps, the
retention of the long pointed form.   Be that as it may, no
one would be likely to predict that the jacamar was one of
the most expert of fly-catchers.

The instinctive activities, which we have now seen to
be something more than local responses to stimuli, and to
involve the general behaviour of the animals which perform
them; and which, while they are correlated with organic
structure, could not in many cases be inferred from the
closest morphological or anatomical examination;—are
characterized, as was said, by the fact that they are
severally common to, and similarly performed by, all
the like members of the same more or less restricted group
of animals.   Knowing the instinctive activities which are
characteristic of the life-history of the great water-beetle or
other organism, you may be sure that they are common to,
and similarly performed by, all the like members of the
species, the qualification *like* members being introduced to
cover the divergencies of instinctive behaviour due to sex.

It must not be supposed, however, that this constancy

* "Chapman on the Birds of Trinidad." *Bulletin Am. Mus. of Nat. Hist.*,
vol. vi., 1894, p. 63.

of behaviour is absolute, and that the instinctive activities are quite invariable. Were this the case, there could be no organic progress so far as instincts are concerned. Evolution would be no longer possible. The constancy is rather to be regarded as analogous to that which we find in those structural characters of animals which are termed specific or generic, as the case may be. When we say that structural characters are constant, we no longer, since the revolution of thought caused by the publication of the " Origin of Species," mean that they are absolutely invariable. We know, or have reason to believe, that these are often subject to variations, many, if not most, of which are slight and inconspicuous. In the same way, the performance of instinctive activities is probably subject to variations of a similar kind. This is, no doubt, difficult to establish on the basis of actual observation, since slight departures from the normal type of activity would be more liable to escape detection than departures from the normal type of structure. We must be guided by analogy, and this certainly does not warrant the assumption that constancy is to be interpreted in any absolute sense.

The next point to notice with regard to the class of activities which we term instinctive is that they are performed under special circumstances, which are either of frequent occurrence, or are vitally essential to the welfare or continuance of the race. They are often of protective value, and very frequently correlated with structural characters which are likewise protective. Thus the hedge-hog, whose body is clad in a spiny skin, instinctively coils himself up when molested, and thus gives effect to his protective structure; so, too, the tortoise instinctively withdraws his head and limbs under the carapace; and the snail retreats within his shell. And in like manner the instincts of the hermit-crab lead him not only to withdraw into his borrowed shell, but to seek and insert himself into one suitable to his size; nay, further, in the case of *Pagurus*, he may even affix to his shell a sea-anemone (*Adamsia*), the distastefulness of which to fishes will prevent his falling a prey to their voracity.

In many familiar cases of mimicry, specific activities are correlated with mimetic structure and appearance. A not uncommon beetle (*Clytus arietis*), which is mimetic of the wasp, has a fussy manner, unlike the usually staid demeanour of beetles, which serves to make the mimicry more effectual. There occurs at the Cape of Good Hope a harmless, egg-eating snake (*Dasypeltis scabra*), which flattens its head, coils as if for a spring, hisses, and darts forward as though about to strike, in a way that closely resembles the characteristic mode of the berg-adder (*Vipera atropos*), of which it is mimetic. It is really quite harmless, subsisting on eggs, the shells of which are broken in the throat by the enamel-tipped processes of the vertebræ, which project into the gullet and form the so-called gular teeth; but its resemblance both in form and behaviour to a venomous snake presumably affords it protection from enemies. Mimetic resemblance may also be of service in stealing upon prey. Thus hunting spiders, which resemble the flies on which they feed, rub their heads in very much the same way as do the flies themselves. These mimetic activities, which are probably truly instinctive in their nature, must not be regarded as consciously imitative; they are, rather, analogous to the mimetic appearance, and, like it, due to natural selection. A great number of other instinctive activities might be adduced in illustration of the fact that they are performed in subservience to the general welfare of the organism, and under circumstances which are of frequent recurrence in the life of the individual and of the species.

Many of these activities are so familiar to the obser-
vant naturalist, constituting as they do the normal life-
habits of the animals which exhibit them, that they are apt
to suffer the common fate of the familiar, and receive less
notice and less attention than the unusual and unfamiliar.
That an insect should exhibit one set of activities as a
larva or caterpillar, and a totally different set of activities
as an imago or perfect insect, seems quite natural, and
what we should expect. But the naturalist, who is something more than a collector, sees in these activities
problems not less difficult of solution than are the problems
of structure with which they are associated. And, in any
consideration of instinct, these familiar activities which
are performed under the ordinary circumstances of normal
life must not be allowed to fall into the background. They
form the largest, if not the most conspicuous, group of
instinctive activities.

But there are other instinctive activities which are
performed seldom or only once, and these are in all cases
of vital importance to the continuance of the race. Of the
many drones which follow the queen-bee in her nuptial
flight, one only is successful in mating with her, and that
but once in his life. And yet, were the sexual instinct
of drones to lapse, even for a single year, the race would
be decimated ; and were it to lapse altogether for but a
few years, the race would become extinct. The instinct is
essential to the preservation and continuance of the race.
And many of these instinctive activities thus but seldom
performed are adaptive with a nicety which is a continual
source of our wonder and admiration. Of such exquisite
adaptation we may take, for example, the instinctive
activities * of the Yucca moth (*Pronuba yuccasella*).

* Described in Kerner's "Natural History of Plants," translated and
edited by Prof. Oliver, vol. ii. p. 156.

The silvery, straw-coloured insects emerge from their chrysalis-cases just when the large, yellowish-white, bell-shaped flowers of the yucca open, each for a single night. From the anthers of one of these flowers the female moth collects the golden pollen, and kneads the adhesive material into a little pellet, which she holds beneath her head by means of the greatly enlarged bristly palps. Thus laden, she flies off and seeks another flower. Having found one, she pierces with the sharp lancets of her ovipositor the tissue of the pistil, lays her eggs among the ovules, and then, darting to the top of the stigma, stuffs the fertilizing pollen-pellet into its funnel-shaped opening.

Now, the visits of the moth are necessary to the plant. It has been experimentally proved that, in the absence of the insects, no pollen can get to the stigma to fertilize the ovules. And the fertilization of the ovules is necessary to the larvæ, which in four or five days are hatched from the insect's eggs. It has been ascertained that they feed exclusively on the developing ovules, and in the absence of fertilization the ovules would not develop. Each grub consumes some twenty ovules, and there may be three or four such grubs. But the ovary contains some two hundred ovules. Of these, therefore, say, a hundred are sacrificed to the grubs of that moth, through whose instrumentality alone the remaining hundred can be fertilized and come to maturity.

These marvellously adaptive instinctive activities of the Yucca moth are performed but once in her life, and that without instruction, with no opportunities of learning by imitation, and, apparently, without prevision of what will be the outcome of her behaviour; for she has no experience of the subsequent fate of the eggs she lays, and cannot be credited with any knowledge of the effect of the pollen upon the ovules. The activities also illustrate what is by no means infrequent in the more complex instincts, namely, the serial nature of the adaptation. There is a sequence of activities, and the whole sequence is adaptive in its nature. A further example of the serial nature of instinct—of the way in which a number of activities are linked into one elaborately adaptive instinctive chain— may be cited.*

A certain beetle of the genus *Sitaris* (one of the *Meloidæ*, to which belongs the common oil-beetle) lays its eggs at the entrance of the subterranean galleries excavated by a kind of mason bee (*Anthophora*). From these eggs the larvæ are hatched in autumn as active little insects very different from the ordinary type of beetle grub, having six legs each armed with a sharp curved hook. In the winter they become sluggish, but resume their activity in the spring. And when in April the drones of the bee emerge and pass out through the gallery, the Sitaris larvæ fasten upon them. There they remain till the nuptial flight of the bees, when, as the insects mate, they pass from the drone to the female bee. Then again they wait their chance. The moment a bee lays an egg, the Sitaris larva springs upon it, and at length breaks its prolonged fast. "Even while the poor mother is carefully fastening up her cell, her mortal enemy is beginning to devour her offspring; for the egg of the Anthophora serves not only as a raft, but as a repast. The honey, which is enough for either, would be too little for both; and the Sitaris, therefore, at its first meal, relieves itself from its only rival. After eight days the egg is consumed, and on the empty shell the Sitaris undergoes its first transformation, and makes its appearance in a very different form. . . . It changes to a white

* From M. Fabre, as given by Sir John Lubbock in his "Scientific Lectures," 2nd edit. p. 45 (1890). I utilized this example in much the same words in "Animal Life and Intelligence," p. 438.

fleshy grub, so organized as to float on the surface of the honey, with the mouth beneath and the spiracles above the surface. . . . In this state it remains until the honey is consumed," and, after some further metamorphoses, develops into a perfect beetle in August.

Here, then, we have a curious and marvellously adaptive life-history, with specialized changes of form and structure, and with correlated modes of activity at each stage. How comes it to perform its varied activities, each step of which is so well adapted to the needs of the stage of life on which it is entering? Parental teaching is altogether excluded, for the parent never sees her offspring; each individual is isolated from others of its kind, so that imitation is also excluded. The activities cannot be performed through intelligence in the common acceptation of the word, for intelligence involves the profiting by individual experience. The larva cannot fasten upon the drone as the result of any previous experience, since it has never done anything of the sort before; nor can it pass to the female bee because experience has taught it that such a procedure brings with it satisfactory consequences. At no stage of the complex process can intelligence, based upon individual experience, be admitted as a factor. If there be experience, it must be the inherited experience of ancestors who have, each in turn, done much the same. Whether we are justified in speaking of inherited experience will be considered in due time. In any case, the procedure, which is typically instinctive in its nature, has its foundations in heredity.

We here touch the very quick of the subject. As we shall use the term, the truly instinctive activity is characterized by a certain amount of definiteness which is hereditary, and which is not acquired in the course of individual experience. A habit, as such, is not, in the restricted acceptation of the term we adopted at the outset, inherited. It is the result of individual acquisition, and is stereotyped by repetition in the course of the experience of the organism which exhibits the habit in question. Now, it is well known that there is a divergence of opinion among biologists as to the answer to be given to the question: Are acquired characters inherited? For us this question takes the following form: Are acquired habits inherited in the form of congenital instincts? I shall not, at this stage of our inquiries, express any opinion in the matter. That must come after a careful consideration of the evidence. But it is clearly essential that we should so define the terms "habit" and "instinct," and the terms "congenital" and "acquired," as not in any way to forejudge the question; nay, rather, in such a way as to facilitate a due grasping of the real nature of the question at issue.

"Habit" has already been defined; it involves individual acquisition. An animal does not come into the world with any tendency to perform ready-made habits. The expression "ready-made habits" is indeed contradictory, for habits are reached by repetition in the course of experience. If they were ready-made, they would not be called habits; if they were habits, they could not be ready-made. The definition of the term "instinct" is occupying our attention at present, and we have just said that what is instinctive is characterized by a certain amount of definiteness which is hereditary, and not acquired in the course of individual experience. Instinctive performances *are* ready-made activities, if the expression be permissible. In other words, they are congenital. Let us, then, use the terms "congenital" and "acquired" in such a way as to be so far as possible mutually exclusive. An activity that is congenital is one the definite performance of which is

c

antecedent to individual experience. Young moorhens, as soon as they are born and have recovered from the shock of birth, can swim with definite accuracy of leg-movements. Here the definiteness is not only congenital, but *connate*, if we use this latter term for a congenital activity which is definitely performed at or very shortly after birth. On the other hand, young swallows cannot fly at birth; they are then too immature, and their wings are not yet sufficiently developed. But when they are some three weeks old, and the wings have attained functional size and value, little swallows will fly with considerable if not perfect skill and power. The definiteness is congenital, for it is not acquired by individual experience; but it is not connate, since it is not exhibited at or shortly after birth. The term *deferred* may be applied to such congenital activities as are performed when the organism has undergone a certain amount of development after birth. The definiteness of the swimming instinct in the moorhen is congenital and connate; the definiteness of the instinctive flight of the swallow is congenital, but deferred. Whether we apply the term "connate" or the term "deferred" to the instincts of fully developed insects— those in the imago stage—depends upon the view we take with regard to the new birth of the insect after its chrysalis sleep.

Let us now turn to the activities the definiteness and the peculiar nature of which may be termed acquired in contradistinction to congenital. If we throw to young chicks several caterpillars, some nice, others nasty, the birds will, in the absence of previous experience, seize them without discrimination. But they will soon eat only the nice ones, and leave the others untouched. Two or three lessons of this kind will suffice. After that, if mixed caterpillars be thrown to them, they will with definiteness and precision select the nice and ignore the nasty. Experience has introduced a differentiation of response, and that of a perfectly definite nature, and it is to this differentiation, as the result of individual experience, that we may apply the term " acquired."

In the animal kingdom there are a great number of skilled activities which are congenital in their definiteness —which have not to be learnt, but are performed with accuracy the first time circumstances and opportunity permit. But in any circus we may see examples of skilled activities which are not congenital, but have been taught to the animals; and any one who has possessed a clever dog will have seen cases of skilled activities which the animal has learnt for himself through the exercise of his intelligence. It is to such activities as these, the performance of which is the result of *individual* experience, that the term "acquired" is properly applicable in the sense in which it is here defined.

It must not be supposed, however, that what is acquired is always entirely new, if by this is meant something altogether disconnected from any instinctive basis. Quite the reverse. In the great majority of cases, what is acquired is a modification of that which is congenital. Of this, perhaps, there is no better example than that afforded by falconry. Here the congenital instincts of certain birds of prey, such as the peregrine falcon, are modified for the purposes of sport; and the modification is always of the acquired type, since in all cases it is a wild bird—either a young one captured fully fledged, or a nestling (eyas) taken from the eyry—that the falconer takes in hand for special training. One cannot breed falcons for the chase. The training requires care, patience, and skill. The newly captured bird has first to be accustomed to man; she is lightly hooded, and provided with bells, jesses, swivel, and leash. She is carried about continuously for several days, and late into the night, being constantly stroked with a bird's wing or feather, very lightly at first. Her early training is largely effected in the dark, and she is only unhooded in a dimly lighted room. She is led to associate certain sounds of lips or tongue with feeding; and at a later stage, certain shouts and tones of voice with the appropriate response. She is trained to the lure—a dead pigeon, or an artificial lure made of leather and feathers or wings of birds and garnished with beefsteak—at first with the leash. Later a light string is attached to the leash, and the falcon is unhooded by an assistant, while " the falconer, standing at a distance of five to ten yards, calls her by shouting and casting out the lure. Gradually day after day the distance is increased, till the hawk will come thirty yards or so without hesitation; then she may be trusted to fly to the lure at liberty, and by degrees from any distance, say a thousand yards. This accomplished, she should learn to stoop to the lure. Instead of allowing the hawk to seize upon it as she comes up, the falconer should snatch the lure away and let her pass by, and immediately put it out so that she may readily seize it when she turns round to look for it. This should be done at first only once, and then progressively, until she will stoop backwards and forwards at the lure as often as desired. Next she should be entered at her quarry. Should she be intended for rooks or herons, two or more of these birds should be procured. One should be given her from the hand; then one should be released close to her, and a third at a considerable distance. If she take these keenly, she may be flown at a wild bird. Care must, however, be taken to let her have every possible advantage in her first flights—wind and weather, and the position of the quarry with regard to the surrounding country, must be considered." With herons and rooks, the falcon is generally kept hooded till the quarry is in sight, when she is at once unhooded and slipped. With game birds the falcon is taught to "wait on" till the game is flushed. " A good game hawk in proper flying order goes up at once to a good pitch in the air—the higher she flies the better—and follows her master from field to field, always ready for a stoop when the quarry is sprung. Hawks that have been successfully broken and judiciously worked become wonderfully clever, and soon learn to regulate their flight by the movements of their master."

These facts and extracts from Colonel Radcliff's article on "Falconry" * will serve to show how the behaviour of a trained falcon is an adaptation and modification of the hawk's congenital instincts as a bird of prey. The finished performance is part instinct and part habit. The basis is instinctive and congenital; the modification is a matter of acquired habit. In domesticated animals that are not only reared, but also bred, by man, there is opportunity for selective mating; and there is opened up the question whether the acquired modification of instinctive behaviour becomes congenital through heredity. Hence in the training of a retriever there may be hereditary effects which are absent in the case of the falcon.

It may be objected, however, that the distinction between "congenital" and "acquired" is one that cannot be sustained, since after all an organism can only acquire that for acquiring which it inherits a potentiality; and that we must in any case come back to heredity in the last resort. The Scandinavian jer falcons (*F. gyrfalco*), for example, will seldom "wait on" well; and merlins will not do it at all. They inherit no faculty for responding to training in this respect. Not only, therefore, is that which

* " Encyclopædia Britannica," 9th edit. vol. ix.

is "congenital" dependent on heredity; that which may be acquired is also, at all events, limited by heredity.

A somewhat similar objection may be urged on slightly different grounds. A great number of habitual activities and acquired modes of dealing with what is frequently presented in experience result from a gradual limitation of what was at first a varied and exuberant output of activity. If we watch a young puppy or kitten learning gradually to deal effectively with some difficulty in its extending environment, we see that it puts forth its activities at first in a somewhat random and indefinite fashion. It tries to effect its object in a number of different ways, many of which are ridiculously inadequate and hopelessly unsuccessful. But gradually it finds that certain efforts are more satisfactory in their results than others; these are repeated, and thus by successive limitations of the originally numerous and relatively in- definite trials the exuberant efforts are narrowed down to those which bring success; these become habitual through repetition, a definite mode of procedure results, and we say that it has acquired a specific and well-adapted habit. Now, such acquisition may be regarded, by those who are sceptical as to the validity of any real distinction between what is congenital and what is acquired, as after all only the selection or rejection of these or those among many congenital activities. Suppose, to put the matter in a somewhat different and at the same time a concrete form, that a baby baboon exhibits a number of con- genital limb movements; each in itself of a relatively definite kind, but without relation to, or co-ordination with, other movements; and further suppose that, as the result of its individual experience, ten per cent. are selected and co-ordinated so as to form an acquired activity for the carrying out of some specific object, while the ninety per cent. are, so far as this particular purpose is concerned, suppressed. The habit thus engendered arises out of the co-ordination of a small percentage of certain given congenital limb movements. But if the selected ten per cent., no less than the rejected ninety per cent., were originally congenital, and if this selected ten per cent. when duly co-ordinated are said to constitute an acquired habit, what becomes of the supposed radical distinction between " congenital " on the one hand, and " acquired " on the other ? The answer to this objection is, that what we have to fix our attention upon is, not the raw material, but what is manufactured out of it. The activity which results from the co-ordination of the selected ten per cent. of originally unrelated movements is, as such, a new product ; and this product is the result of acquisition, and is not, as a definite co-ordinated activity, congenital. Just as a sculptor carves a statue out of a block of marble, so does acquisition carve an activity out of a mass of given random movements. Or just as an architect builds a cathedral out of an indefinite mass of material by selecting, shaping, and bringing into relation the given parts, so does acquisition build an habitual response out of a given number of indefinite movements by selecting, modifying, and bringing them into relation. It is the definite, co-ordinated, responsive activity that is acquired.

Now, there are certain activities which are congenitally definite, which are inherited ready-made, of which the co-ordination is practically perfect at birth. Instance the swimming of a young moorhen when first it enters the water, or the spinning of a cocoon by a silkworm without previous practice or experience. The definiteness and co-ordination are here not of individual, but of ancestral origin. And there are other activities the definiteness and co-ordination of which are acquired through experience, and are thus not of ancestral, but of individual origin. The one group comprise congenital activities; the other group, acquired activities. And whether the definiteness individually acquired in one generation contributes to the definiteness of ancestral origin in succeeding generations, is the subject of discussion among biologists.

It must not be supposed that the distinction between what is congenital and what is acquired—a distinction which we are endeavouring to draw with the utmost clearness—is invalidated by the fact that there are a great number of activities, such, for example, as the perfected flight of birds, which are of double origin, being in part congenital and in part acquired. Such cases do indeed show that imperfect instincts may be perfected by habit and individual acquisition of skill. But they render the more necessary a careful distinction between the factors which co-operate to produce the ultimate result. And only when the distinction is thus duly emphasized does the question, whether the acquired perfection of one generation tends to lessen the congenital imperfection in the next generation, stand out in its true significance. It is interesting here to compare the flight of birds with the flight of insects. In the latter class we find many cases in which the instinctive factor in flight is relatively much more highly developed towards congenital perfection than it is in the former class, at any rate so far as most birds are concerned. The question therefore arises, Is the greater relative perfection in the instinctive flight of some insects due to the inheritance of acquired skill on the part of their ancestors? Or is it due to the fact that there has been among insects more elimination of those who failed in congenital power of flight, and hence a survival through natural selection of those in which the instinctive flight was better developed? Or is it due to some other cause?

At present we will not attempt to answer such questions as these. We are concerned merely in drawing as clearly as possible a distinction which shall enable us to put the questions in a definite and intelligible form. It is a matter of no small importance accurately to focus the point of such questions.

The distinction between that which is congenital and that which is acquired may be further illustrated from a structural point of view. There is an inherited organic mechanism through the possession of which an animal is fitted to perform certain more or less definite and adaptive activities without learning, with little or no practice (though even in these cases practice helps to make perfect), through no teaching, by no imitation, and without any individual experience on which intelligent choice of the best mode of procedure could be based. This is due to what may be termed *congenital automatism*. On the other hand, there is an organic mechanism which is gradually developed during the individual lifetime, through the due co-ordination and persistent repetition of certain selected activities. These activities, by constant repetition, themselves become automatic as habits. We may term the working of this organic mechanism, which is thus developed during the course of individual life, *acquired automatism*. The biological question is—Does the acquired automatism of one generation contribute, through inheritance, to the congenital automatism of the next?

There is still, however, the difficulty suggested but not removed a few pages back, that after all an animal can only acquire that for acquiring which it inherits a potentiality; and that we must in any case, even when individual acquisition is under consideration, come back to heredity in the last resort. This is indubitably true; and it shows that the more or less definite congenital activities do not by any means exhaust the hereditary possibilities. All that an animal owes to heredity may, indeed, be classified under two heads. Under the first head will fall those relatively definite modes of activity which fit it to deal at once, on their first occurrence, with certain essential or frequently recurring conditions of the environment, and this forms the group here termed "congenital." Under the second head will fall the power of dealing with special circumstances as they arise, and this we may term *innate capacity*. The former may be likened to the inheritance of specific drafts for particular and relatively definite purposes in the conduct of life; the latter may be likened to the inheritance of a legacy which may be drawn upon for any purpose as need arises. If the need become habitual, the animal may, so to speak, instruct his banker to set aside a specific sum to meet this need as often as it arises. But this arrangement is a purely individual matter, and no wise dictated by the terms of the bequest.

In this classification instinctive activities, as we propose to define them, fall under the first head. They display some share of that hereditary definiteness which is characteristic of what we have termed " congenital activities." It must be remembered, however, that, as already mentioned, there is unfortunately no common and accepted agreement so to define the term "instinctive." Professor Wundt, indeed, divides instincts into two classes : (1) those which are congenital, and (2) those which are acquired. So that the distinction we are drawing will by no means be accepted by him and his followers. Where opposing views are in the field, it is necessary to carefully weigh the advantages and disadvantages of each, and to adopt one or the other. I am quite convinced that, from the biological point of view, it is more satisfactory to restrict the term "instinctive" to those activities which are in greater or less degree congenitally definite, and it is in this sense that the phrase "instinctive activities" will be used in this work. No doubt there are in many cases difficulties of interpretation; but these must be met as they arise in the further prosecution of our studies.

It may be convenient to indicate the nature of the suggested classification in tabular form :—

INHERITED.

Congenitally definite activities, under which those termed "instinctive" are comprised.	Innate capacity, involving (*a*) a power of association, and (*b*) hereditary susceptibilities to pleasure and pain.

ACQUIRED.

(*a*) Confirmation, or (*b*) Modification, of congenitally definite or instinctive activities so as to render them habitual by repetition. (*c*) Suppression of congenital activities.	Particular application of innate capacity; (*a*) Occasional and under special circumstances; (*b*) Frequently repeated, with the consequent formation of acquired habits.

We may now sum up what has been advanced in the foregoing discussion, and say that from the biological point of view (and it is from this standpoint alone that they have been so far considered) instincts are congenital, adaptive, and co-ordinated activities of relative complexity, and involving the behaviour of the organism as a whole. They are not characteristic of individuals as such, but are similarly performed by all like members of the same more or less restricted group, under circumstances which are either of frequent recurrence or are vitally essential to the continuance of the race. While they are, broadly speaking, constant in character, they are subject to variation analogous to that found in organic structures. They are often periodic in development and serial in character. They are to be distinguished from habits which owe their definiteness to individual acquisition and the repetition of individual performance.

CHAPTER II.

SOME HABITS AND INSTINCTS OF YOUNG BIRDS.

MUCH stress has been laid, in the foregoing introductory chapter, on the distinction between the definiteness which is congenital and the definiteness which is individually acquired. There would seem to be certain activities the definite performance of which is antecedent to individual experience, and these were termed instinctive. There are others which reach definiteness only through a process of learning, through the exercise of intelligence, or through imitation, their definite performance becoming more or less automatic and stereotyped by individual repetition, and these were termed acquired. So far as our present inquiry is concerned, it is on the definiteness that we must fix our attention. And it is a matter for careful and unprejudiced observation to decide whether the definiteness of behaviour, under given circumstances, is congenital or acquired. This question of fact may, for the present, be kept quite distinct from the question of origin. When some of the facts have been given, it will be time to inquire whether the congenital definiteness is due, on the one hand, to the natural selection of slight congenital variations, or, on the other hand, to the inheritance of the adaptive modifications which result from individual acquisition. But the first thing is to collect facts observed with all possible accuracy.

Nor need we trouble ourselves much at present—not otherwise, that is to say, than incidentally—with the subjective interpretation of the facts. We need not now stay to inquire whether, on the one hand, the performance of a truly instinctive activity—one the definiteness of which is congenital—is a merely organic response (be it accompanied by consciousness or not); or whether, on the other hand, there are innate ideas or inherited memories by virtue of which consciousness guides or directs the activity into a definite channel. This question is closely connected with that of origin, inherited memory and inherited acquisition being often associated in one interpretation of the facts—that adopted by those who may be termed transmissionists. This again is a matter the discussion of which may be profitably deferred.

We have to concentrate our attention, then, on the facts established by careful and critical observation, and it will be convenient for many reasons to limit our field at first to the readily observable habits and instincts of young birds. Since they are easily hatched in an incubator so that all maternal influence is avoided; and since many of them are active soon after birth; since, too, certain species can be reared without serious difficulty, and subjected to conditions which are pretty well under control;—on all these grounds they afford satisfactory material for the investigation with which we are now concerned.

Studies of the domestic chick have been made by several observers, notably by Douglas Spalding,* by Professor Preyer,† by Professor Eimer,‡ and more recently by Dr. Wesley Mills.§ Spalding's observations have been widely

* *Macmillan's Magazine*, February, 1373, vol. xxvii., "Instinct."
† "The Mind of the Child," part i., "The Senses and the Will," 2nd ed., 1884, Eng. trans., by H. W. Brown.
‡ "Organic Evolution," pp. 245–254, Eng. trans., by J. T. Cunningham, 1890.
§ *Transactions R. S. Canada*, sect. iv., 1895, p. 249.

quoted, but in some cases their accuracy has not been confirmed by later observers.

The eggs from which the subjects of my own investigation were hatched were either artificially incubated from the first, or were transferred from the hen to the incubator a few days before they were timed to emerge, so that in no case was the behaviour of the young influenced by older birds. They were kept under observation in a small pen or enclosure surrounded by wire netting, or in a room set aside for that purpose, and were occasionally allowed the run of a little garden plot.

Previous to hatching, the little fellows may often be heard chirping within the egg. Young moorhens do so in some cases for as much as forty-eight hours, and ducklings as much as twenty-four hours before they finally emerge, and this in the case of strong and healthy birds. The beak must then have pierced the air-chamber within the egg, and direct air-breathing must have taken the place of embryonic respiration. The eggshell, when they thus begin to chirp within it, is generally, but not always, broken or chipped at one point of its surface. This chirping is a truly congenital activity, and has not to be learnt. One young moorhen, lying silent in the chipped shell, responded by chirping to my low whistle. So that even then they can hear, or at any rate are influenced by an auditory stimulus. Mr. Hudson, referring to "several species in three widely separated orders," tells us * that, according to his observations, "when the little prisoner is hammering at its shell, and uttering its feeble *peep*, as if begging to be let out, if the warning note is uttered, even at a considerable distance, the strokes and complaining instantly cease, and the chick will then remain quiescent in the shell for a

* "Naturalist in La Plata," 1892, p. 90.

long time, or until the parent, by a changed note, conveys to it an intimation that the danger is over." Here we have a remarkable connate response to definite stimulus.

In some cases the shell is finally rent by the struggles of the little bird, in whom air-breathing probably provokes increased activity. But some birds, ducks for example, chip the egg along a circle near the broad end. When they emerge, the down is wet and draggled in appearance, and the little new-born things are comparatively helpless for some hours, having, as a rule, little power to hold up their heads, and none to stand firmly. I noticed that newly hatched plovers lay in the drawer with bill on the ground and outstretched neck in a well-known protective attitude. Like the eggs, they assimilate well in colour with their natural surroundings. Some young moorhens, hatched out in a drawer lined with cotton-wool, had taken a good deal into their beaks during the first five or six hours—so much, indeed, that in one case it was in some danger of choking.

There would seem to be some instinctive shrinking from one's hand when the birds are for the first time taken from the drawer after hatching, and this seems to be the more marked the longer they have been left to recover from the shock of birth. There was, however, little sign of shrinking in plovers or lapwings. Chicks and ducklings lie quiet longer than partridges and pheasants, which soon begin to move about. Any instinctive fear which they may show soon passes by, and after a very little experience they come to the hand instead of shrinking from it. Still, we may probably regard the shrinking as congenital, but more marked at a slightly deferred period of life. And perhaps there may be in this a special adaptation. The hen, for example, is a somewhat fussy being, and, in the absence of any instinctive knowledge of her as their natural protector (for it is probable that there is no such instinctive knowledge), very strong connate shrinking on the part of the chicks would lead them rather to avoid her than to submit to her ministrations. Hence it comes that the young birds accommodate themselves to a foster-parent even so strange as a human being, if he take them in hand early enough. There is also from the first an instinctive tendency to nestle into any warm, soft place. When there are several little birds in the incubator drawer, they cuddle together and burrow under each other in a very comical manner. And when one has older and younger birds, the little ones get in under and between the legs of their seniors in a way that appears to be somewhat embarrassing to the latter. This was, for example, especially notable with two recently hatched moorhens, which persistently tried to cuddle down under the lanky legs of two older birds of the same species. So, too, in a mixed brood of several species I had under observation, a little guinea-fowl and a still younger pheasant tried to cuddle down under a wild duck and a tame duck, a day or two older than themselves, with a touching confidence that was not at all appreciated by the greedy ducklings, eager only for food. Dr. Mills introduced to his chicks two pigeons (a white pouter, and a black owl), to test whether the chicks would show any instinctive fear. Not at all; the little birds nestled under them !

This instinctive action is, of course, under nature, in adaptation to the corresponding instinctive behaviour of the mother-bird, who takes them under her wing. But with hand-reared birds the instinctive tendency acquires a new direction, and undergoes modification. Chicks, pheasants, partridges, plovers, moorhens, and other young birds, whether wild by nature or of domesticated breeds, would all run to my hands, after a very short time,

D

nestle down between them, and poke out their little heads confidingly between my fingers. Here, then, there is a congenital and instinctive tendency, to nestle in any warm place, modified in accordance with acquired individual experience. It was pretty to see three little partridges, two French and one English, following me about the room wherever I went. And when the instinctive tendency is thus modified, its natural end seems to lapse; for chicks even a few days old seem to have completely lost any instinctive tendency they may have possessed to run to and cuddle under the hen. As to the existence of any such instinctive response to the sight of the hen, or to her clucking, there is difference of opinion.

Spalding describes * how a chick, which had been blindfolded at birth, was placed, twenty minutes after it had been unhooded, "on rough ground, within sight and call of a hen with a brood of its own age. After standing chirping for about a minute, it started off towards the hen, displaying as keen a perception of the qualities of the outer world as it was ever likely to possess in after-life. It never required to knock its head against a stone to discover that there was 'no road that way.' It leaped over the smaller obstacles that lay in its path, and ran round the larger, reaching the mother in as nearly straight a line as the nature of the ground would permit. This, let it be remembered, was the first time it had ever walked by sight."

Other chicks, which had been placed in a bag immediately they were hatched and kept there for a day or two, ran eagerly to the clucking of a hen hidden from their view in a box nine or ten feet distant. This observation was repeated on nine different chicks. But Spalding draws our attention to the fact that this

* *Loc. cit.*, p. 289.

instinctive response to a specialized auditory stimulus was completely lost at the end of ten or twelve days.

The results of my own observations may now be briefly described. I took two chicks ten days old to the yard whence I had received the eggs from which they had been hatched, and opened the basket wherein they had been conveyed, about two yards from a hen which was clucking to her brood. Though they were not in a frightened condition, as shown by the fact that they jumped on my hand and ate grain off it, scratching at my palm, they took no notice whatever of the clucking of the hen. I then placed them with another hen in a small fowl-house; but they took little heed of her, neither running to her nor seeming frightened, or, if at all, but little. Three other chicks were taken when they were thirteen days old to the yard, and were put down outside a fowl-house in which a hen was clucking to her brood. They also took no notice of the sound, but scratched about quite unconcernedly. Subsequently they were placed with the hen, who seemed inclined at first to drive them away, but afterwards looked more kindly on them, though they did not keep close to her like the others. I went over on the following day, and when I bent down and held out my hand, one of my little friends ran to it and nestled down confidingly. So far my observations confirm what Spalding says concerning the loss of the instinctive response, or, at any rate, its absence after the lapse of a few days. But the following case shows that the instinctive recognition of the hen, if indeed it exist at all, is very soon lost. I took a chick at two and a half days old (that is to say, at about the same age as Spalding's birds) to its own mother, which had three chicks. These followed her about, and ran at once to her when she clucked and pecked on the ground. The little stranger took no notice whatever of the clucking of its, till then unknown, mother, and did not show any tendency either to go to the hen or to follow the three chicks. He pecked about independently and unconcernedly, eating grain, and seizing small stones, but came to my hand when I held it out towards him, and cuddled down in it. When the hen took her three chicks under her wing, the stranger was placed close to her. She clucked and seemed anxious to entice and welcome the little fellow, seizing an oat-husk and dropping it before the chick, which, however, took no notice whatever, but walked away and stood in the sun. After about forty minutes he seemed more inclined to go with the other chicks, but still ignored the existence of the hen. Thus I have not found any truly instinctive response to the clucking of a hen; but, as before noticed, Spalding recorded a different result. And Mr. Hudson's observations on the effects of warning notes on unhatched birds indicate a truly congenital response in their case. We need more evidence.

We may now turn to the instinct of pecking, and the congenital definiteness of orderly movements which it involves. As the observations of Spalding, Eimer, Preyer, and others have conclusively proved, the pecking at grain and other small objects is a definitely congenital activity, and one, be it noted, which involves remarkable nicety and complexity of co-ordination. The aim is, however, seldom quite correct at first, though very nearly so, the object, if not struck, being only just missed, though the accuracy was somewhat exaggerated by Spalding. In some cases the tendency seems to strike a little short of the object. Moving the grain or egg-fragments with a pin, or dropping some before the chick, causes the edible material more readily to catch the eye. Most noteworthy is the fact that the young birds only strike at objects which are well within striking distance; they have not to learn this distance by experience. To peck at an object of a certain size, just within easy reach, is a definitely congenital response, and not the result of acquired skill. In nearly all cases, as one might expect, the simpler process of striking is more accurate than the more complicated process of striking and seizing; and this, again, than the yet more elaborate process of striking, seizing, and swallowing. Nevertheless, this yet more complicated activity, or train of activities, is performed so soon, and with so few trials—often at the third or fourth attempt—that one must regard the whole as essentially congenital in its definiteness, and look upon the few preparatory efforts as merely the steadying of the inherited organic apparatus to its work.

Of the birds which I have had under observation, partridges, both English and French, pecked earlier and with better aim than any others, but soon desisted if what they pecked at was not satisfactory. Plovers (my observations were on the common peewit or lapwing) were slow to peck, and their co-ordination seemed relatively poor. Chicks and guinea-fowl were about on a par; pheasants somewhat less keen. Ducklings—those of wild ducks and tame ducks being, so far as I could note, equal in this respect—peck early and with fair aim, but they do not seize and swallow so readily. They mumble what they seize, and often shake it out of the bill unswallowed. Moorhens show a somewhat different instinctive tendency. From the first they crouch down with the head and neck held back, and the skinny little wings working to and fro; in this attitude they open their beaks more like the callow young of jackdaws or other nursling birds than the young of fowls or pheasants. They soon strike, however, with fair accuracy of aim, at objects held above them;

but it is some time before they will pick up food from the ground. I tried with two moorhens the experiment of feeding them as little as possible from the hand, so as to induce them to eat independently, but with fatal results. Mr. Crisp, who has had good opportunities of watching these birds under natural conditions in the moat beneath the walls of Playford Hall, in Suffolk, informs me that the parent birds always feed the young from their beaks during the first few days of life. The instinctive attitude quite bears out the accuracy of this observation.

When they are a little older, and have had some practice, their keenness of eye, both at long and short distances, and their accuracy of aim are alike wonderful. One, about ten days old, after nestling awhile in my hand, singled out and seized in his bill several not very conspicuous hairs on the first joint of my fore-finger. There was also a speck of white on my hand, which caught his eye, and at which he pecked with complete accuracy of aim again and again. A few days after, one pecked at a minute black speck on my hand, though it was but a quarter of an inch from the tip of his bill. Shortly afterwards, in the garden, he spied a small ant moving on the wall about four feet distant, ran, and seized it. The field of vision is very soon completely ordered for practical use.

I took a young pheasant, which had been hatched some time in the night, from the incubator drawer at nine o'clock in the morning. He was very unsteady on his legs, so I held him in my hand, and tried to induce him to peck at a piece of egg-yolk held in a pair of forceps. He did not do so; but he followed, with his head, every movement of the object in a narrow circle about two inches in front of his beak. Simple as the action seems, it shows a striking example of congenital co-ordinated movements accurately related to movements in the visual field, the whole performed without any possibility of learning or practice, and less than half an hour after the bird had first seen the light of day. On the other hand, two nestling jays, brought to me when they were about ten days old, were quite unable to follow in this way food moved slowly over their heads. They merely gaped for it to be put into their mouths. When they began, after a day or two, to follow an object with the head and eye, the movements were at first jerky. In a week, when I swept the food through a circle a foot in diameter in front of their cage, it was followed smoothly and evenly. It was curious to see the two jays following it thus, their heads moving in unison through a small circle corresponding to my wider sweep. Here a certain amount of individual learning and practice, absent in the case of the pheasant, was required.

Chicks, pheasants, and other birds which are active shortly after birth may be induced to peck by tapping on the ground with the finger-nail, a pencil, or penholder, thus simulating the pecking action of the hen, and may thus be induced to seize objects which they would otherwise leave untouched. Mr. S. E. Peal* states that the Assamese, when they find newly hatched pheasant chicks in the jungle, teach the little ones to peck and pick up food by sharply tapping among the crushed rice and egg on which they feed them, and say that without this many of them would die. Professor Claypole informs me, on the authority of a friend who had practical experience, that young ostriches hatched in the incubator will not pick up food for themselves unless the ground be tapped so as to suggest the action of pecking. But on young moorhens this has no effect, and I could not find much response, if any, in plovers.

* *Nature*, April 9, 1895.

The facts above noted possibly gave origin to the supposition to which Darwin gave his support,[*] that pecking is, in young chicks, primarily suggested through the sound of pecking. But both Spalding and Professor Preyer showed [†] that sound does not necessarily play any part in initiating the pecking activity. And my own observations fully confirm theirs. It is apparently the sight of the artificial pecking, and the movement thus caused among the grains of food, rather than any sound made, that has suggestive value.

With regard to the objects at which domestic chicks peck, in the absence of any parental guidance, one may say that they strike at first with perfect impartiality at *anything* of suitable size; grain, small stones, breadcrumbs, chopped-up wax matches, currants, bits of paper, buttons, beads, cigarette-ash and ends, their own toes and those of their companions, maggots, bits of thread, specks on the floor, their neighbours' eyes—anything and everything, not too large, that can or cannot be seized is pecked at, and, if possible, tested in the bill. Similarly with young pheasants, guinea-fowl, and moorhens. I watched the latter for an hour the second or third time they were put out in my little garden. They pecked at everything of suitable size they could lay bill on. There does not seem to be any congenital discrimination between nutritious and innutritious objects, or between those which are nice and those which are nasty. This is a matter of individual acquisition. They soon learn, however, what is good for eating, and what is unpleasant, and rapidly associate the appearance with the taste. A young chick two days old, for example, had learnt to pick out pieces of yolk from

---

[*] "Expression of the Emotions," 1st edit., 1872, p. 47. On the authority of Mowbray.

[†] *Op. cit.,* pp. 237, 238.

others of white of egg. I cut little bits of orange-peel of about the same size as the pieces of yolk, and one of these was soon seized, but at once relinquished, the chick shaking his head. Seizing another, he held it for a moment in the bill, but then dropped it and scratched at the base of his beak. That was enough; he could not again be induced to seize a piece of orange-peel. The obnoxious material was now removed, and pieces of yolk of egg substituted, but they were left untouched, being probably taken for orange-peel. Subsequently, he looked at the yolk with hesitation, but presently pecked doubtfully, not seizing, but merely touching. Then he pecked again, seized, and swallowed.

To some other chicks I threw cinnabar larvæ, distasteful caterpillars conspicuous by alternate rings of black and golden-yellow. They were seized at once, but dropped uninjured; the chicks wiped their bills—a sign of distaste —and seldom touched the caterpillars a second time. The cinnabar larvæ were then removed, and thrown in again towards the close of the day. Some of the chicks tried them once, but they were soon left. The next day the young birds were given brown loopers and green cabbage-moth caterpillars. These were approached with some suspicion, but presently one chick ran off with a looper, and was followed by others, one of which stole and ate it. In a few minutes all the caterpillars were cleared off. Later in the day they were given some more of these edible caterpillars, which were eaten freely; and then some cinnabar larvæ. One chick ran, but checked himself, and, without touching the caterpillar, wiped his bill—a memory of the nasty taste being apparently suggested by association at sight of the yellow-and-black caterpillar. Another seized one, and dropped it at once. A third subsequently approached a cinnabar as it crawled along, gave the danger

note, and ran off. Then I threw in more edible caterpillars, which again were eaten freely. The chicks had
thus learnt to discriminate by sight between the nice and
the nasty caterpillars. Similarly, moorhen chicks rapidly
discriminated between small edible beetles and soldier
beetles. Such discrimination is, however, not congenital,
but acquired. The young birds do not for some little time
avoid pecking at their own fresh excrement, though this is
obviously distasteful.

The cinnabar caterpillars are, as I have said, conspicuously marked with alternate yellow and black rings.
It would seem that the end of this conspicuousness is to
render association in the individual experience of young
birds more rapid and more certain ; there does not appear
to be any congenital and instinctive avoidance of such
caterpillars with warning colours. Young moorhens
found the conspicuously marked burnet moth distasteful,
the obnoxious part being the wings, for the body from
which the wings were removed was eaten with apparent
relish, while the severed wings were rejected with evident
signs of distaste. I was desirous of ascertaining whether
the different appearance of brandlings (*Lumbricus fœtidus*)
and other small worms was sufficient to enable the moorhens to distinguish them, but this was apparently not the
case. The experiment showed, however, the marked influence of the *first* experience. For the moorhen which was
given a brandling first was long before he would touch any
worm, while that which was given a brandling after several
less highly flavoured worms, though he was rendered a
little suspicious for a time, picked up each cautiously and
rejected or swallowed it according to the taste. A few days
later, however, both moorhens would eat brandlings when
they were hungry.

My observations with regard to the effects of giving

to young birds distasteful insects were made solely with a view to ascertain whether there was any instinctive avoidance on the part of the birds. Of this I have not found a single instance. Cinnabar caterpillars (*Euchelia jacobiæ*) were tried and avoided after a few trials by all the birds on which I have made observations, though one hungry jay ate five in succession, never again eating another, though he had frequent opportunities. The brown pupæ of this moth were eaten by jays with apparent relish. All avoided large woolly-bear caterpillars (*Arctia caja*); but whereas jays, ducks, and moorhens ate small caterpillars of the wood tiger moth (*Nemeophila plantaginis*) and the cream-spot tiger moth (*Chelonia villica*), the chicks, pheasants, and guinea-fowl to which they were given found them distasteful. Jays ate freely the pupæ of the currant moth (*Abraxas grossulariata*), but on the following day took them less readily, and with some wiping of the bill. One of the jays also ate the large larva of the buff-tip moth (*Phalera bucephala*), which the other jay rejected, as did ducklings and chicks. After wiping it to and fro across his perch, he tore it, eating the inside with apparent relish, and leaving the skin for a time. This he subsequently swallowed. Two days later he ate another in the same manner. Moorhens, as already mentioned, found the wings of the burnet moth (*Zygæna filipendulæ*) distasteful. Soldier beetles and ladybirds were invariably tested, and avoided as the result of experience. The net result of these observations is that, in the absence of parental guidance, the young birds have to learn for themselves what is good to eat and what is distasteful, and have no instinctive aversions.[*]

I am not, of course, prepared to say that in no case

* My thanks are due to Mr. G. C. Griffiths for kindly sending me larvæ and pupæ.

is there such instinctive aversion. A far more extended series of observations is needed to justify such a sweeping assertion. The birds on which the observations were made have, under natural conditions, parents who certainly afford them some guidance in the matter of feeding. Such guidance would in some degree prevent the incidence of natural selection, and would diminish the elimination of those which, without such guidance, might eat to their destruction. There are, however, birds, like the megapodes, which are hatched out in mounds apart from parental influence, and never know a mother's care. They may show instinctive avoidances which our well-cared-for birds do not possess.

That the parent bird does in most cases afford guidance is unquestionable. And there seems to be an instinctive tendency on the part of the young to wait upon her bill, or rather upon any bill. I have observed a young pheasant and a young guinea-fowl following ducklings, and apparently waiting for the help that did not come; for the bird that waited for anything eatable from a duckling's voracious beak would assuredly wait in vain. Still, the ducklings are untidy feeders, and grains of meal would adhere near the base of the beak; and these the guinea-fowl would pick off with care, till—and this was soon the case—he grew to be independent.

There does not seem to be any marked instinctive response to the sight of water as such. Prof. Eimer * placed on a board a large drop of water. At first his chicks took no notice of it; but when it was made to tremble by shaking the board, one of the birds immediately drank from it with perfect success in the well-known fashion of adult fowls. Spalding says † that his

* *Op. cit.*, pp. 247, 248.
† *Macmillan's Magazine*, February, 1873, p. 288. Cp. Darwin as quoted in "Mental Evolution in Animals," p. 229.

chicks, though thirsty, did not recognize water by sight, "except, perhaps, in the form of dew-drops on the grass; and they had, to some extent, to learn to drink. . . . They pecked at the water, or rather at specks in the water, or at the edge of the water." Dr. Mills says,[*] "When water is presented to the chicks they peck at some drops on the side of the tin containing the water, and accidentally get the beak into the water, when drinking follows." I set before my chicks a shallow vessel containing water. Several of them ran repeatedly through the tin, but took no notice of its contents. Then, after about an hour, one of them standing in the vessel pecked at its toes, and at once lifted its head and drank freely with characteristic action. Another subsequently pecked at a bubble near the brim, and then drank. The touch of water in the bill at once led to the characteristic responsive and congenitally definite action. I found, indeed, that the best way of inducing them to drink was to place some grains of food in the tin of water. They then pecked at the food, and incidentally discovered the nature of water. As an example of the association on which the intelligent procedure of animals is so largely founded, it may be worth noting that a chick which had drunk but once while he was standing in the shallow tin, a little later ran through the water, and then stopped to drink. Wet feet seemed to have suggestive value through association in previous experience.

Ducklings showed no more instinctive acquaintance with the nature of water than chickens. They walked several times through the water, but took no heed of it. On dipping the beak of one of them beneath the surface, it then drank repeatedly, shovelling up the water with characteristic action. Its companion subsequently imitated its behaviour, and then drank freely. Pheasants, too,

[*] *Trans. R. S. Canada,* Sect. iv., 1895, p. 250.

seemed to take no heed of water in a shallow vessel. They pecked, however, at drops on my finger-tip, or on the end of a toothpick, and for long preferred to take it in this way to drinking from the vessel. Presumably in the natural state they depend largely for water on the dew-drops that bead the vegetation. Moorhen chicks liked to take water from my finger-tips. But when they were dipped in a bath, by holding them in the hand and gradually submerging the palm, as soon as the water reached the bird's body he bent down his head and drank.

It has already been noted that if food is moved about before newly hatched birds, it more readily catches their eye. The hen, as we may see in any poultry-yard, lifts and drops before her chicks the grain or other food which she wishes them to eat. Moving insects, grubs, or caterpillars more readily attract their attention than objects which are still, and if small are struck at. A chick a day or so old will catch a running fly at from the seventh to the twelfth shot. Pheasants are quite as sharp; but ducklings do not catch running flies so readily, perhaps because they do not walk so well. Even protective coloration is of little value if there is movement, so sharp are the eyes of young birds. The caterpillar of the small white butterfly (*Pieris rapæ*) on a nasturtium leaf, with which its clear green colour assimilated well, was picked off by a moorhen chick the moment it moved its head. Recently hatched stick insects (*Diaphcromera femorata*), which Professor Poulton gave me, were snapped off the lime leaves directly they moved. As in the case of palatable and distasteful insects respectively, there does not seem to be any instinctive differentiation of response according as the insects are armed with stings or not. That is a matter of individual acquisition.

The following, however, is an account of one of

Spalding's observations: " A chicken that had been made
the subject of experiments on hearing (having been blindfolded at birth) was unhooded when nearly three days
old. For six minutes it sat chirping and looking about it;
at the end of that time it followed with its eyes the movements of a fly twelve inches distant; at ten minutes it
made a peck at its own toes, and the next instant it made
a vigorous dart at the fly, which had come within reach of
its neck, and seized and swallowed it at the first stroke;
for seven minutes more it sat calling and looking about it,
when a hive-bee, coming sufficiently near, was seized at a
dart, and thrown some distance much disabled." He also
states that a duckling one day old caught a fly on the
wing.

First, with regard to the accuracy of aim shown in these
observations, I cannot but think that such success in
catching flying insects at the very first shot is unusual! In
any case, my own observations tell a different tale. During
their third, and again on their fifth and sixth day of life
special experiments were made with a view to testing this
point. Two or three flies were placed under a tumbler in
a good light. The birds pecked at them as seen through
the glass. One by one, they were then allowed to escape.
The chicks made a dash at each in turn, but never
succeeded in catching any on the wing, though they caught
one or two as they crawled out, before they had taken
flight. I tried also with tumblers covered with cardboard
lids, which could be removed when the birds had seen the
insects and were eager to seize them. It may be said
that the conditions were unnatural, and did not give the
birds the best possible chance. But I have watched chicks,
ducklings, pheasants, guinea-fowl, and moorhens strike
repeatedly at flies buzzing round them or flying near them
in the open air, and have never yet seen one caught on

the wing by a bird younger than ten days or a fortnight.
The wild duck, tame duck, and chick I had, together with
other birds, in a room, dashed repeatedly at flies which
settled on the floor. The wild duck caught one for the first
time when it was seven days old; the chick succeeded
when he was nine days old. I never saw the tame duck
successful. Nor have I ever seen a chick, pheasant, or
duckling, when only two or three days old, catch at the
first shot, even a running fly—one, that is to say, the
wings of which had been clipped. I must therefore repeat
that young birds in my experience do not show that
congenital accuracy of aim which Spalding's observation
implies; hence his results, until they are confirmed by
other observers, must, in my opinion, be regarded as
unusual and tending to give an exaggerated view of the
inherited skill.

Secondly, with regard to the difference of behaviour
towards the fly which was swallowed, and the bee which
was thrown aside disabled. The implication is that there
is an instinctive discrimination between the edible fly and
the hurtful bee, and that, too, when these insects were on
the wing. It is possible that the buzzing of the bee made
the difference in the behaviour in the two cases; but all
my own observations are against the view that there is any
truly congenital power of discrimination. This, however,
was not Spalding's view. He regarded a fear of bees as
instinctive, but only imperfectly so, by which it would
seem that he meant that it had not yet reached the stage
of infallible avoidance. To quote his own words, "the
chicks were uncertain, shy, and suspicious." It may
be well, however, to give the whole passage. "When a
week old, my turkey came on a bee right in its path—the
first, I believe, it had ever seen. It gave the danger chirr,
stood a few seconds with outstretched neck and marked

expression of fear, and then turned off in another direction. On this hint, I made a vast number of experiments with chickens and bees. In the great majority of instances the chickens gave evidence of instinctive fear of these sting-bearing insects, but the results were not uniform, and perhaps the most accurate general statement I can give is that they were uncertain, shy, and suspicious." Now, here, so far as observation goes, I am able to confirm the facts as thus generalized, but I differ from Spalding in their inter-pretation. As I understand him, the shyness and sus-piciousness were of bees *as such*, there being an imperfect congenital avoidance of this dangerous insect because it was instinctively recognized as dangerous. My own observa-tions lead me rather to the following conclusions: First, that there is a congenital differentiation of response according as the moving objects, or even freshly introduced inanimate objects, are large or small; in other words, that there is some congenital "shyness and suspiciousness" of *any* largish thing moving towards them or thrown to them. But, secondly, that this becomes very much more marked through individual experience. For example, a young chick a day or so old which will peck at a small fly held in a pair of fine forceps, will hesitate and shrink from a large bluebottle held thus, especially if it buzzes; while a little bird which will run eagerly to small bits of a chopped-up match, will shrink away from a whole "Bryant and May;" and in these cases there has been but little experience by which the difference of behaviour could be guided. I have seen half a dozen chicks, on their fourth day of active life, uttering the danger note round a large carabus beetle which lay sprawling on its back, and though one chick at last pecked at it with a little dash, and threw it on one side, after this neither he nor any of the others dare go near it. There can be no question, however, that such

E

differences are emphasized through experience. A large
fly with clipped wings was thrown among some two-days-
old chicks. Only one dared approach it, and he gave the
danger note. Presently, however, he followed and caught
it, after several failures. Shortly afterwards another was
given them; the one who had learnt by experience that
the fly was harmless and nice to eat ran and caught it at
the second shot. While small worms are picked up with
avidity, large worms are left alone by quite young birds,
and often evoke the alarm note. None of the chicks on
their fifth day dared go near a particularly large worm.
Bits of red-brown worsted, somewhat resembling worms,
were seized with eagerness and eaten with surprising
avidity, so long as they were not more than a couple
of inches long. Of a four-inch bit the chicks were afraid,
until one, bolder than the rest, seized it, whereupon
the others chased him for the prize till he escaped to a
secluded corner and swallowed it. On their eighth day the
chicks stood timidly round a lump of sugar I had thrown in
among them, uttering the danger note, and then ran at it,
pecking rapidly and withdrawing in haste. Young moorhens were at first shy of large worms, but soon ate the
biggest I could find. A little pheasant which would run to
my hand for wasp larvæ placed upon the palm, one
morning gave the alarm note, and would not as usual jump
upon my fingers. Four or five of the grubs had stuck
together so as to form a large mass of which he was afraid!
Moorhen chicks were at first afraid of the common yellow
underwing moth and of the gamma moth, though both were
eaten freely after I had given them dead moths.

No doubt the response to the sight of a moving
object may look at first blush like instinctive recognition. Plovers seized small worms with an avidity which
looked like an inherited recognition of natural food, but of

somewhat larger worms they seemed afraid. And my belief is that the instinctive response is not to a worm, as such, but to a small moving object,—a larger moving object evoking a quite different response.

Pheasants and partridges, when they seized a worm for the first time, shook it and dashed it against the ground; one of them did so, indeed, with such vigour that he shook himself over, and thereafter could not for some time be induced so much as to look at a worm. They also, even more markedly than chicks, showed a tendency to bolt with such a treasure as a caterpillar or a worm. This was marked in the case of two pheasants, one much larger than the other, though of the same age; for though the smaller one never attempted to rob his larger companion of a worm or insect, yet the latter always bolted off to some little distance with it. He sometimes tried to bolt with one of his companion's toes by mistake, when one or both would topple over. These modes of behaviour appear to be congenital.

Very interesting is Spalding's observation of the special manner of catching flies adopted by the young turkey, for it would seem to bear all the distinguishing marks of a truly instinctive activity. "When not a day and a half old," he says, "I observed the young turkey slowly pointing its beak at flies and other small insects without actually pecking at them. In doing this its head could be seen to shake like a hand that is attempted to be held steady by a visible effort. This I observed and recorded when I did not understand its meaning. For it was not until after that I found it to be the invariable habit of the turkey, when it sees a fly settled on any object, to steal on the unwary insect with slow and measured step until sufficiently near, when it advances its head very slowly and steadily till within an inch or so of its prey, which

is then seized by a sudden dart." Further observations
are needed on the behaviour of turkeys to larger insects
and to bees.

Returning now to bees, I have not a single instance of
their avoidance by young birds from anything like instinctive knowledge of their hurtful nature. Here is
some of the evidence. To some five-days old chicks, one
of which, bolder than the rest, would eat large flies with
relish, I threw in a bee. Most of the chicks were afraid,
as they were of large flies. The bolder chick, however,
snapped it up and ran off with it. Then he dropped it
and shook his head, wiping his bill. Probably he tasted
the poison, and was not stung; in any case, he was quite
lively and unconcerned in a few minutes; but he did not
touch the bee again. Later in the day I put beneath a
tumbler a large fly and a small humble-bee with a sting.
Two of the chicks ran round the tumbler, pecking at the
insects. I let the bee escape. The bolder chick seized it,
dashed it against the ground, and swallowed it without
hesitation. To another group of chicks I first gave hive
bees, which were seized, but soon let alone, and then the
droneflies (*Eristalis*), which so closely mimic the hive bee.
They were left untouched. Their resemblance to the bees
was protective. Later I gave drone flies again, and
induced a chick to seize one by pecking at it with my
pencil. He ran off with it, chased by others. It was taken
from him and swallowed. The other drone flies were then
left untouched, but one was subsequently eaten. Older
chicks run with a dart at a humble-bee, or a large beetle,
dash it rapidly on the ground, and throw it aside disabled.
But they will do just the same with a largish pellet of
brown paper. The mode of behaviour is congenital; but the
object that calls it forth does not appear to be recognized
by anything like inherited memory. To some ducklings

a bee was given; one of them seized and swallowed it and perhaps was stung. He kept on scratching his beak, first on one side, then on the other, and seemed uneasy, but was all right again in half an hour, though he did not seem keen after another offered to him; nor would he take any notice of a drone fly. Two or three days later, however, he took a disabled humble-bee to the water, mumbled it there for a while, and then ate it. My experience with moorhen chicks is of a similar character. On giving a humble-bee to two of them one seemed shy of it; the other ate it eagerly. Later, when they were a fortnight old, I threw them two bees, which were seized at once and without hesitation, and shaken violently. One of the birds was probably stung, for he shook his head, scratched the base of his bill, and went again and again to the water and drank. He was all right in about three-quarters of an hour, but for about that time scolded a good deal. The other ate his bee without any ill effects. A day or two after they were given a humble-bee, from which the sting had been removed, but the bird that had been stung would not go near the insect; the other seized and ate it. The next day two drone flies were given to them. The stung bird would not go near them; the other ate both. He subsequently ate one of the flies (*Volucella*), which mimics the wasp; there was no sign of instinctive avoidance. I experimented one day, after testing that his avoidance of cinnabar larvæ still held good, by giving him a wasp from which the sting had removed, being desirous to see whether the black and yellow of the wasp suggested the nastiness associated with the black and yellow of the cinnabar. But it was not so; the wasp was snapped up and eaten.

I have not, in any one instance, found any instinctive avoidance of wasps. The sting was usually removed before the experiment. But several young wasps having crawled out˙ of a nest containing larvæ and pupæ, and having fallen on to the floor, where a wild duck, a tame duck, a chick, a guinea-fowl, and a pheasant were roaming in search of food, the ducks at once snapped them up and ate them. All except the pheasant (which would not touch even largish flies) subsequently ate a large number of the sleepy wasps, and seemed to enjoy them. The jays also ate several, crushing them to a pulp in the extreme point of the bill before swallowing them.

It would be wearisome to recount at length further observations, all pointing with sufficient definiteness to one conclusion: namely, that, though there is at first some congenital shyness of largish active, and especially buzzing, insects, this shyness is not congenitally particularized, and, in the long run, acceptance or avoidance is almost entirely due to the acquired results of individual experience. It is therefore clear, if this conclusion holds, that in experiments on the relative palatability of insects or larvæ with either warning or protective coloration, we must not look for instinctive avoidance, and that the results will largely depend on the nature of the previous experience of the bird (and the same is probably true of other animals) to which they are offered. There are, of course, individual differences of apparently a congenital kind. Some birds are constitutionally shyer than others. Much also depends on the nature of *initial* experience. A bird that has in early days seized a bee with ill effects is shy for a long time, not only of bees, but of moths, large flies, and beetles, while one which is so stung at a later stage, is made, perhaps, a little more cautious generally; but the main effect is a particularized one concerning bees or the bee-like drone fly. In several cases I have noticed that the sting, or possibly a taste of the poison, of the hive bee does not serve as a warning against humble-bees so long as they do not buzz, but, on the other hand, may give rise to the avoidance of even a large fly if it makes a buzzing noise. Some difference in the results in different animals may, perhaps, be due to the fact that in some cases the bee, the bitter experience of which gave the initial avoidance, buzzed, and in some cases did not.

It seems, therefore, that the tendency to peck at small objects, always within striking distance, is a congenital and instinctive activity which involves great nicety and no little complexity of motor co-ordination; that in presence of largish moving objects there is hesitation, and probably instinctive shyness and timidity; that apart from this there is no instinctive discrimination; that what shall be selected for eating and what rejected is a matter of individual experience; and that, by repetition of the selective process, the eating of certain materials, and not of others, passes into a more or less fixed habit.

I will conclude this chapter with a brief description of a few observations made on nestling birds.

The callow young of these birds are fed by the parents, either on grubs, worms, or insects, or other such food which they collect, or on food which is prepared for them, or in some cases formed by a special mode of secretion. They simply open their mouths, gaping widely to be fed; but the swallowing reflex is congenitally adequate. A spotted fly-catcher, about a day old, with eyes not yet open, would stretch out its neck and widely gape its beak on the auditory stimulus of a low whistle, gulping down greedily the little bits of raw beef on which it was fed. Swallows in the nest will respond at once to a low whistle by similar gaping actions. The eyes of the fly-catcher were not open till the third day after I received it. It was placed in a small "chip" box lined with cotton-wool, and kept in the corner of the incubator drawer. So soon as it had taken a morsel or two of food at intervals of about thirty to forty minutes, it would energetically thrust its hind quarters over the edge of the box and void its excrement. Jays and other young nestlings also show this instinctive procedure, which prevents their "fouling their own nest." The excrement is enclosed in a sort of skin, and can be lifted with a pair of forceps without breaking this pellicle. The old birds in many cases carry away the excrement in the bill, and drop it at a distance from the nest. A friend of mine, who loves birds, and has been accustomed to observe their habits for years, noticed swallows flying in and out of the porch of his house, and, to induce them to build, he caused shelves to be put up there. On these shelves swallows built their nest. He noted that the young birds, when old enough to quit the nest and rest on the shelf, after being fed by their parents, were nudged and pushed until they turned round and voided excrement, which was immediately seized by the parent bird with the tip of the beak, carried away, and dropped outside.

Nestling jays, which were brought to me when they were about ten days old, showed no sign of fear, and fed greedily on what I provided, thriving well, and growing up into fine birds. The following observation, made on the ninth day after receiving the birds, is worth recording as a good example of deferred instinctive procedure. I offered one of them a June-bug or summer chafer (*Rhizotrogus solstitialis*). It was refused. The other bird seized it at once in the bill, bent down its head, and tried on the perch to put his foot on it. After trying this unsuccessfully two or three times, he hopped down on to the floor of the cage, and dropped the beetle, seized it again as it crawled off, and, after two or three attempts, swallowed it, tossing it back from the point of the bill into the throat. This was the first time he took food from the ground, or swallowed it in this manner.

At a later date, when both had learnt to pick up their own food, I gave them a small dead bird, which they at once fell upon and tore to pieces, eating every morsel. I had at the time two young fly-catchers, which could just feel their wings in short flights. The cage in which the jays were kept was outside the window of the room, and when the fly-catchers were being fed the window was closed. After their meal the little birds would take short flights in the room, and if one reached the window-pane, both jays became much excited. A fatal day came when I carelessly omitted to close the window. One of the fly-catchers, without waiting to be fed, flew off as soon as his cage was opened, and, before I could avert the calamity, reached the jays' cage and put his head through the wire network. Like a lance the jay was on him, and the head was nearly wrenched from the body. The bird died at once, almost without a flutter.

On another occasion a small frog was placed in the jays' cage. One of the birds hopped down, but the frog shrieked so, that both birds were apparently frightened. I had not the heart to leave the frog in the cage, and gave it liberty. Nearly a fortnight later (some days after the fly-catcher tragedy), I put in a small toad, about an inch and a half long. One jay seized it with the tip of his bill and threw the toad aside, leaping up on to his perch again. The toad remained perfectly motionless, resting on all fours, with the body raised well off the ground, in a seemingly strained attitude, and continued thus for nearly twelve minutes. At first one of the jays kept hopping down from his perch, with wings well up over his back, nearly, but not quite, striking the toad with his bill, and rebounding, as it were, to the perch. Then he desisted, and eyed the toad. After seven or eight minutes, he turned on his perch, and very soon the toad dropped on its belly and rapidly crawled away, hiding in a crack between the board and the side of the cage, from which position he was removed and set free. The procedure of the two creatures —bird and amphibian—was a very pretty example of animal habit, with apparently a good deal of instinctive basis.

The fly-catchers I had under observation took the raw beef on which I fed them from the points of a pair of forceps with a rapid snap of the bill. Is this because they are naturally fed on live insects ? Shortly after the tragic end of one of them, the other died; but for two days he had taken food from the forceps, fluttering on the wing.

CHAPTER III.

LOCOMOTION IN YOUNG BIRDS.

WHEN young birds are hatched in an incubator drawer they seem at first to be exhausted by the effort, and require some time to recover from the "catastrophe of birth." I have generally left them for twelve hours or so, by which time, if strong and healthy, they generally begin to move about and get into the corners of the drawer. If then removed and placed on the floor or ground, chicks, partridges, pheasants, guinea-fowl, and plovers are able to walk with such accuracy of inherited co-ordination that there can be no question as to the truly instinctive and congenital nature of the definiteness shown by these activities. Ducklings and moorhens are more unsteady on their legs at first, the leg-movements of the former being sprawly, and the body not well raised from the ground. A chick, pheasant, or partridge, can stand on one leg and scratch the side of his head with the other foot on his first day of life with only a little wobbling, but a duckling topples over or tilts backward on to his tail ; the double co-ordination of standing on one foot and scratching his head with the other is too much for him. The clever way in which a little pheasant chick, only a few days old, will squeeze through a wire netting is not only exceedingly pretty, but is remarkable as showing nice control over the locomotor apparatus. Little moorhens seem to have a tendency to clamber up on to anything, such as a cloth heaped up on the ground, and use their skinny wings in a peculiar alternating hand-over-hand fashion which is also seen in young dabchicks and in the South American hoactzin (*Opisthocomus cristatus*).

This bird has, when quite young, the thumb or bastard wing armed with a claw, a second claw being developed on the digit of the wing corresponding to our index finger. The nestlings crawl about almost like young quadrupeds, and can hold on to the nest or twigs by means of the clawed wings.*

If the skinny wing of a newly-hatched moorhen be examined, the thumb or pollex is found to be relatively large, and also armed with a claw; and though I have not observed that this claw is of much use in climbing, still the wings are used in a manner very different from that which is seen in pheasants or partridges. These birds, too, have a tendency to leap up on to one's foot or a low hassock (and, in the case of a little partridge, on to my fox-terrier's back as he lay!) which reminds one of the way in which they climb on to the mother bird's back. But the scrambling up of the moorhen chick is differently performed, with a curious hand-over-hand action. One need hardly point out that such a mode of clambering would be of use to the little bird under the natural conditions of its life, and would help it to climb into the loosely compacted nest. At a later period, when my sole surviving moorhen was about six weeks old, he was taken to a farm near which ran a little beck. The manner in which he scrambled up and down the bank and ran rapidly to and fro among the rushes, threading his way with neatness and ease, was noteworthy, since he had

---

* See J. J. Quelch, *Ibis* for 1890, pp. 327, 335; also W. P. Pycraft, *Natural Science*, vol. v. p. 358; and Fredk. A. Lucas, " Report of U.S. National Museum for 1893," p. 662, where the young birds are figured.

hitherto no experience of obstacles of this kind. It looked like a bit of congenital moorhen nature, and told, perhaps, of its relationship to the land-rail and the water-rail.

Very soon such young birds as plovers, partridges, pheasants, guinea-fowls and chicks will begin to run. On their second day of life they will run freely, and one cannot but be struck with the manner in which they can guide their course, either to seize their food or to escape from another bird. Quite curious is the way in which a little guinea-fowl will do his best to evade one's grasp when one wishes to put him to bed, running backwards and sideways in a manner I have not noticed in other birds. As a further example of the way in which young birds can very soon make use of their legs, I transcribe one or two notes with respect to French partridges. At twenty-four hours old they were placed in a "rearer" with a warm chamber and an open run, separated by an opening guarded with strips of flannel. In the course of a few hours they learnt how to run in and out of the warm chamber, and in the chamber to nestle round the warm pipe covered with cotton-wool. At thirty-four hours old, while I was giving one food, I left the other in the run, placing a cigarette-box $3\frac{1}{4}$ inches high before the opening to the warm chamber. He jumped up on to it, though it was twice his own height, and got through the curtain of flannel strips into the chamber. I then placed the other in the run. He made a jump at the box, and missed; jumped again, and successfully landed on the top. He then ran round on the box, avoiding the edge, and in a minute jumped through the curtain and joined the other, which was "peeping" inside. Next evening he jumped out of the rearer, a height of more than 7 inches.

It is quite possible that under natural conditions the little chicks find the use of their legs more rapidly than incubated birds. A writer in the *Magazine of Natural History*, quoted by Yarrell, found a sandpiper's nest* in which there were three young chicks, and an egg through which the bill of a fourth was protruding. "Young as they were, on my taking out the egg to examine it, the little things, which," says the writer, "could not have been out of their shells more than an hour or two, set off out of the nest with as much celerity as if they had been running about for a fortnight." Other observations of like import might readily be quoted. But enough has been said to show that the co-ordination for walking and running is congenitally definite.

Next as to swimming. Ducklings, a day or two old, dropped into a tepid bath, kicked vigorously and excitedly for a few seconds, but in a minute were swimming with easy, rapid motion, and pecking at the marks on the side of the bath. The movement of the legs showed great nicety and accuracy of co-ordination. I compared a wild duck and a tame duck, both about fifteen hours old, but could detect no difference in swimming power. Both swam at first with rather rapid strokes, but well. One, the wild duck, while swimming kept putting its bill to the joint of one leg, and seemed to find the presence of water awkward. It did not, however, lift the leg, as an older bird would have done. What struck me most in such young birds, on the first occasion of their being in the water, was their power of either staying in one spot, paddling rapidly, or going ahead at a good speed, and turning readily in any direction.

Young moorhens, taken to the bath when the down was scarcely dry after hatching, and before they could walk

* Vol. ii. p. 609, from *Mag. Nat. Hist.*, vol. vi. p. 148.

with any steadiness, and gently lowered into the water on
the palm of the hand, swam off with fair ease. The only
difference in their leg-movements from those of somewhat
older birds was that the strokes were rather slower, more
sprawly, and not quite so neat. The scarce-dry down, too,
soon gets wet, and the bird sinks deeply in the water.
Under natural conditions the young moorhen takes to the
water almost at once. Mr. F. A. Knight tells me that he
has several times disturbed moorhen chicks a day after
hatching (having seen, that is to say, the unhatched eggs
the previous day), and observed them scramble into the
water and swim away. On one occasion, however, the birds
were less clever swimmers, and Mr. Knight's companion
"righted" two of them with her parasol. Mr. Knight
also noted at the time (oh! that men would always be
careful to note at the time, and take to heart the ex-
cellent precept of the immortal Captain Cuttle!) that
one of the young moorhen chicks that he thus disturbed
dived under a log of wood. Now, I did all in my power
to make my little moorhens dive; hustled them in the
bath, clapped my hands, banged the door, and boxed their
ears, but without effect. I played them a few chords on
the violin, but even that did not scare them. They seemingly regarded all this as among the inevitable incidents
of education. I put up a barrier across the bath, penning
them into a confined space, and placing on the other side
their favourite raft, made out of an old cigar-box, on to
which they always climbed as soon as possible, thinking
they might dive under the barrier to reach their raft.
And here it may be parenthetically remarked that young
water-birds, ducks and moorhen chicks, which are only
occasionally given a swim, take to the water less eagerly
than those which under natural conditions are from the
first accustomed to be constantly swimming; ducklings

even seem to shrink from the water, if for some days they are not given access to it.*

Tempted by the raft, then, my moorhen chicks tried to scramble over the barrier, but would not attempt to dive under it. I lifted the barrier, so as to leave half an inch of space between it and the water, and so long as the bird could put its beak and head through, he would make a shift to bring the body after; but when the space was insufficient for this, the little bird would not attempt to get under the barrier. So all these early attempts to induce my little charges to dive were abortive. When the last of the brood was taken to the beck near a farmhouse on the Yorkshire moors, I hoped he would exhibit his natural powers as a diver; but for some time he did not do so. One day, however, when he was about nine weeks old and becoming pretty well fledged, he was swimming in a narrow part of the stream, with steep banks on either side, when an ungainly, rough-haired pup came bungling down, and made an awkward feint towards the bird. Plop! down he went out of sight in the twinkling of an eye; and after a moment I saw his head appear, just peeping above water beneath the bank. Though long deferred, here was the instinctive activity in congenital purity and definiteness, and absolutely true to type, for this was the very first time he had ever dived, nor had he ever seen any bird do so. I take it that the failure to make him dive in the bath was, perhaps, partly due to the unnatural surroundings—though it must be remembered that at first he did not dive in the beck—but chiefly to my inability to frighten him, so accustomed was the bird to me and my strange ways; for his tameness, both with myself and others, was in marked

---

* The same is true of the gosling. See Lewes's "Problems of Life and Mind," Prob. i. chap. ii. § 22, note; also T. R. R. Stebbing, "Essays on Darwinism," p. 73.

contrast with the extreme shyness of such birds in their natural haunts. In Professor Newton's "Dictionary of Birds" we are told * that, "though often frequenting the neighbourhood of men, the moorhen seems unable to overcome the inherent stealthy habits of the Rallidæ, and hastens to hide itself on the least alarm ; but under exceptional circumstances it may be induced to feed, yet always suspiciously, with tame ducks and poultry." My little friend Tinker, as we called him, had, however, overcome all constitutional shyness, and was as tame as the tamest of barn-door chicks.

Analogous instances of what, from the description given, would seem to be truly instinctive activities are those of the dipper and of the hoactzin. The way in which the dipper, or water-ousel, dives and runs along the bottom of a stream, aided by his wings, but clutching with its claws the stones at the bottom, has often been described. I have, however, never seen an old bird attempt to escape in this way ; when disturbed, he flies off. The Duke of Argyll describes a case from his own observation of a young dipper, on being disturbed, dropping from the nest, and, when it reached a pool, diving instinctively. It may be well to give in full the passage in which his Grace describes the facts.† " A pair of dippers built their nest last year at Inverary, in a hole in the wall of a small tunnel constructed to carry the rivulet under the walls of a pleasure-ground. The season was one of great drought, and the rivulet, during the whole time of incubation and of the growth of the young in the nest, was nearly entirely dry. One of the nestlings, when almost fully fledged, was taken out by the hand for examination, an operation which

* See p. 590.
† *Contemporary Review*, July, 1875, "On Animal Instinct," vol. xxvi. p. 352.

so alarmed the others that they darted out of the hole, and ran and fluttered down the tunnel towards its mouth. At that point a considerable pool of water had survived the drought, and lay in the path of the fugitives. They did not at all appear to seek it; on the contrary, their flight seemed to be as aimless as that of any other fledgling would have been in the same predicament. But one of them stumbled into the pool. The effect was most curious. When the young bird touched the water there was a moment of pause, as if the creature was surprised. Then instantly there seemed to wake within it the sense of its hereditary powers. Down it dived with all the facility of its parents, and the action of its wings under the water was a beautiful exhibition of the double adaptation to progression in two very different elements, which is peculiar to the wings of most diving birds. The young dipper was immediately lost to sight among some weeds, and so long did it remain under water that I feared it must be drowned. But in due time it appeared all right, and, being recaptured, was replaced in the nest."

The hoactzin, the curious gallinaceous bird whose powers of climbing have already been noticed, has when young the power of swimming and diving. The nests are built over the water, and when one of the little birds fell into the water, Mr. Quelch observed that as soon as his hand was placed close to it the hoactzin rapidly dived into the dark water, in which it was impossible to see it, and would rise at distances of more than a yard away.

Mr. Hudson tells us * that he was once examining one of the eggs of the jacana (*Parra jacana*), lying on the palm of his hand, when " all at once the cracked shell parted, and at the same moment the young bird leaped from my hand and fell into the water. . . . Stooping to pick it up

* " Naturalist in La Plata," p. 112.

to save it from perishing, I soon saw that my assistance
was not required, for immediately on dropping into the
water it put out its neck, and with the body nearly submerged, like a wounded duck trying to escape observation,
it swam rapidly to a small mound, and, escaping from the
water, concealed itself in the grass, lying close and perfectly motionless like a young plover." With regard to
the submersion of the body, we must remember that the
down of a freshly hatched bird would be still wet. I have
again and again noticed that young moorhen chicks, even
when the down has dried, if they are dropped into the
water, are (and in this they differ from ducks) completely
wetted, and swim with but little of the back above the
surface. This would, I should suppose, be the case with
the just-hatched jacana when it fell from Mr. Hudson's
hand into the water.

Ducks not only swim, but dive very shortly after birth.
A wild duck, full of life and spirits, placed in my bath
when not six days old, at once dipped his head, and
then dived, swimming some distance along the bottom,
apparently from sheer exuberance of vital power. Ducks
that build in trees take their little ones to the water,
carrying them in some cases in the bill. Acerbi, quoted
by Yarrell,* says of the goosander, "As soon as the eggs
are hatched, the mother takes her chicks gently in her bill,
carries and lays them down at the foot of the tree, when
she teaches them the way to the river, in which they
instantly swim with astonishing facility." The hooded
merganser, the eider-duck, the wood-duck, and other
members of this group of birds, are said to carry their
young in this way. Yarrell says † the same of the
sheldrake. But Sir R. Payne Gallwey, quoted by Mr. H.

---

* Yarrell, "British Birds," vol. iii. p. 398.
† *Op. cit.*, vol. iii. p. 237.

Cornish in his "Wild England of To-Day," * states that he saw one, " when the tide was low, and she was unable to lead her brood to the sea, carry them on her back, each duckling holding on by a feather, having, while she lay down, climbed up and ensconced themselves with the greatest care." The young are skilful swimmers.

It would be interesting to know whether they take to the water instinctively; that is to say, whether the sight of water is in itself a sufficient stimulus to cause them to enter the water and swim. Mr. John Watson, on the authority of a keeper of long experience, says † of sheldrakes, that " the ducks, immediately they were hatched, seemed to be able to smell the salt water, and would cover miles to gain it." It would be of interest to put this beyond question by direct observation. I have not been able to experiment with ducks so fully as I could wish. A brood of ducklings, hatched out under a hen, which I watched some years ago, seemed to come to the side of the pond by chance; they drank from the water, and then some of them left it; others waded further in, dipping their breasts and head under, and then they went further in and swam. Since the parent birds seem, under natural conditions, to lead their young to the water, it is not improbable that the instinctive tendency may not have been ingrained in the congenital nature. But it is a question which can only be answered by further direct observation.

The horned or Sclavonian grebe (*Podicipes auritus*) has a protective habit or instinct which is worth noting. Mr. Proctor, quoted by Yarrell,‡ shot one as it emerged after diving, " and was surprised to see two young ones, which, it seems, had been concealed beneath the wings of the parent bird, drop upon the water. I afterwards shot

* P. 64.   † "Nature and Woodcraft," p. 192.   ‡ Vol. iii. p. 414.

several birds of this species," he adds, " all of which dived with the young under their wings. The young were placed with their heads towards the tail, and their bills resting upon the back of the parent bird." It must be remembered that the grebes and divers do not use the wings for progression under water.

Before leaving the activities connected with swimming, attention may be drawn to the curious habit observed by Mr. Thomson, head keeper at the Zoological Gardens. " Birds which sleep floating upon ponds or tarns," says Mr. Headley,* commenting on this habit, " are in danger of drifting to the bank and falling victims to any beast of prey. To prevent this the ducks and others have the habit of sleeping with one leg tucked under the wing, while with the other they keep gently paddling so that they revolve in a circle. In summer-time, when they have had a long day, they will begin this early, when there is still some light, and then is the time to watch them. This remarkable habit is a kind of sleep-walking turned to good account, and is, no doubt, perfectly compatible with complete unconsciousness." It would be interesting to ascertain if this habit be truly instinctive, and how the paddling in a circle would prevent their drifting ashore. That the locomotor activities concerned in swimming and diving are congenital, though no doubt subject to improvement and modification by practice and individual acquisition, admits, I think, of no question.

Passing to the powers of flight possessed by birds, it is clear that, if a truly instinctive activity, it is, in the great majority of birds, of the deferred type. Spalding kept young swallows caged until they were fully fledged, and then allowed them to escape. " One, on being set free, flew a yard or two close to the ground, and then rose in

* " The Structure and Life of Birds," pp. 171, 172.

the direction of a beech tree, which it gracefully avoided. It was seen for a considerable time sweeping round the beeches, and performing magnificent evolutions in the air high above them. The other, which was observed to beat the air with its wings more than usual, was soon lost to sight behind some trees. Titmice, tomtits, and wrens," says Spalding, " I have made the subjects of a similar experiment, and with similar results." * Professor Preyer writes as follows : † " The young redstarts which I have observed daily before they were fledged, receive no instructions for flying. But they exercise their wings in the nest before the first attempt at flight, often spreading them and making them whir. The first excursion is slower than the flight of the parents ; the young creature flies downward, but it never hits against anything, and after a few days the certainty of its flight is worthy of admiration. Confidence comes with practice."

The following experiment, to which Dr. Van Dyck, of Beyrout, drew my attention, may readily be performed. If a chick a day or two old be placed in a basket, held firmly in the hand, and then lowered rapidly through the air, the fledgeling will stretch out his little immature wings in such an attitude as would make them break his fall were they fully developed ; or will, if he be a little older, flap them with flight-like action, in either case showing an instinctive response. I do not find that moorhen chicks do this for some weeks, the early movements of the wings, which are very skinny and unfledged, being, as before mentioned, peculiar and alternating ; they are held out forwards over the back, and at the sides of the thrown-back head, when food is offered or when they scold each

---

* *Nature*, vol. xii. p. 507.

† " The Mind of the Child," part i. p. 239. Translated by H. W. Brown, New York.

other, or when they encounter some stranger, such as, for example, a chick, or even a little one of their own kind, whose wings or toes they will seize and worry, or perhaps an impertinent sparrow who invades their garden precincts.

My first experiments with more fully fledged birds were on house-martins. Two were taken from different nests. In one the wings were already well developed, and it flew round and round the room. In the other the wing feathers were shorter, and the wings as a whole blunter. This latter one could only flutter along the ground. I then allowed it to flutter over a table, and, when it reached the edge, it flew to the floor with definite progression, alighting awkwardly about four feet from the table. It also flew down from my hand held above my head, but had to be shaken off, as it was loth to start of itself, clinging tightly to my finger. Seeing that it could only flutter along the ground, it was very improbable that this bird had ever left the nest before it was brought to me, but of this I had no direct proof.

I asked my friend, Mr. H. F. Howard, who had kindly procured these martins for me, to watch a nest containing three young swallows, whose parents had built on a ledge specially placed there for the purpose in the porch of his uncle's house. In the fulness of time they came to the edge of the nest, standing there extending and fluttering their wings. One of them, about a fortnight old, or a day or two more, we took to the study. It clung to my finger with its sharp claws, but on being detached, a foot or so from the floor, flew off. Tossed into the air, it flew round three sides of the room, but did not rise much, striking the window-blind about four feet from the floor, and then coming to the ground. In further trials it alighted awkwardly on the edge of a shelf, and clung there, swallow-fashion, with tail against the ledge. Experiments with a second bird were to the same effect. Both seemed to be "feeling their wings;" and we believed that we could see some improvement in the art of flying even in the short time that the swallows were under observation. With the third nestling we made no experiments. When the others had been returned to the nest, we stood back a little and watched them, but were not prepared for what occurred. One got up on the edge of the nest, paused a moment, and then dived down and flew off through the outer door. Where it alighted we could not see, but we searched all round in vain, my fox-terrier Tony assisting eagerly in the search—so that it must have gone some distance, and probably alighted in a tree or shrub. The new experience of aerial locomotion was, it would seem, so satisfactory (and one can well imagine that it would bring with it a sense of novel and delightful power) that it had to be repeated.

Mr. Howard, who watched the further behaviour of the birds, tells me that the second swallow flew off about two hours later. He searched for the truants, and after some time found them perched on the bough of an ash tree, fifteen or twenty feet from the ground. The old birds, much excited, were feeding them and endeavouring to induce them to return to the nest; but all in vain. They then tried to induce the third swallow to leave the nest, but though he fluttered his wings, he could not quite summon up courage to fly. By ten o'clock the parent birds had gone to roost with their family scattered. Early next morning, however, all three were in the nest, and remained there all day. At about twelve o'clock on the following morning one flew out again, and was away till nightfall; and later the second took wing, though it returned at intervals during the day. It was not

till the third morning after our experiments with the two
that their companion took wing—or, to be accurate, that
all three young birds left the nest, for we had not marked
in any way the one that was left. They returned that
night, were absent the two following nights, but returned
again to the nest on each of the two succeeding ones.
After this Mr. Howard left the house.

In the following year my friend, Mr. Howard's uncle,
having reason to believe that one of a brood of young
swallows in his porch had died, procured a ladder and
ascended it to ascertain where the body was lying, but
found that it had disappeared, having evidently been carried
away by the parent birds. The three remaining young
swallows lay crouched against the wall, eying him for a
few moments, when one of them suddenly dashed past and
flew out of the porch, and was followed a second afterwards
by the remaining two birds. They flew into the garden,
and alighted in some shrubs, where they were found a few
minutes afterwards by the old birds, who immediately
proceeded to entice and induce them to fly into an adjoin-
ing ash tree (that in which the young birds were found
perching the preceding year), by flying backwards and
forwards to and from it. In the course of half an hour all
three young birds were safely perched on a high branch,
where they remained all day, and were fed by the parents,
but in the evening two of the young birds were again in
the porch.

These swallows had been carefully watched at intervals
every day, and, beyond occasionally stretching a wing and
preening it, had never made an attempt to use their wings
in flight before their sudden dash for freedom into the
open.

My friend, on a former occasion, was taken to see a
nest of young linnets in a low hedge. He stood watching

them for some minutes, and thought he would come again
and look at them, but whilst leaning over the nest, one of
them suddenly rose and flew; and all the rest followed in
the same direction, looking like thistle-down blown away
by a sudden puff of wind, and, like that, never more to
return to the same spot.

Both the jays and fly-catchers which I brought up from
quite an early stage, began to use their wings as they
hopped from perch to perch. This involved, however, but
little exercise of the power of flight, and little or no
guidance. The first time the fly-catchers were thrown into
the air in a room, they descended on to the floor in a
gentle curve. Their wings were not strong enough for
sustained and guided flight. The jays were more advanced
in development when they were first given a wider area
than their cage afforded. They flew round the room with
well-directed flight. One tried to alight on a shelf, and,
missing it, came to the ground. The other aimed for the
top of a picture, and, though it alighted awkwardly and
with some scrambling, yet contrived to maintain its hold,
and stood there panting.

Such birds as chicks, pheasants, and guinea-fowl use
the wings to assist them in running and in leaping up on
to and down from any low objects in their run. Individual
practice thus co-operates with the development of congenital
power. They appear to use the wings with some freedom
before they are sufficiently developed to sustain the weight
of the body.

These observations, now given in sufficient detail, confirm those of Spalding and Prof. Preyer. It is beyond
question that some birds are able, in the absence of
previous experience, to fly for considerable distances with
an accuracy which is purely congenital, if deferred. No
doubt there is some preparatory fluttering and flapping

of the wings in the nest, which serves to afford preliminary experience in co-ordination ; but the co-ordinations
of actual flight, with its more or less definite and guided
progress, must be regarded as far more delicate and
intricate than those for stationary wing-exercise on the
brink of the nest.   No doubt, under normal circumstances,
the parent birds accompany and encourage the young in
their flight.   No doubt imitation plays some part in flight-
development, though probably rather in affording a
stimulus to start on the wing, than as giving any
assistance in the details of wing-usage.   Still, such
observations as those which have been given show an
amount of congenital definiteness which cannot be over-
looked.   It forms the foundation of an activity which is
perfected by practice and experience.   For we may here
apply what Miss Hayward says in another connection in
"Bird Notes." *   "Birds inherit a great deal, but not
everything; and perhaps, as with ourselves, what they
inherit has to be cultivated."

It may, perhaps, be said that the young birds, before
they fly themselves, have ample opportunities of watching
the flight of their parents and other old birds.   This is true
enough.   But who ever learnt to do a difficult thing, even
passably well, by merely watching it done superbly by
another?   Let any one who has never played billiards or
lawn-tennis watch for a week the most skilled exponents
of the art, and catch with the eye, if he can, all the delicate
adjustments which mark the play of the master.   Then let
him take cue or racquet in hand, and see what he makes
of the game without previous individual practice.   He is
helpless.   The movements which looked so easy, the
delicate turns which seemed so natural, will not come to
the beginner, no matter how long he has watched their

* P. 80.

performance by others. And to suppose that a young bird can learn to fly as well as the little swallows flew, merely by watching their parents, is to suppose that which practical experience and the teaching of psychology alike show to be intrinsically improbable.

There is, however, a case—perhaps one of the most remarkable at present known—where a bird whose parents, we may note, take no interest in its welfare, flies almost as soon as it is hatched. This is the megapode. The family of the *Megapodidæ* are peculiar gallinaceous birds, of the Australian region. They deposit their eggs in large mounds, which are heaped up by the birds for that purpose (whence the popular name of "mound-birds," or "mound-builders"), or in holes in the warm sand. Many hens lay their eggs in the same spot, and take no further interest in their welfare, or that of the chicks which are hatched from them. The eggs are of relatively enormous size, and are laid at considerable intervals of time. From each there emerges a young bird which is already well fledged. I could scarcely believe that the stuffed specimen Mr. Chapman showed me in New York was that of a bird only just hatched. Dr. Worcester, who has had opportunities of studying *Megapodius cumingi* in the Philippine Islands, informs me that the newly hatched bird has often to make its way through six feet of earth before it reaches the surface. "It is a common occurrence," he says, in a letter from which he kindly allows me to quote, "in digging into mounds for eggs, to meet the young birds on their way to the surface. If not seized before they can free themselves they will invariably escape, as they fly actively and promptly. I once made an unsuccessful attempt to seize a newly hatched bird while digging in a mound, and it flew several rods into thick brush, escaping without difficulty."

Speaking of the allied Maleo (*Megacephalon rubripes*) of Celebes, which lays its eggs in warm volcanic sand, Mr. A. R. Wallace says,[*] " The young birds, on breaking the shell, work their way up through the sand and run off at once to the forest; and I was assured by Mr. Duivenboden, of Ternate, that they can fly the very day they are hatched. He had taken some eggs on board his schooner, which hatched during the night, and in the morning the little birds flew readily across the cabin."

Here, then, we have birds in which the instinctive co-ordination for flight is not, as in the great majority of birds, more or less deferred, but is connate. And there is in this case no opportunity for either parental instruction or the imitation of older birds.

A congenital basis of flight may therefore be taken as established. And on this basis is built the finished and most admirable product. For no one would be likely to contend that the consummate skill evinced in fully developed flight at its best—that activity which is performed sometimes with perhaps the maximum, at other times it would seem with the minimum, of animal effort— the hurtling flight of the falcon; the hovering of the kestrel; the wheeling of swifts; the rapid dart and sudden poise of the humming-bird; the easy sweep of the seagull; the downward glide of the stork, which has been observed to slide down an inclined plane of air with a descent of about one foot in five from the high rock on which the town of Constantine is built, and reach the ground at a distance of more than a mile from its starting-point;[†] or even the easy descent from the house-roof of a pigeon, with never a vibration of the wings, till just as it turns to windward in alighting;—no one, I say, would be likely to contend

[*] " Malay Archipelago," edit. 1894, p. 204.
[†] Britonniére, quoted in the " Dictionary of Birds," p 203.

that the exquisitely nice adjustments necessary for all the varieties of bird-flight are purely instinctive. In their finished form they are the result of practice and individual acquisition, but they are unquestionably founded on a congenital basis.

"As soon as he has the use of his wings," says Mr. Headley,[*] "a young gull may be seen for a good part of the day busily practising. And the great proficients in the art—eagles, vultures, storks, and albatrosses—have acquired their skill by experimenting on all varieties of currents." I have no doubt that Mr. Headley is right. One has only to watch with care the flight of birds to see how easily, and with what nicety and accuracy, they feel the wind and adapt their wing-spread to its force and direction. A hawk or a gull may be seen sailing round the coast-line or along a hill-ridge, utilizing the strong upthrow of air which the natural obstacle produces. In a light wind the wings of a tern or a gull are widely spread; but with a fresher breeze the wing is partially flexed so as to make a more acute angle where the wing bends near the middle of its length. Compare the way in which the sparrow leaps from the ground and whirs off, having no difficulty in rising, with the laboured start of the cormorant or the duck, which only by much effort succeeds in rising from the water and getting up speed. The albatross, with all his splendid powers of flight, flaps long over the surface of the sea ere he can rise freely; and he always starts against the wind. Observe, again, how the lark can rise in a vertical line from the meadow, how well he balances his body, and how skilfully he adjusts his rapid wing-strokes for mounting directly upwards. It cannot be doubted that all this specialized skill in flight is perfected by the individual not without much practice,

* "The Structure and Life of Birds," p. 232.

no matter how deeply the congenital ability to fly is founded in heredity.

Individual differences in the manner of flight are partly congenital as particularized modes of activity, partly enforced by congenital differences of structure. When, for example, a falcon is flown at a heron overhead, the quarry, as soon as he sees the hawk, flies upwards, the falcon following. The difference in mode of flight is then well seen. The heron, with his large concave blunt wings and light body, rises in narrow circles. The hawk, with her long pointed wings and relatively heavy body, sweeps through a wide spiral, more than making up for the greater distance she has to cover by her rapidity of flight. This continues until the falcon has gained sufficient advantage to enable her to stoop at the quarry.

The different modes of flight in correlation with different types of wing; the problems connected with soaring and sailing flight; these are tempting themes. But they are beyond our present purpose, and I have nothing new to say on them. That the bird of skilled flight is able to feel in some way the strength and varying direction of the air-currents seems beyond question. Is it the pressure on the feathers of the breast that affords the necessary data which the bird utilizes in the acquisition of that experience which through much practise makes flight perfect? We do not know. We can only say that the experience, however gained, is a factor in that acquired power which is founded on a congenital basis due to hereditary transmission.

CHAPTER IV.

FURTHER OBSERVATIONS ON YOUNG BIRDS.

Our consideration of the instinctive activities of walking,
running, swimming, diving, and flying serves to bring out
the fact that, in such cases, what is inherited is a congenital co-ordination of motor responses under the
appropriate conditions of stimulation. Not only is there
inherited a given structure of leg or wing, but a nervous
system through which there is an automatic distribution of
outgoing currents to the several muscles concerned; so
that, without learning or experience, they are called into
play with nicely graded intensity, and exhibit complex
contractions and relaxations in serial order, thus giving
rise to instinctive behaviour of an eminently adaptive
nature.

In discussing the activities concerned in feeding, we
found that there was a similar congenital co-ordination
of motor responses for pecking at a small object within a
suitable distance. But, from the observations, it seems
that the selection of certain of these objects and the
rejection of others is a matter of individual experience.
We were not, however, prepared to found a sweeping
generalization on a limited number of observations on a
few species, and freely admitted that there may very
probably be cases where particular sensory stimuli give
rise to appropriate congenital responses; in other words,

that there may be, in some birds, instinctive avoidance of certain objects when they are first presented to sight.

We have now to consider the evidence for instinctive fear of particular animals or objects. For the present, however, the matter must be regarded from the purely observational point of view. We will not now attempt to determine what is the nature, or what the manner of origin, of the emotional state as such. That must be deferred to a future chapter. What we have to seek is evidence of instinctive response, such as shrinking from an object in such a way as to show an inherited dread of it.

The reader will remember that there is no instinctive fear of bees or wasps as such, but that there is a shrinking response, probably instinctive, from *any* largish strange object, especially if it moves vigorously or makes some such noise as buzzing. This leads one to suspect that the instinctive dread is not of any particular object of sight, but rather of certain modes of activity. I have trained my fox-terrier to remain passive and undemonstrative in presence of the birds, though his trembling muscles as he stands over them shows that he is exercising no little control. None of the birds have shown the slightest fear of him under these conditions. Pheasants, partridges, and plovers would peck at his nose as he smelt at them, and run in between his legs. A wild duck, three days old, nearly broke down his self-control as it mumbled at his lips. A chick, two and a half days old, when introduced to the dog, who sat up with his head held down, sniffing at the little fellow, ran in and out round his forepaws, and then crept daintily in under the dog's body and cuddled down in the warmth. Opening the door softly to call one of my servants, who was in the next room, and whose feelings would, I knew, be touched at the sight, I saw that Tony, so soon as my back was partly turned, had seized the

G

chick (matters having really gone too far!) and had gently carried it a yard or so across the room. He dropped it at once, and looked sufficiently sheepish; but the chick was quite unhurt, and apparently not much, if at all, frightened, showing no fear of the dog half an hour later. Neither chicks, pheasants, nor jays—not even the little fly-catchers—showed any signs of dread of a kitten, nor did chicks of an older cat.

The moorhen chicks, though not afraid of me, always struck their odd attitude and scolded, or seemed to scold, when I picked them up. They liked to be caressed in the hand, and would come to my call, and their scolding as I gently grasped them was probably only an energetic demand for worms. They struck the same attitude before the dog when he smelt at them; but, when he lay down, would peck at his toes and the points of his ears with consummate impertinence. He took one or other of them in his mouth two or three times, but quite gently. The one which was taken to Yorkshire came up one afternoon when the dog was lapping from the tin which contained the birds' water, and pecked vigorously at his nose, following it up with a dab which narrowly missed his eye. On another occasion the moorhen hopped on to and sat on the edge of the basin in which was the terrier's sopped biscuit, and pecked the dog when he came for his share. It must be mentioned that Tony is very gentle in his ways, except where rats, rabbits, and such fair game are concerned, and never acted aggressively towards the birds. The moorhen was not afraid of the large gentle sheep-dogs on the farm. But how a blundering, vigorous puppy scared him and made him dive we remember.

While there are, no doubt, specific and individual differences, some birds being naturally shyer and more timid than others, there is not apparently much difference in the young of wild and tame birds. The wild and tame duck brought up together, and with other birds, showed no distinguishable difference in this respect. Dr. Rae, however, a careful observer, says,[*] " If the eggs of a wild duck are placed with those of a tame one under a hen to be hatched, the ducklings from the former, on the very day they leave the egg, will immediately endeavour to hide themselves, or take to the water, if there is any water, should any person approach, whilst the young from the tame duck's eggs will show little or no alarm, indicating in both cases a clear instance of instinct or 'inherited memory.' " My own observations, so far as they go, do not corroborate this statement. I have mentioned with what impudent familiarity the wild duck treated my fox-terrier, and must repeat that I have observed but little difference in instinctive timidity between the young of wild and domesticated birds. Mr. Charles A. Allen says [†] of the young of the black duck (*Anas obscura*), which he observed under natural conditions, " They showed no fear, and would cuddle under one's hand very confidingly."

The little birds soon get thoroughly accustomed to their surroundings, and are then shy of any new and strange object placed among them. My jays were wont to bathe in a shallow tin ; but when I introduced a white basin into the cage, they were much scared, jumping and fluttering to and fro, and uttering their harsh note. The first time I placed the shallow tin in a room where there was a mixed brood—wild duck, tame duck, chick, guinea-fowl, and pheasant—the three latter were curiously afraid, standing and looking at it with outstretched necks, and uttering

[*] *Nature*, July 19, 1883. Quoted in "Mental Evolution in Animals," p. 196.

[†] "The Nesting of the Black Duck on Plum Island" : *The Auk*, vol. x. (1893), p. 57.

the alarm or danger note, as they did also when I threw among them a large ball of screwed-up paper. Of a Java sparrow, too, in a cage they seemed afraid. The ducks, wild and tame alike, seemed to show any disquiet they may have felt less markedly—perhaps because they have no danger note which can be readily noticed. But they did not go near the tin for more than an hour. I have omitted to try the effect of introducing the dog to their notice for the first time at a comparatively late period—after they are ten days or so old. I should expect them then to show signs of timidity; not because he is a dog, but because he is new and strange to their experience. For in some respects timidity increases with increased experience of the ways of this wicked world.

Very noticeable is the effect on chicks of any sudden noise—a sneeze, a clap of the hands, a sharply struck chord on the violin, or the sudden pitching among them of a piece of screwed-up paper. They scatter and crouch, or sometimes simply crouch down where they are; the constant piping " cheep-cheep " ceases, and for a moment there is dead stillness, each bird silent and motionless. In a minute or so up they get, and resume their cheeping notes. Plovers, when they hear a sudden noise, also crouch at once. The effect on pheasants is somewhat different. I have seen them stop dead and remain silent at a sudden sharp knock at the door. While two of them, thirteen days old, were walking about and uttering a contented peeping sound, a loud chord was struck on the violin. Both stopped dead; the peeping noise ceased, and one of them who was walking with his leg just lifted from the ground remained for half a minute in this attitude, with neck stretched out, as if struck quite still and mute in the attitude in which he chanced to be when the sharp sound fell on his ears. Then he took a few steps, and again stopped quite still for about the same period.

Mr. F. A. Knight well describes this mode of behaviour in the pheasant chick. He tells * how an old bird, seen on Exmoor, "silently emerging from the tangle of the hedge, stalks across the path with slow and stately pose, moving her head jauntily, as if with the conscious pride of motherhood. A yard behind her follow in single file the little members of her family, struggling manfully through the jungle by the hedgerow. Two of them have just got clear—tiny, fluffy balls of down, not many days out of the shell—when the old bird, suddenly aware of danger, utters two sharp notes of warning. Instantly the two small figures are still, as if they were turned to stone. They do not even move so much as to crouch down in the grass. One of them had just turned its head—perhaps to look for its companions—and so it stands, motionless. A new-comer would have little chance of making out the tiny forms among the stones and herbage of the bank. We pass within a yard of them, and still they make no sign. Meanwhile the old bird has vanished through the opposite hedge, and, when the danger has passed, will rejoin her little charges."

The effect of a sudden startling noise on moorhen chicks is different. It seems to make them run away to some corner. I was observing one day some little plovers and a young moorhen, all about a week old, when the door slammed. The effect was curiously different. The plovers dropped where they stood; the moorhen chick started so violently, and began to run with such vigour, that he toppled over and lay struggling on the floor. A day or two before, the moorhens and plovers were placed together in the same enclosure for the first time. The former, which were five days old, at once gave the danger or alarm note. One ran away; another showed fight and pecked

* "By Moorland and Sea," p. 168.

at one of the plovers, but timidly withal. In a quarter of an hour or so they were all in happy agreement. Of my quiet dog these little moorhens showed no fear, but of vigorous young plovers they seemed somewhat afraid !

The following observations of Spalding's have often been quoted : "When twelve days old one of my little *protégés,* while running about beside me, gave the peculiar chirr whereby they announce the approach of danger. I looked up, and behold a sparrow-hawk was hovering at a great height overhead. Equally striking was the effect of the hawk's voice when heard for the first time. A young turkey, which I had adopted when chirping within the uncracked shell, was, on the morning of the tenth day of its life, eating a comfortable breakfast from my hand, when the young hawk, in a cupboard just beside us, gave a shrill chip, chip, chip. Like an arrow the poor turkey shot to the other side of the room, and stood there motionless and dumb with fear until the hawk gave a second cry, when it darted out at the open door right to the extreme end of the passage, and there, silent and crouched in a corner, remained for ten minutes. Several times during the course of that day it again heard these alarming sounds, and in every instance with similar manifestations of fear."

With regard to the first observation, on the effect of a sparrow-hawk overhead, it may perhaps fairly be questioned whether the reaction was in response to the particularized stimulus of the sight of a hawk as such. I noticed that a moorhen chick was startled and cowered in the reeds when some geese flew at a considerable height above him. Miss Hayward noted a case in point. A robin, she says,* " was piping on the edge of my veranda as usual, asking for a bit of bacon ; but when I went to the window, opened it,

* "Bird Notes," p. 105.

and threw the bacon to him, instead of picking it up, he stood quite still, with his eye laboriously turned towards the zenith; and so he remained staring. . . . Then I opened the window wide and looked up; and there passing over the house and flying at a great height was a heron. That was what the robin was watching." Although a heron may occasionally make a meal of a robin, I question whether we may legitimately infer that there was any instinctive recognition of an enemy as such. At the same time, it is commonly believed that fowls in a yard evince an excitement when a hawk flies overhead, which they do not show when a rook passes over. It is, however, probable that such discrimination, if it be a fact, is due to the hen handing on the traditional fear of a hawk by uttering a warning note, as her parents had done when she was a chick. If so, chicks hatched in the incubator should show no such discrimination. Those who have shot under a kite know that game-birds are deceived by a passable but very inexact imitation of a bird of prey.

So, too, with regard to the cry of a hawk which startled Spalding's young turkey. I have seen young birds startled by such a variety of strange and unusual sounds, that I am inclined to believe that had Spalding struck a loud chord on a violin, his turkey would have behaved in much the same way; that, in a word, there is in this observation no evidence of instinctive knowledge of the hawk as a bird of prey, and therefore dangerous, but an instinctive response to a sharp, unusual sound.

To ascertain whether there was any instinctive avoidance of a snake-like animal on the part of young pheasants, I procured a large blind worm and set it in front of the incubator drawer in which the birds passed the night. On opening the drawer, the pheasants hopped out almost on to the top of the blind worm, which was fairly active; but they took no notice of it. Presently, however, one of the birds pecked at its eye, and then again and again at the tongue as it played in and out of the blind worm's mouth. This observation naturally leads one to surmise that the constant tongue-play in snakes may act as a lure for young and inexperienced birds; and that some cases of so-called fascination may be simply the fluttering of birds round this tempting object. I distinctly remember, when a boy, seeing a grass-snake with head elevated and quite motionless, and round it three or four young birds fluttering nearer and nearer. It looked like fascination; but it may well have been that each hoped to be the first to catch that tempting but elusive worm! Presently they would, no doubt, be invited to step inside.

Mr. F. Howard Collins tells me that when cruising in the Mediterranean off the south-east coast of Spain, and out of sight of land, during half a gale, a dove took refuge on his yacht, evidently blown off the shore by the wind. The bird displayed at no time any fear or alarm whatever at the men on board, who took it into the forecastle, where from the first it seemed quite at home, and remained there quite contentedly, hopping about, picking up food, and roosting, and all this although more than a dozen men were constantly passing to and fro. No cage or restriction was used. It remained on board some six months, until the cruise was ended, and then was taken ashore by one of the men, with whom it lived at least a year or more. Whether the tameness arose from that common cause, hunger and starvation, or from the fact that the bird had never previously seen a man, must remain unknown.

All these observations seem to lend support to Mr. Hudson's contention that fear in birds is, in reference to particular animals, a matter of "experience and tradition." *   There is probably no instinctive fear of man, and if one move gently and quietly, one may feed young fledgelings in the nest.   There is probably no instinctive fear of a cat, and if she creep up stealthily she may get close to young birds, unless they hear the alarm note of their parents or other birds.   What does seem to evoke an instinctive response is the rapid approach of any quickly moving vigorous animal, or even a leaf driven by the breeze.   "A piece of newspaper," says Mr. Hudson, "carried accidentally by the wind is as great an object of terror to an inexperienced young bird as a buzzard sweeping down with death in its talons." As experience is gained, it is the unusual which evokes the response which indicates fear.   A plover will drop and crouch on hearing the crisp crunch of a paper bag crushed in the hand.

With birds reared under natural conditions by the parents, their alarm note serves as a warning, and, as Mr. Hudson well describes, tradition hands on the fear of particular enemies and dangerous animals.   "Hawks," he says, "are the most open, violent, and persistent enemies birds have ; and it is really wonderful to see how well the persecuted kinds appear to know the power for mischief possessed by different raptorial species, and how exactly the amount of alarm exhibited is in proportion to the extent of the danger to be apprehended." These differences, however, would seem to be neither the result of heredity nor of merely individual acquisition, but of racial experience handed on by tradition through the instrumentality of danger notes.

Here too, however, as in the case of response to the sight of materials which may serve for food, or which are,

* "Naturalist in La Plata," chap v. p. 53.

on the other hand, distasteful, we must avoid the error of a too sweeping generalization. No doubt there may be cases in which instinctive fear is evoked at the sight of particular objects of alarm. To deny this would be going beyond the evidence, and would savour strongly of dogmatizing on negative premises. Where tradition is necessarily excluded, as seemingly is the case with the megapodes, it may be that the instinctive avoidance of any rapidly approaching animal, whether it be harmful or harmless, is insufficient to guard the young from destruction; and there may be ingrained in the megapode constitution through natural selection a congenital fear of such animals.

We must now pass to the notes emitted by young birds. Whatever may be the case with the elaborated song of birds, which is regarded by Mr. C. A. Witchell and others as for the most part the result of tradition and imitation, there can be no question that the sounds emitted by many young birds are truly instinctive, and that some of them are fairly differentiated from the first. In domestic chicks I could distinguish at least six notes. First the gentle " piping," expressive of contentment, heard on taking the little bird in one's hand. A further low note, a sort of double sound, seems to be associated with extreme pleasure, when, for example, one strokes the chick's back and caresses it. Very characteristic and distinct is the danger note—a sound difficult to describe, but readily recognizable. This is heard on the second or third day. If a large humble-bee, a black beetle, a big worm, a lump of sugar, or in fact anything largish or strange, be thrown to the chicks, the danger note is at once heard. Then there is the cheeping, piping sound, expressive apparently of wanting something. It generally ceases when one goes to them and throws some grain, or even stands near them. My chicks were accustomed to my presence in the room,

and generally were restless when I left them; and under
such circumstances they made this sound.   Then there is
the sharp squeak when one seizes them against their
inclination.   Lastly, there is the shrill cry of distress,
when, for example, one of them is separated from the rest.
A chick that was brought up with ducklings always cried
thus when they were taken away for a swim.   I have very
little doubt that all these sounds have, or soon acquire, a
suggestive value of emotional import for the other chicks.
Certainly the danger note at once places others, both of
their own kind and of different species, on the alert.   But
the suggestive value seems to be, in part at least, the
result of association, and the product of experience; though
this is a point upon which it is difficult to speak with any
certainty.   With pheasants a gentle piping note of contentment, and a shriller cry of distress were differentiated
from the first.   On the sixth day an alarm or danger note,
much like that of the domestic chick, was heard when the
little pheasant came suddenly upon a piece of paper the
size of a half-crown; and afterwards, if I seized in my
forceps a worm from one of the pheasants, he would utter
the note and show fight.   Another bird uttered the note
when he saw a Java sparrow in a cage.   The complaining
note of the partridge is uttered six or seven times quickly
in succession, followed by a pause.   The note of the plover
is high-pitched and much like that so familiar in the older
bird.   So, too, the guinea-fowl in down utters from the first
notes quite characteristic of its kind.   Its danger note, also,
is not unlike that of the domestic chick.   The piping of the
ducklings is comparatively monotonous, and I have not
heard in them any danger or alarm note.   Moorhen chicks,
as above noted, cheep in the egg before they are hatched.
On the first day two notes were marked—a calling note
lower in pitch than that of the chick, and rather harsh

and raucous; and a "tweet tweet" of pleasure, something
like the contented note of a canary bird. At the end of a
week there seemed to be five distinguishable notes or types
of note. First a harsh "crek crek" when asking for food,
when excited in any way, or angry; this was always
uttered in crouching attitude, with head thrown back and
the wings held out and forward, waving about in the
curious and exceedingly characteristic manner before
noted; secondly, a querulous call, expressive of discomfort;
thirdly, a sharper, quicker sound of pain, when, for
example, a moorhen's wing was seized by one of his
neighbours; fourthly, a gentle, persistent sound of contentment; and, lastly, the canary-like "tweet tweet" of
perfect contentment. That, at any rate, the harsher note
is of suggestive value there seems no doubt; for I have
again and again seen one thrown into the characteristic
attitude on hearing the "crek crek" of its companion.

That suggestive warning notes are of great value to
birds in their free life can scarcely be doubted. Miss
Haywood says,* "I have frequently seen a bird that was
feeding quietly at the window unaware of my presence at
the other side, turn sharply round on hearing the warning
note of the robin, and look about it for danger." So, too,
it is a matter of familiar knowledge that, under natural
conditions, the various sounds made by the hen are of
suggestive value to her chicks; but how far the several
tones produce a congenitally definite response, or how far
the play of individual experiences reaches in this matter,
it is hard to say. Mr. Hudson, however, states, as the
result of personal observation, that a young bird hammering in the shell will cease in its efforts on hearing the
warning note of the parent bird. And he also states that
the warning cries of the foster-parent have no effect on

* "Bird Notes," p. 39.

the young cow-bird (*Moluthrus*) at any time. On the whole I am disposed to believe that the warning cry evokes a truly instinctive response.

Let us now turn to some apparently insignificant but not uninteresting activities, some of which constitute distinctive traits in the several kinds of young birds, and all of which, though they may be perfected in definiteness through individual practice and guidance, have a sufficiently definite congenital basis to be regarded as fundamentally instinctive.

A duckling a few hours old will scratch the side of his head. It is true, he may topple over in the process through insufficient co-ordination; for the simultaneous performance of poising on one leg and having a good scratch is no easy matter. But let not either the familiar simplicity of the act of scratching, nor some observed difficulty in carrying it out, blind us to the fact that this is a congenital activity, and that of no little complexity, indicating a quite definite inherited organic nexus. A local irritation (I have produced this artificially with young birds, and found the response quite definite) sets agoing a most complete set of movements in the hind limb of that side, the result of which is that just that particular spot is scratched; or sometimes the bill is applied to the point of irritation in the body, *which is definitely localized* in the absence of previous practice or the establishment of "local signs." Similarly, a young moorhen chick that had seized a piece of lettuce, which stuck in its mouth and projected at the hinder end of the gape, scratched at it rapidly and vigorously and with perfect definiteness. And a recently hatched pheasant, fed by hand, whose bill had got clogged with food, wiped it on the ground with exceeding precision and neatness. These may perhaps be regarded rather as reflex actions than as instinctive activities. As we have seen, the line is hard to draw. In any case, they indicate that accuracy of response, implying great nicety of organic mechanism, which is at the root of all instinctive activity.

The preening of the down is definitely congenital. I have seen a little plover, hatched in the evening, and taken out of the incubator drawer for the first time next morning, bend back his head and apply the bill to the down of throat and breast. In moorhen chicks the specialized way in which, after a bath, they wring the water out of the fluffy down-feathers and shake it from the bill with a little jerk of the head is noteworthy, though I have not observed its performance for the first few days. Both chicks and pheasants and other young birds, when they are freshly released from the basket in which they sleep, run with little spurts indicative of the energy accumulated during a period of inactivity and repose; ducklings and moorhen chicks sometimes do the same. Quite different, however, is the little dance with which somewhat older chicks, and especially young moorhens, greet their liberty and the freshness of the morning air. Ducklings stretch their necks and flap their immature wings, and then race round in mere exuberance of spirits. And the way in which they preen, rubbing the bill to and fro over the breast, applying it to the tail and rubbing it and their whole head across and along the back, notes them as ducks to the manner born. The scratching of the ground by chicks and pheasants is definitely congenital. They did this in some cases on the third or fourth day, while in others it was deferred till the eighth or ninth, the conditions being closely similar, and the surface that of newspaper with generally a little sand strewn on it. I noticed that some scratched very vigorously on the smooth surface of the empty tin in which they generally found water. Keenness after food is a predisposing cause. I have described how a little pheasant, which was fed on wasp grubs from my hand, would, when he had finished them all, leap upon my palm and scratch for more. But though the scratching is unquestionably congenital, its continuance is dependent upon experience of some good accruing from the action. A chick placed in a rearer at night, in the run of which there was sand and earth and pieces of coke or charcoal, together with some grain and other food, would scratch here for chance grains buried in the earth; but when, in the day, he had the run of the room, on the floor of which only a sprinkling of sand and grit was scattered (the grain being therefore readily visible), he rarely scratched after the first day or two. Experience had guided the originally congenital activity in accordance with circumstances. I did not notice the guinea-fowl scratch the ground. Its tendency seemed rather to thrust the beak sideways through the earth. Very curious was the way in which the little plovers thrust their bills deeply into the soil and ploughed it forwards in a way quite different from that of rasorial birds. Sand-dusting in chicks is also definitely instinctive, and was observed generally about the eighth day. There was only a little sand strewn over the newspaper or floor, so not much good came of the operation. Still they persisted in it for a quarter of an hour at a time, squatting down, ruffling themselves, and fluttering their wings in the most approved fashion. The ducklings thoroughly enjoyed a dip. Each morning, at nine o'clock, a large black tray was placed in their pen, and on it a flat tin containing water. To this they eagerly ran, drinking and washing in it. On the sixth morning the tray and tin were given them in the usual way, but without any water. They ran to it, scooped at the bottom, and made all the motions of the beak as if drinking. They squatted in it, dipping their heads and waggling their tails as usual. For some ten minutes they continued to wash in non-existent water, the coolness of the tin to their breasts perhaps giving them some satisfaction. Then I gave them water. The next day the experiment was repeated with the dry tin. Again they ran to it, shovelling along the bottom with their beaks, and squatting down in it. But they soon gave up the attempt to find satisfaction in a dry bath. On the third morning they waddled up to the dry tin, and sadly departed. One of my moorhen chicks, about a week old, showed, once and once only, a slight dipping up and down of its breast in the tin, but soon desisted; nor was he seen again to do anything of the sort, though he and the others enjoyed standing in the water. Some five weeks later, one of the birds was taken to a farmhouse in Yorkshire, and, on the first morning after his arrival, was carried down to the beck. When he reached the part of the stream where it ran and broke over the pebbles, he stopped, ducked, and took an elaborate bath, dipping his head well under, flicking the water over himself, ruffling his feathers, and behaving as such birds do when they bathe. Each day he did the same, with a vigour which increased up to about the third morning, and then remained constant. Whether this was the same bird which before made an abortive attempt, I am not certain, but probably not. In any case, the definiteness of the first regular bath was very marked. When the moorhen chicks were just a month old, I noticed for the first time the characteristic upward flick of the tail, then still quite black and downy, the white under tail-coverts of the adult bird not appearing (as seven yellowish-white feathers on each side, which were spread by the bird when specially happy) for another month.

With regard to bathing, the following observation on

jays is worth noting. Ten days after receiving them as nestlings about a week or week and a half old, I placed in their cage a shallow tin containing water. They took no notice of it, having probably never seen water before, for they were fed chiefly on sopped food, which gave them all they required. Presently one of them hopped into it, whether purposely or by accident it is difficult to say, squatted in it, bending his legs, and at once fluttered his feathers, as birds do when they bathe, though those of the breast scarcely touched the water. The other seized the edge of the tin in his bill, and then pecked at the inside, thus wetting his beak. He too fluttered his feathers in a similar fashion, though he was not in the water at all. A little later the first again entered the tin, and dipped his breast under water; this was followed by much fluttering and splashing. The bird took a good bath, as did the other shortly afterwards, and then spent half an hour in a thorough grooming, with much fluttering of wings, the crest feathers being constantly raised and lowered, expressive of an emotional state.

Mr. H. T. Charbonnier tells me of a similar observation of his own. A magpie about five weeks old, which he had reared from quite an early stage of its life, when placed in a cage and supplied with a pan of water, made one or two pecks at the surface, and then, outside the pan without entering the water at all, proceeded to go through all the gestures of a bird bathing, ducking its head, fluttering its wings and tail, squatting down, and spreading itself out on the ground. It afterwards and by degrees acquired the habit of bathing really, and seemed always anxious for a bath in rainy weather.

The inquisitiveness of the jays was well marked. Soon after being placed in a cage, they examined every corner, every projecting bit of wire, and every mark on the wood at the sides and the glass above. Any new object introduced was carried about and curiously examined. A wax match was soon torn to shreds. After hopping about with an object for a time, and trying to tear it to pieces, they would take it to a corner of the cage, and try and hammer it in with vigorous blows of the beak. Again and again, as it caught their eye, they would return to it, hammer at it for a while, and then hop off. Under natural conditions they would no doubt have buried it. Many little, apparently instinctive, traits were observed, such as the attitude assumed in sleeping, with the head turned, and the bill buried in the feathers, and the lifting of the head over the wing when they wished to scratch the head; but further details would only prove wearisome.

I have already, perhaps, presumed too largely on the reader's patience. The diary-notes—themselves selected from a considerable body of observations recorded day by day—may well appear in many cases to savour of triviality. It is only, however, by careful and minute observation that we can hope to gauge the length to which heredity runs. In anatomical investigations we must pay patient attention to details of structure; and in investigations into the phenomena of habit and instinct, we must not shrink from the labour and the expenditure of time involved in daily and almost hourly observation, if we would attempt to distinguish between what is inherited in a relatively perfect condition, and what is acquired by experience or through imitation.

Such observations as have been given in this and the preceding chapters require to be extended to other species, and over longer periods of time. If what is here set down should induce others to take up a mode of investigation which will be found full of interest, and in which much still remains to be done, one of the objects in placing on record the details of my own work will be fulfilled. There are many activities and modes of behaviour which are generally assumed to be instinctive and due to heredity, but which may be the result of tradition, handed on by example from parents to offspring. Partridges, for example, when they jug, nestling close together at night, would seem, from the appearance of the droppings, which are generally deposited in a circle of only a few inches in diameter, to arrange themselves in a circle, tails inwards and heads outwards. Is this behaviour instinctive or is it traditional? The young of the colin (*Ortyx virginiana*), we are told,* "when the shades of evening approached, crowded together in a circle on the ground, and prepared themselves for the slumbers of the night by placing their tails all together, with their pretty mottled chins facing to the front in a watchful round-robin." The fact that these birds behave thus, apparently instinctively, would lead one to surmise that the behaviour is instinctive in the partridge. My own birds died at too early an age for this point to be determined.

We may now summarize some of the general conclusions to be drawn from our observations as follows :—

1. That which is congenitally definite as instinctive behaviour is essentially a motor response or train of motor responses. Mr. Herbert Spencer's description of instinct as compound reflex action is thus justified.

2. These often show very accurate and nicely adjusted congenital or hereditary co-ordinations.

3. They are evoked by stimuli, the general type of which is fairly definite, and may, in some cases, be in response to particular objects. Of the latter possibility we have, however, but little satisfactory evidence.

4. There does not seem to be any convincing evidence

* Yarrell, "British Birds," *sub. spec.*

of inherited ideas or knowledge (as the term is popularly used); that is to say, the facts can be equally well explained on the view that what is inherited is of the nature of an organic response.

5. Association of ideas is strong, and is rapidly formed as the result of individual acquisition.

6. Acquired definiteness is built, through association, on the foundation of congenital responses, which are modified, under experience, to meet new circumstances.

7. Acquired definiteness may pass, through frequent repetition, into more or less stereotyped habit.

CHAPTER V.

OBSERVATIONS ON YOUNG MAMMALS.

THE most systematic observations on young mammals with which I am acquainted are those of Dr. Wesley Mills.[*] They deal with the sensory endowments, instinctive activities, the early habits of the dog, pure-bred and mongrel, the cat, the rabbit, and the guinea-pig; and are recorded in the form of diaries, to which comparisons of the results obtained are appended, and from which conclusions are drawn and clearly set forth. The observations on the guinea-pig supplement and extend those of Prof. Preyer published in his work on the " Mind of the Child."[†] Spalding contributed to the British Association in 1875 a paper [‡] in which he described a few observations on young pigs. And Mr. W. H. Hudson has recorded [§] some interesting observations on the sheep and deer of South America.

Just as the young of different kinds of birds are hatched out at different stages of development—the megapode being able to fly shortly after birth, and the domestic chick emerging from the shell in a far more advanced stage of development than the pigeon or the rook—so is it with mammals. Not to do more than mention monotremes, like the duck-bill (*Ornithorhyncus*) that lays eggs from which

[*] *Trans. Roy. Soc. Canada*, sect. iv. (1894), pp. 31–62 ; and 2nd series sect. iv. (1895–6), pp. 191–252.

[†] Part i., " The Senses and the Will." Eng. trans. by H. W. Brown. New York, 1893.

[‡] " Habit and Acquisition." See *Nature*, vol. xii. p. 507.

[§] " The Naturalist in La Plata," chap. vi.

very immature young emerge, or marsupials, like the kangaroo, in which the young are brought forth in an immature condition, and are then transferred to a pouch; there is much difference even among the placental mammals with which we are familiar. The day-old puppy is far more helpless than the day-old lamb; the new-born kitten is much more immature than the new-born guinea-pig. And in comparing the activities, or the sensory endowments, of the young at birth, this fact must be taken into consideration.

The puppy and the kitten, for example, can do little more than crawl for some days after birth, and are slow in attaining definite and accurate co-ordination of the hind limbs. Rabbits, rats, and mice move about in a sprawling, feeble way; and though a rabbit a day or two old can stand for a moment, yet when he shifts his position he only crawls awkwardly. Cattle, sheep, and deer, however, can stand and walk very soon after birth. "Though both the red and fallow fawns can follow the hinds within a few minutes after birth," says Mr. Cornish,* "the careful mothers hide them in the tall fern and nettles, and it is only the older fawns that are seen in the open ground or trotting with the herds. When the fawn is born, the mother gently pushes it with her nose until it lies down in the fern, and then goes away and watches from a distance, only returning at intervals to feed it, or, if the wind changes or rain threatens, to draw it away to more sheltered ground."

"I have had frequent opportunities," says Mr. W. H. Hudson,† "of observing the young, from one to three days old, of the *Cervus campestris*, the common deer of the pampas, and the perfection of its instincts at that tender

---

* "Wild England of To-day," pp. 124, 125.
† "The Naturalist in La Plata," pp. 110, 111.

age seems very wonderful in a ruminant. When the doe
with fawn is approached by a horseman, even when accompanied with dogs, she stands perfectly motionless, gazing
fixedly at the enemy, the fawn motionless at her side ; and
suddenly, as if at a preconcerted signal, the fawn rushes
directly away from her at its utmost speed, and, going to a
distance of six hundred to a thousand yards, conceals itself
in a hollow in the ground or among the long grass, lying
down very close with neck stretched out horizontally, and
will thus remain until sought by the dam. When very
young it will allow itself to be taken, making no further
effort to escape. After the fawn has run away, the doe
still maintains her statuesque attitude, as if resolved to
await the onset, and only when the dogs are close to her
she also rushes away, but invariably in a direction as
nearly opposite to that taken by the fawn as possible. At
first she runs slowly, with a limping gait, and frequently
pausing as if to entice her enemies on, like a partridge,
duck, or plover when driven from its young ; but as they
begin to press her more closely her speed increases,
becoming greater the further she succeeds in leading them
from the starting-point."

Of the sheep on the pampas, the same author tells us *
that the first instinct of the newly born lamb is to struggle
up on its feet; its second to suck; and its next important
instinct, which comes into play from the moment it can
stand on its feet, to follow after any object receding from
it, and, on the other hand, to run from anything approaching it. " If the dam turns round and approaches it from
even a very short distance, it will start back and run from
her in fear, and will not understand her voice when she
bleats to it; at the same time it will confidently follow
after a man, dog, horse, or any other animal moving from

* *Loc. cit.*, pp. 106-108.

it. A very common experience on the pampas, in the sheep country, is to see a lamb start up from sleep and follow the rider, running close to the heels of the horse." "This blundering instinct is," however, "quickly laid aside when the lamb has learned to distinguish its dam from other objects, and its dam's voice from other sounds."

Speaking of the old native breed of sheep, which, descended from those introduced three centuries ago, have in great measure lost the qualities which make sheep valuable to man as a food and wool-producing animal, but have, on the other hand, to some extent recovered the vigour of a wild animal, Mr. Hudson says,* "I have often seen a lamb dropped on the frosty ground in bitterly cold windy weather in midwinter, and in less than five seconds struggle to its feet, and seem as vigorous as any day-old lamb of other breeds. The dam, impatient at the short delay, and not waiting to give it suck, has then started off at a brisk trot after the flock, with the lamb, scarcely a minute in the world, running freely at her side."

Some other mammals, belonging to different groups, are fairly active very soon after birth. Guinea-pigs, seventeen hours old, placed on Dr. Mills's study table, ran so fast as nearly to reach the edge before they were caught. Hares are said to run almost as soon as they are born. Mr. Hudson, in the chapter just quoted, describes how quite young bats were able (though they could not fly) to "work their way upwards through the leaves and slender twigs in the most adroit manner," until they reached a considerable height, "when they proceeded to hook themselves on to a twig and assume the inverted position side by side." If we may credit "the experienced hunter," whom Thunberg quotes, a hippopotamus calf, only just born, escaped from the Hottentots who rushed

* *Loc. cit.*, pp. 108, 109.

upon it, "and at once made the best of its way to the river." One would like confirmation of this observation, but it is not readily obtainable. There is an oft-quoted statement of Spalding's of which confirmation should not be hard to get. He put a new-born pig in a bag, keeping it there for seven hours, and then placed it outside the sty, ten feet from its mother. It ran straightway to the sty, went along the outside of it, and tried to get to the sow, though to reach her it had to struggle under a bar, a feat it successfully accomplished. Spalding supposed that it was guided by the maternal grunting ; but, as Prof. Preyer points out, guidance by the sense of smell is not excluded. If Spalding be correct, there is shown an accurate sensing of the direction from which the sound proceeded.

I have consulted those who have opportunities for observing, and asked them to repeat the observation. But, beyond some strong expressions of scepticism, I have so far obtained no decisive evidence. Mr. Mann Jones tells me that "an accurate observer (ex-agriculturalist, sawyer, miner, and poacher) says, 'The word "walks" should not be used for the young of the pigs we know in Devon. Until thirty-six to forty-eight hours after birth, they at first sprawl, and later on stagger, when they move.' This," adds Mr. Jones, "accords with my own observations on the breeds he refers to." Other breeds seem to be more active soon after birth. Confirmation of Spalding's experiment is, however, desirable.

Now, when a guinea-pig, startled by such a sound as a low whistle, runs off rapidly within a few hours of birth, we have a case of instinctive response well-nigh in perfection. That there is not similar behaviour on the part of the puppy and the kitten is, in large measure, due to their incomplete physical development. As this development proceeds, and the limbs gain strength, the instinctive activity of locomotion, thus necessarily "deferred," may manifest itself. But since the manifestation is—unlike the deferred instinctive dive of the duck or the moorhen—gradual, and since, under normal conditions, the gradual development is accompanied by a good deal of individual practice, the walking or running, though founded, no doubt, on an instinctive basis, is not purely congenital. It is, in part at least, the result of acquisition. The habit is in such cases of double origin, partly instinctive, and partly acquired. This is so in a great number of cases; and in them it is difficult to assign their due shares to instinct and to habit. It is just for this reason that there has been so much diversity of opinion in the matter. Spalding,* in combating the views of "that school of psychology which maintained that we and all other animals had to acquire, in the course of our individual lives, all the knowledge and skill necessary for our preservation," went too far in the opposite direction in asserting "that the progress of the infant is but the unfolding of inherited powers." Such unfolding there is, but it is under the guidance of individual experience. The regular flexions and extensions of the legs, "which appear even months before the first successful attempt to walk, when the child, held upright on the floor, is pushed forward," are instinctive, as Prof. Preyer † points out, and as Prof. Mark Baldwin ‡ has also shown. But under normal circumstances the walking of the child is not solely an instinctive activity: acquisition largely co-operates. Like the finished flight of birds, it is a joint product of instinct and acquisition. In the precocious guinea-pig instinct predominates;

* *Nature*, vol. xii. pp. 507, 508.
† Preyer, *op. cit.*, p. 271.
‡ "Mental Development of the Child and the Race," p. 82.

in the immature kitten acquisition appears to be the chief factor.

A very interesting observation is that which Dr. Mills summarizes as follows: "I have found, in the case of all puppies, and several other kinds of animals examined (the cat and the rabbit, for example), that even on the first day of birth they will not creep off a surface on which they rest if elevated some little distance above the ground. When they approach the edge they manifest hesitation, grasp with their claws, or otherwise attempt to prevent themselves falling, and it may be cry out, giving evidence of some profound disturbance in their nervous system." And he adds, "It is interesting to note that a water-tortoise I have had for some years, will at any time walk off a surface on which it is placed," and fall to the ground. The newly born animals on which Dr. Mills experimented were still blind, so that the effects were not due to sight, but probably to the lack of support experienced when the edge of the surface was reached; and they exemplify a very interesting mode of apparently instinctive behaviour. Spalding's observation on a two-days-old pig may be quoted for comparison. "When placed on a chair, it knew the height to require considering, went down on its knees, and leapt down." The expression "knew the height to require considering" is unfortunate and open to criticism. But the kneeling preparatory to leaping down is a matter of direct observation, and not of inference. Mr. Mann Jones, in a letter with which he has favoured me, says, "The going down on the knees (*i.e.* bending the wrist joint) is the ordinary resting position in both young and old pigs, and the only inference warrantable from the action is that the muscles were tired by standing. I doubt whether any mammal," he continues, "ever 'leapt' from such a position. If the pig attempted to get down from the chair without first getting on its feet, it would merely slip off. Practical men to whom I have spoken deprecate the use of the word 'leapt' as totally inappropriate." When I suggested to a worthy farmer that he should repeat the observation for me, his indirect reply, "But who will pay for the pig?" sufficiently indicated what, in his opinion, would be the result of the experiment. If any pig-breeder should read these pages, he may perhaps be induced to try some such experiment.

As control over the limbs is gradually acquired the locomotor activities are perfected. But here constitutional differences are shown. Both at the age of three months and in adult life, the power of motor control in the cat, and the delicacy and accuracy of co-ordination, are greater than in the dog; and in the adult dog they are greater than in the adult rabbit. The control in the cat over the fore limbs is especially marked in correlation with their use in climbing and in seizing prey. The kitten finds it easier to climb up than to descend. On its 101st day, for example, Dr. Wesley Mills's kitten, taken by surprise, climbed a tree just at hand to a height of some thirty feet. But it feared to descend, and was, after a time, lowered down at the end of a pole. A kitten in a tree, apparently unable to come down, is not an unfamiliar sight. The tendency to climb seems to be an innate proclivity in the cat; as does also its alertness in the dusk of evening. So, too, in the rabbit, spasmodic, jerky, jumpy movements are early seen; scratching at the surface still earlier; the characteristic wiping of the face with the fore paws quite as soon (second day); and at a later period (about the fifteenth day) the squatting up on the hind legs, and the mode of running characteristic of its kind. Quite different is the scuttling run of the guinea-pig. Dr. Mills does not note any instinctive tendency in the rabbit to burrow. But

Mr. Drane observed * that a tame hare persistently tried to burrow in his bed. The carriage and movements of the tail in the dog and the cat, each after its kind, exemplify congenital tendencies ; and the socially dependent nature of the dog, as compared with the self-sufficiency of the cat, is early seen. In the kitten the arching of the back, the characteristic response which we interpret as the accompaniment of fear or anger—opened mouth, guttural hissing, and a final spit—are undoubtedly congenital traits ; as are also the licking of the fur (paw, sixteenth day ; neck and chest, twenty-second day, in Dr. Mills's kitten), the washing of the face (twenty-ninth day), and the stretching after the manner of an old cat (thirty-first day). Congenital but deferred is the purring of the cat (fifty-fourth day) ; congenital, too, would seem to be the tendency in the kitten, much more markedly than in the puppy, to crouch and stalk a moving object of small size, the response being, it would seem, evoked by any such moving object. I could detect no difference in the reaction to a clockwork mouse and the real animal. Still, I have no doubt that the *smell* of a real mouse is not without its effect. Dr. Mills's observation, in fact, show this to be so. So, too, the smell of game will set a game-dog on the *qui vive.* When I am incubating pheasants' or partridges' eggs, my fox-terrier takes an olfactory interest in the drawer which he does not show to the same degree with hens' eggs or those of ducks. This is still more the case with the young birds. Such difference of behaviour is, no doubt, partly due to association and experience ; but in greater degree, it is generally believed, to what is given through inheritance.

Starting at very different levels of physical development,

* *Trans. Cardiff Naturalists Society*, vol. xxvii. part ii., 1894–95.

the guinea-pig and the rabbit agree in their rapid attain-
ment of maturity in such powers as they possess. The
guinea-pig, very soon after birth, is able to care for itself,
and capable of maintaining an independent existence ; the
rabbit at birth is "blind, deaf, incapable of any considerable locomotive power, and, generally speaking, in a
perfectly helpless condition." Yet, starting at such
different levels, these two animals both run so rapidly
through the early stages of the unfolding of what is congenital, accompanied by the learning by experience of what
is of chief value to their relatively simple life, that at the
end of three or four weeks there is "little to note by way of
further advance." "After the first month of existence,"
says Dr. Mills, "comparison with the dog, cat, and allied
creatures ceases to be suggestive. The rodents are left
quite behind. They seem capable of little education,
either by man or by nature. In other words, they get
little by experience beyond that which strengthens their
instincts and emphasizes their simple psychic life." On
the other hand, Mr. Mann Jones has found that some
rabbits are capable of a good deal of education, and are
by no means lacking in intelligence. Of rats, too, his
experience is of a similar kind. And Mr. Drane has given
an interesting account of what may be done with the hare
as a pet.

With regard to the development of sensory power, the
guinea-pig soon after birth shows so clearly that it sees,
hears, tastes, etc., that it would be hazardous, in the
opinion of Dr. Mills, to assert that these functions do not
exist at birth. This, too, seems to be the case with the
hare. Development by use there no doubt is, but the steps
towards perfection are taken with great rapidity. The
congenital element predominates.

All young mammals seem sensitive at birth, or very

shortly after, to warmth and cold, and show a tendency
to seek the warmth—of the mother's body, for example.
Sensitiveness to touch seems also quite early developed.
When the mouth or nose of a kitten, on the second day,
was touched, and especially when the inner surface of the
nostrils was irritated, withdrawal of the head followed.
With young rabbits, on their first day, the slightest touch,
or even a light puff of air from the mouth, causes much
disturbance; they move in an irregular, ill co-ordinated
way, but evidently are greatly affected. A fly crawling
across the face caused jerky movements of the head
as a whole, and of the ears. When solutions of Epsom
salts and of common salt were placed in the mouth of
a rabbit not twenty-four hours old, to test its power of
taste, there was some movement of the paws to wipe it
away. On the seventh day it used the paws fairly well
to get rid of any irritant, such as a feather, put against
the mouth. The period that elapses between stimulus
and response varies. In the dog and cat, for example,
there is a much longer "latent period," in the case of
the reflex started by a pinch, than is shown by the rabbit.
On the sixteenth day a kitten was seen to use the hind
leg to scratch the ear or head; and such a reflex is seen
in the dog at about the same time (seventeenth day).
In both these animals, as before noted, the co-ordinated
movements of the hind limbs develop somewhat slowly.
A Himalayan rabbit, on the other hand, used its hind
leg to scratch itself as early as the second day. There
can be little doubt that such reflexes, whereby local irri-
tations are connected with limb-movements effective for
their removal, are congenital in their nature, and form
the basis of further and more accurate localization of the
point of irritation, and of further adaptation of the movements necessary for its removal.

Prof. Preyer's experiments seem to show that young guinea-pigs both taste and smell at a very early age— counted by hours rather than days. With its eyes bandaged, the little animal avoided oil of thyme and camphor, and licked at sugar, but not at glass or wood. Dr. Mills also found that a guinea-pig, on its first day, sucked at a feather dipped in sugar-solution, but turned away from one dipped in aloes. A couple of them were put in a box with some brown sugar, peppermint rock, salt, and camphor. They licked at the salt only once; but they went again and again to the sugar. In the rabbit taste and smell seemed to be well developed by the seventh day. In the dog and cat, Dr. Mills is not prepared either to affirm or deny that taste and smell are present at birth, but if they do exist he is sure that they are of the feeblest, are of very little use to the animal, and play but a very subordinate part in its life during the blind period. Still his kitten, on the second day of life, sniffed and became uneasy when Dr. Mills rubbed his hands well on a St. Bernard and then placed them near the little cat's nose. By the twentieth day smell had become of great suggestive value in the dog.

The rabbit, kitten, and puppy are born with the eyes closed, so that sight is impossible. In the rabbit the eyes open on the tenth, eleventh, or twelfth day; in the kitten, on the eighth or ninth day; and in the puppy, on about the eleventh to the thirteenth day, there being well-marked individual differences. The eyes of the guinea-pig are open at birth; and at the end of seventeen hours these precocious animals see well and exhibit the winking reflex. This reflex is seen feebly in the kitten on the eleventh day, in the rabbit on the fourteenth day, and in the puppy on the fifteenth day; in each case, that is to say, two or three days after the eyes are opened. It seems to be but slowly developed in the dog and cat, and is never so marked as with man. For some days after the eyes are open, the time being longer for the dog than the cat, Dr. Mills found it difficult to get evidence of anything like distinct sight, and, in the dog especially, sight seems at this stage quite subordinate to smell. In the rabbit, too, on the sixteenth day, Dr. Mills can say no more than "I think they begin to distinguish objects by sight." In these cases experience seems to play an important part in the development of anything like distinct vision.

The rabbit, like the kitten and the dog, appears to be deaf at birth; but one moved its head and ears on the tenth day (twelfth in the case of the Himalayan rabbit) when a dog-whistle was sounded. The kitten showed signs of hearing on the eighth day; but it was not till the seventeenth day, or thereabouts, that puppies responded in a definite way to sounds; the responsive ear-movements in the two animals being somewhat different. The hearing soon becomes delicate and accurate as to direction. In such observations it is, of course, necessary to remember that it is only by the answering movements that one can obtain any evidence of sensation. It may be that there are sensations, but that answering movements are not yet developed in response to them; on the other hand, what we interpret as a felt sensation may be at first only a physiological stimulus.

Much has been written on the instinct or reflex of sucking. There is no doubt that the lip and mouth-movements for sucking may be initiated in a just-born infant or young mammal by inserting any suitable object into the mouth. Prof. Preyer found that with young guinea-pigs, only eight to sixteen hours old, and separated

I

from the mother after two hours, concentrated water-solu-
tions of tartaric acid, soda, and glycerine, introduced into
the mouth through glass tubes, were swallowed just as
eagerly as milk and water, with vigorous sucking.   He
found, too, that the empty tube, placed on the end of the
tongue, occasioned just such sucking.   And he believes
that, under the influence of hunger, touch, as a reflex
stimulus, overpowers any taste-stimuli acting at the same
time.   It is certainly probable that the act of sucking is
a reflex started by the appropriate sense-stimuli, and, as
such, is of a purely congenital nature.   But what leads the
infant to the nipple of the mother's breast, or the new-
born animal to the teats of its dam ?   In the case of the
human infant, it finds its way very imperfectly and in-
adequately, being, under ordinary circumstances, guided in
its random efforts by the mother.   Prof. Preyer believes
that, in the case of animals, they are at first guided to the
teats by the sense of smell.   He states that puppies,
rendered incapable of smell by the severance of the
olfactory nerve, could no longer find the mother's teats
so long as they were blind.   They crept about on her belly,
trying to suck everywhere.   Blind puppies in the normal
state, on the other hand, find the teats at once.   Dr.
Mills, however, expresses a different opinion as the result
of his observations.   " I have not changed my opinion,"
he says, " as expressed in my first paper on the dog,
that the puppy, and, I will now add, the kitten, find the
nipple of the mother by touch rather than smell, and
that they are drawn towards the belly of the mother by
the warmth of the part."   This also is the opinion of
Mr. Mann Jones.   " So far as my observations go," he
says in a letter from which he kindly allows me to
quote, " I am inclined to think that the heat of the
mother's belly determines the approach of the young to

the teats; but many would fail to find them in good time, were it not that sows, bitches, and cats push the young with their noses (or even, in the case of the two latter species, with their paws) towards or into the warm area, when they get outside it. Further, I have seen both bitches and cats get up and again lie down so as to bring the teats into closer proximity to the mouth of any young which failed to find them. It has been noticed by a man who is a remarkably good observer and has had much to do with animals, and also by myself, that when a lamb is weakly and fails to find the teat, the mother not infrequently uses its shoulders, head, and neck as a lever to place the lamb on its legs; and, having accomplished this, straddles over the lamb, and brings the teats against its lips; and these efforts are continued until the little animal sucks."

Of the pampas sheep Mr. Hudson says, "When born the lamb's first impulse is to struggle up on to its feet; its second to suck, but here it does not discriminate like the newly hatched bird that picks up its proper food" —a conclusion, by the way, from which my own observations lead me to dissent—"for it does not know what to suck. It will take into its mouth whatever comes near, in most cases a tuft of wool on its dam's neck, and at this it will continue sucking for an indefinite time. It is highly probable," Mr. Hudson says, "that the strong-smelling secretion of the sheep's udder attracts the lamb at length to that part; and that without something of the kind to guide it, in many cases it would actually starve without finding the teats."

Mr. Mann Jones, in the letter from which I have quoted, says, "A lady, who observed closely, assured me that in some breeds of pigs the young so often fail to find the teat by their own unassisted efforts, that many would probably have died if assistance had not been given; and she had seen many instances where the teat had at length to be placed in the mouth of the young pig to prevent starvation.

"So far as I have been able to observe, the direct action is most ready where the difference between the temperature of the mother and that of the atmosphere is greatest. Young pigs, pups, and kittens are impelled towards the mother by the irregular action excited by the difference of temperature much more decidedly when it is great."

We are considering, it must be remembered, the very beginnings of this activity which is of such essential importance to the young mammal. There can be no question that experience plays its part in the further development of the act; and that here, as elsewhere, practice makes perfect. Whether the gentle rhythmic pressure of the fore paws on the mammary glands is partly instinctive, it is difficult to say. No doubt experience renders the act more effectual. Darwin believed that a habit of such rhythmic pressure is engendered. We may often see a kitten or older cat gently pounding at a cushion as she lies dozing and purring.

To revert to the initial establishment of the behaviour characteristic of the suckling; in the absence of further evidence, we may perhaps accept the view that the young are drawn to the mother by the sense of warmth, and come in contact with the teats either as the result of random movements and vague attempts to suck something (other parts being often sucked as well as the teats), or in response to stimuli affecting the sense of smell, or through some external guidance.

The suggestive value of smell is of great importance both to animals of the hunting type, such as the dog or the cat, and of the hunted type, such as the rabbit; and it is therefore of interest to ascertain how far the effects of certain odours are congenitally definite. There is an oft-quoted observation of Spalding's in this connection. "So old," he says,* " is the feud between the cat and the dog, that the kitten knows its enemy even before it is able to see him, and when its fear can in no way serve it. One day last month, after fondling my dog, I put my hand into a basket containing four blind kittens, three days old. The smell my hand carried with it set them puffing and spitting in a most comical fashion." Experiments of my own have led me to question whether the reaction is so particularized—so specially a response to the smell of a dog as such—as Spalding believed. A whiff from a bottle of ammonia, and some straw from a pigsty, produced much the same effect. Dr. Mills, too, says that he has been very much impressed by the fact, that at an early age the kitten, when suddenly disturbed in any way, reacts much as if a dog had come upon it, though in a less marked manner. " Nevertheless," he adds, balancing the evidence, " the behaviour of a kitten, even a few days after its birth, towards even the smell of a dog on the hands, is very suggestive of an instinctive fear or dislike of a dog. At the same time, I have seen a kitten act much the same way when an irritant was placed near its nose, or, after it could hear, when it was startled by a noise." Even Dr. Mills himself, when he appeared before his kitten, on its twenty-seventh day, in a somewhat startling coat—" light in colour, with pronounced vertical stripes "—caused the animal to open its mouth, and, on his going nearer, to hiss. Mr. Mann Jones tells me he has " often introduced young kittens to dogs, and *vice versâ*, and that there was no sign of repugnance on the part of the younger animal, nor of the

* *Nature*, vol. xii. p. 507.

older if not accustomed to 'badger,' as the result of keeping bad company."

There can be no doubt that the mode of response —the opening of the mouth, the guttural hiss, followed, if the disturbance is yet stronger, by an explosive "spitting"—when the kitten is startled or affected by a strongly disturbing stimulus is congenital and eminently characteristic. That it is called forth in a kitten when it is a few weeks old (and accompanied by an equally characteristic arching of the back and raising of the fur) on sight of a dog, especially one approaching her, is a matter of familiar observation. But I have seen the same response to a large rabbit. In kittens of this age—say three weeks to a month—I have not found that the smell of the hand, after fondling a dog and getting the dog to lick it, evokes more than a curious sniffing. Even if the smell of a dog call forth instinctive behaviour, accompanied by emotional disturbance, this must be regarded as an organic response, accompanied, indeed, by certain conscious states affording data to experience, but not reviving those purely mythical states of consciousness spoken of as ancestral memories. To say that through smell a kitten "knows its enemy even before it is able to see him," is to put the matter picturesquely, but not satisfactorily from the point of view of scientific interpretation. At most there is a congenital response of a useful kind, at once anticipating the results of experience and affording a basis for experience to work upon.

In any observations on instinctive antipathy, all influence of the parent must be excluded. I once carried a blind puppy to a litter of kittens to see if they would show signs of such antipathy, the cat being away. Not getting any response, much to my surprise at that time,

I repeated the experiment. Unfortunately, the cat was there, and I long bore on my lip the mark of her claw. The kittens were much disturbed, and there was ample opportunity for the establishment of an association between this uneasiness, due to the old cat's behaviour, and the smell of a dog.

I have seen my fox-terrier smell at a young lamb, about a fortnight old, that was lying in a field, and the lamb showed no signs of fear, even when the two animals were nose to nose, till the ewe came up bleating fussily; then the young thing started up and ran to its dam. I take it that many popular notions concerning instinctive fear are erroneous and exaggerated, and that what Mr. Hudson showed for birds—that the fear is mainly due to experience and tradition—is also true for mammals. With regard to one such popular notion, this is what Mr. Selous says: * " I think it is a mistake to say that oxen and horses have an instinctive fear of the smell of a lion. I have always found that a shooting-horse, trained to carry meat, will allow you to pack a reeking lion-skin upon him with as much indifference as an antelope-hide, so long as he has never been frightened or mauled by one of the former animals; this, at least, is my experience."

Still, there may be an instinctive basis in some cases where animals are by nature enemies. And we must remember that what is instinctive often forms merely the foundation upon which what is acquired is built in the course of individual development. Dr. Mills puts this very clearly. " The whole history of the kitten," he says, " is an illustration that, however strong instincts may be in an intelligent animal, its psychic life is determined by experience, *i.e.* there come to be almost no pure instincts— instincts unmodified by experience, if such a thing is

* " Travel and Adventure in Africa," p. 126.

conceivable, as the language of some writers would seem
to imply. Each day of this kitten's life showed me a
progress dependent on experience, and the same applies
to the dog; but I must add that, for the first eight or ten
weeks, the kitten seemed to get the most out of its experience." Of course, the development of experience is
in accordance with, and in large degree determined
by, the innate character of the animal. This, too, is fully
realized by Dr. Mills; for he says, in commenting on
and comparing the diaries of the pure-bred dog and the
mongrel, that "heredity is, was, and ever will be stronger
than environment." The hereditary factor in the development of acquired experience must never be for-
gotten.

But though, as Dr. Mills says, in an intelligent animal,
there come after a while to be "almost no pure instincts,"
that which was given as instinct having been utilized,
modified, and adapted through experience and acquisition,
yet the fundamental distinction between that which is
congenital and instinctive, on the one hand, and that
which is acquired through individual experience, on the
other hand, remains unaltered. Nor does the fact that
all acquisition is rendered possible by an innate faculty
for acquiring—nay, more, for acquiring in this way or that
in accordance with hereditary character—diminish a whit
the value of the distinction. The instinctive action is
prior to experience; the acquired action is due to experience. And this distinction holds, no matter how hard
it may be to decide whether this action or that is in the
main instinctive or in the main acquired. The final
products of individual development may be, and no doubt
generally are, of twofold origin, partly instinctive and
partly due to acquisition; but this, I repeat, does not in
any way serve to annul the distinction between the

two several elements in the final product. If we add water to our whisky, there is no longer pure whisky; the whisky has been more or less modified, but the spirit is still there none the less, and we cannot neglect its presence. So, too, if we add the water of experience to the whisky of instinct, we have a joint product of which so much comes from the bottle and so much comes from the jug. And when Dr. Mills contends that in the kitten "its psychic life is determined by experience," we must take him to mean that the whisky of instinct is, as a matter of fact, always more or less watered down in the course of individual development.

When animals are brought up by their parents, it is often a matter of difficulty to determine how far any specially characteristic behaviour is due to the influence of the parent, whose behaviour is similar, and how far it is due to instinct. But when the young are separated from their parents at an early age, the instinctive basis is often rendered more clear and obvious. The following observations of Mr. Charles F. Batchelder, which he has kindly given me permission to quote, are of interest in this connection.

" The nest in which our grey squirrel (*Sciurus carolinensis leucotis*, Sapper) rears its young is usually built among the higher branches of some large tree. It is a bulky mass of sticks and leaves, entirely covered above, and entered only by a small passage through the side of the structure. In the middle is a cavity, softly lined, where the young are born, and where they spend their infancy, cut off from sight of the outside world.

" From such a nest, near the top of a tall white pine (*Pinus strobus*, Linn.), on May 12, 1877, I obtained two young grey squirrels, out of a litter of four. They were so young and feeble that, as they clung to my rough woollen coat, it was no easy matter for them to climb, even with the good foothold that it afforded. It was evident that they had never ventured so far as the outside of their nest; and up to that time they certainly could have had no opportunity of making the acquaintance of the ground, which lay far below them, and concealed from the nest by a screen of thick branches.

"When I had brought them home, starvation seemed to threaten them, for they did not know how to eat solid food, nor would they lap milk. To overcome this difficulty, I improvised a nursing-bottle by putting a quill through a hole in the cork of a small wide-mouthed bottle, which I filled with a mixture of cream and hot water. This they took to readily. After a few days they learned to drink milk from a saucer, and gradually, through bread and milk, they were introduced to more solid viands.

"After they had lived some time on such food as biscuits and bread-crusts, I gave them one day some hickory-nuts, one of the staple articles of diet of an adult grey squirrel, whose powerful teeth take but a few moments to penetrate the thick, hard shells. They examined the nuts attentively, evidently looking upon them as unusually interesting novelties, and at last the more enterprising of the two set to work on a nut, as if he wished to find out what prize it might contain. With hitherto unexampled patience he laboured over it, until at last, after more than half an hour's diligent gnawing, he gained access to the kernel. With a few days' practice they acquired skill and speed in extracting these hard-shelled delicacies; and after that they lost all interest in such things as biscuits, and hickory-nuts formed the principal item on their bill of fare.

"These squirrels were often taken from their cage for hours at a time, and given the freedom of a room. Here they got abundant exercise, climbing and jumping over the furniture, racing up the window-curtains, and leading, as well as they could, well-regulated squirrel lives. It was here, when they were a month or two old (unfortunately, I have no record of the exact date), that they first displayed a very interesting instinct. Many a time I saw one or the other of them take a nut, when there were more than he could eat, look about the room until he found a suitable place, then put the nut down on the carpet in some sheltered corner, such as against the castor of a sofa-leg, or in the corner of the carved foot of a bureau. He would press the nut down on the carpet, and then go through all the motions of patting the earth over it, after which he went about his business as if that nut were safely buried.

" I have neglected to mention that in a state of nature the adult squirrels of this species do not, as a rule, in times of plenty, gather hoards of nuts ; but take the superfluous ones and bury them singly, at a depth of an inch or two in the ground, digging a little hole, if necessary, pushing the nut into the hole, covering it, and then pressing and patting the earth over it. They bury so many that they could hardly remember exactly where each was put ; but they have no trouble in finding most of them by their sense of smell, which seems to be very acute. One is often to be seen running about on the ground, sniffing here and there, and stopping now and then to dig, when he rarely fails to unearth a nut.

" I was interested to observe that my young squirrels were satisfied to bury their nuts in the nearest approach to a hole that they could find on the ground (carpet), and were not disturbed by the fact that when the process was completed the nut still remained plainly visible. It is also interesting to note that (as I have shown in some detail above) at the time they were removed from their parents they not only had never seen the operation of burying a nut, but were totally unacquainted with the properties both of earth and of nuts."

In this case the untaught instinctive procedure is all the more marked since it effected no good purpose. So far as it goes, too, it would seem to be pure congenital whisky undiluted by the water of experience. On the other hand, the way in which Dr. Mills taught his kitten habits of cleanliness is an equally instructive object-lesson in acquisition through association, accompanied, however, by some instinctive traits, such as the pawing of the sand.

I have drawn largely on the observations which Dr. Mills has placed on record in the papers to which reference has been given. Let me assure the reader that much remains of equal interest and importance. The diaries should be carefully read by all students of animal habit and instinct. Especially interesting are the observations on the so-called "play instinct," the outcome of an excess of vital energy finding expression in varied activities, all of them more or less directly correlated with those which are of importance in subsequent life, and giving opportunity for the development of the motor control so essential to that life. Interesting, too, is the marked effect on development of allowing a mongrel puppy, hitherto brought up in comparative seclusion, to mix with other dogs. "His advancement was literally by leaps and bounds." The less social nature of the kitten, so far as members of its own kind were concerned, is also noted. "The behaviour of one kitten," says Dr. Mills, "has less influence on the others than that of one puppy on its fellows." The length of time required by the kitten— much more marked than is the case with the puppy—to learn how to lap milk successfully, and, later, to eat solid food, seems to show that there is here more acquisition than instinct. The very early spontaneous attempt at eating in the rabbit, and the fact that, though the dog is so essentially a carnivorous animal, yet until a certain stage of development is reached, the puppy "is no more excited by meat than by any object whatever, show in the clearest way that there is an order in psychic as in physical development," both in the race and in the individual. Enough has, however, been quoted to illustrate the nature of instinctive response and of acquired habit as exemplified by young mammals.

Those who are familiar with the life and ways of domesticated and wild species will be able to recall to mind a number of instinctive traits. The way in which the dog turns round before lying down, the way in which he holds up his paw when excited and on the scent, the manner in which the mother cat carries her kitten, the strange instincts of cattle which Mr. W. H. Hudson has so well described and discussed, the numberless characteristic traits which animals, each after his kind, display, would fill a volume. Concerning all such, I would beg the observer to note carefully how far they are unmistakably and indubitably congenital, and how far they may result from individual acquisition through experience or imitation.

CHAPTER VI.

THE RELATION OF CONSCIOUSNESS TO INSTINCTIVE BEHAVIOUR.

THERE is scarcely anything more wonderful in the whole range of biological phenomena than the series of changes which take place during the incubation of the egg. On the surface of the central mass of yolk, when the egg is laid, there is a little patch of somewhat lighter colour. Placed under the hen, or in the drawer of an incubator and kept at a temperature of about 104° Fahr. for three weeks or so, such a transformation occurs that there emerges a little chick which, in about twenty-four hours, will be actively pecking at small objects, selecting some and rejecting others. Unless we are prepared to assert that birds are throughout their lives unconscious automata, mere machines of marvellously cunning make, we must regard the little chick, a day old, that is every moment gaining fresh experience of the world into which it is born, as endowed with consciousness. It not only seems to feel, but to shape its actions in accordance with what it has already felt in the few hours of its active life; seeking the repetition of certain experiences and avoiding the recurrence of others. It appears to be guided by some such consciousness as that by which we too are guided in our own actions. The consciousness may lack much of that complexity which human consciousness presents; it may be wanting in certain features which for us are distinctive; it may be altogether more naïve and rudimentary. But it suffices as a means of guidance amid the comparatively simple conditions of the chick's life.

Now, if, on the one hand, it cannot be said without extravagance that the egg with which we start is endowed with consciousness; and if, on the other hand, it cannot be said without extravagance that the day-old chick is an unconscious automaton; there must be some intervening moment at which this consciousness has its origin. When is this, and how does it arise? If we attempt to answer this question with anything like thoroughness, we shall open up the further question, From what does consciousness take its origin? And this would lead to a difficult and, for most of us, not very interesting discussion. We should have to decide whether consciousness arises out of merely material and physical conditions within the developing chick; or whether it is somehow introduced from some external source; or whether it arises out of something associated with the material egg which, though not yet consciousness, developes into consciousness. These problems we will not here attempt to solve. The probabilities appear to me to be in favour of the third alternative; on which view the question takes the more practical form, When does consciousness become effective?

By effective consciousness, I mean that which enables an animal to guide its actions in the light of previous experience. It is clear that, on the hypothesis indicated, we cannot deny that there may be sentient states (if one may so term them), which merely accompany organic or other processes, but which are not thus effective in the guidance of life. They are of no practical value, however, unless they afford data by which the animal is able to profit by his experience. In the series of changes, for example, which take place in the duly fertilized egg, there may be sentient states of this kind. But there is no

reason to suppose that the sequence is in any material
respect guided by such accompanying sentience, if it exist.
It is just because the actions of the chick do seem to be
guided by the results of experience, that we may fairly
infer the presence of effective consciousness.

We have reason to suppose that this effective consciousness accompanies the functional activity of the higher
brain-centres, probably those of the superficial layer or
cortex of the cerebral hemispheres. These are in connection with certain other nerve-centres, the lower brain-
centres, and those of the spinal cord; and these, again,
with various parts of the body through the intervention of
nerve-fibres, which are divisible into two great groups—the
afferent nerves, which transmit currents inwards from the
several parts of the body to the nerve-centres; and
the efferent nerves, which transmit currents outwards from
the nerve-centres to the several parts of the body.

Now, it is the business of the lower centres to co-
ordinate the functional activities of the body by means of
outgoing currents along the efferent nerves; and this co-
ordination, effected by the lower centres only, sometimes
reaches extraordinary complexity and delicacy. It would
seem, however, that their co-ordinating influence lies
wholly within the sphere of organic and physiological
action. There may be sentience, in the sense above alluded
to, but there is no effective consciousness. The co-
ordinating activity of these lower centres, in so far as it
is not guided and controlled by the influence of the higher
centres with their accompaniment of effective consciousness, we may describe as automatic; and we will restrict
the phrase " animal automatism " to organic activity that

* I say "restrict," because Prof. Huxley has used the phrase in a far
broader sense. For a discussion and criticism of his usage, see the *Monist* for
October, 1896.

results from the co-ordinating influence of these lower nerve-centres. An automatic act, then, is one which is performed without the immediate and effective intervention of those organic processes in the cerebral cortex or elsewhere which are accompanied by consciousness.

The higher brain-centres, therefore, are those the functional activity of which is alone, so far as we know or may safely conjecture, accompanied by effective consciousness, in the sense in which we are using the term. They are the centres of guidance and control; or, to speak more accurately, if somewhat pedantically, they are the centres in which occur those organic processes which exercise an influence on the lower centres, and which have conscious accompaniments. They are called into play, directly or indirectly, by the incoming currents of the afferent nerves; and they exercise their influence on the lower automatic centres, either (1) by increasing their activity, or (2) by checking it, or (3) by increasing here and checking there, and thus modifying the activity in accordance with the effects of incoming currents.

So much technical description seems to be necessary as a preliminary to a consideration of the question,—What is the relation of consciousness to the performance of instinctive activities? This question may be put in another form: What is the relation of automatism, as we have defined it, to the performance of these instinctive activities? Let us leave generalities, and take a particular case, fixing our attention on the very first occasion on which a chick pecks instinctively at a grain of food or other such object at suitable distance. The logical possibilities are as follows:

1. The action may be completely automatic.

2. The action may not be completely automatic, but in some degree *guided* by consciousness.

K

If completely automatic, it may be either—

A. *Accompanied* by consciousness.

B. Unaccompanied by consciousness.

Combining these and stating them in a more convenient form for the purpose of discussion—

1. The chick may be an altogether unconscious automaton.

2. It may act under the guidance of consciousness, and not altogether automatically.

3. It may act automatically, but its automatic response may give rise to consciousness, in the light of which its future action may be guided and controlled.

Let us assume, to begin with, that the first possibility expresses the facts of the case, and that the chick is, so far as the activity in question is concerned, a completely unconscious automaton. It may be conceded that the first peck can be quite adequately explained on this view; response following stimulus under conditions which are purely organic and wholly within the sphere of the merely automatic co-ordination of the lower centres. It may, indeed, be urged that it is not reasonable to suppose that the chick pecks at the grain without seeing it, and this implies the presence of consciousness. But, in the first place, we are not in a position to affirm that there is anything more than a physiological stimulus of the retina; and, in the second place, even if we were, it would still be conceivable that, though the incoming effects of the retinal stimulus give rise to the sight of the grain, the outgoing nerve-currents which call the muscles into co-ordinated activity (and it is this co-ordinated response that constitutes the instinctive activity as such) are not only automatic, but unconscious. Indeed, there is much to be said in favour of the view that the outgoing nerve-currents, and the molecular processes in the lower nerve-centres to which they are proximately due, have no conscious accompaniments in the case of the first performance of an instinctive act. Still, looking at the instinctive response as a whole and in all its bearings, there seem good reasons for supposing that, if it be automatic, it at any rate in some way affords data to consciousness; and that if the chick be an automaton, it is not merely an unconscious automaton. But how, it may be asked, can the observer decide whether consciousness be thus present as an accompaniment, though, so far, without guiding influence? Only by watching the subsequent behaviour of the bird. We are forced, then, to consider the after-effects in order to determine whether the first peck is accompanied by consciousness or not. And if we do thus watch the bird in its subsequent efforts, we find that they rapidly improve in accuracy, and soon have all the appearance of being under guidance and control, so that they can be modified or checked according to the nature of the object, nice or nasty, as the case may be. Now, we may safely lay down this canon: *That which is outside experience can afford no data for the conscious guidance of future behaviour.* When we say that conduct is modified in the light of experience, we mean that the consciousness of what happened, say yesterday, helps us to avoid similar consequences to-day. If the happenings of yesterday were unconscious, they could afford no data for to-day's behaviour. If, then, the first peck is unconscious, it is as such completely outside the experience of the chick, and can therefore afford no data for subsequent guidance and control. Similarly, the second, third, and succeeding pecks, so far as automatic and unconscious, afford no data to experience. But observation shows that the activities concerned in pecking are not only guided to further perfection, but play a part in that active life of the little bird which cannot without extravagance be interpreted as unconscious; for only by appealing to consciousness can they be thus guided. Hence we seem forced to reject the hypothesis of unconscious automatism on the grounds that the activities in question do afford data to experience, can be modified, and are therefore subject to voluntary control, by giving rise to sensations and feelings which enter into the conscious life of the chick.

Let us assume, then, in accordance with the second possibility, that the very first peck is carried out under the guidance of consciousness. Now, guidance and control are based on previous experience. A chick, for example, will seize the first soldier-beetle he meets with; but after one or two trials of this distasteful morsel, though he may run towards one, if he catches sight of it moving at some distance from him, he checks himself so soon as he sees clearly what it is. He controls his tendency to peck at it in the light of his previous experience of its unpleasant taste. It is clear, however, that the first time a chick pecks there is no individual experience in the light of which the activity can be guided or controlled. Hence we can only admit the second possibility on the hypothesis that experience is inherited. But though it is quite conceivable that the effects wrought by experience are transmitted in some way, at present unexplained, through heredity—that, for example, the acquired skill of one generation may become congenital in the next—this is something very different from the inheritance of experience itself. Unless we are prepared to admit some form of metempsychosis; unless we believe that the individual remembers that which happened to its parents or grandparents;—we must hold fast to the fact that the conscious experience of the individual is limited to the events of its own lifetime. Remembering, then, that the phrase "inherited experience" is merely a condensed expression for the hereditary organic effects, if such there be, wrought through experience, we are forced to conclude that in the case of the first peck the chick has no experience in the light of which its action could be guided and controlled. If consciousness be present it is not yet effective. And our second hypothesis is thus placed out of court.

We are, therefore, thrown back upon our third possibility—that the automatic response gives rise to consciousness in the light of which the chick's future activities may be guided and controlled. On this view the first peck—and it must be remembered that we are concentrating our attention on the very first occurrence of an instinctive response in the course of individual life —though it is an organic and automatic response, nevertheless affords data to consciousness; it thus provides the initial experience by which subsequent efforts at pecking may be guided and controlled. Is not this, however, it may be asked, in contradiction of what was stated a few pages back, that there is much to be said in favour of the view that the outgoing currents as such have no conscious accompaniments in the case of the first performance of an instinctive act? No. The contradiction is only apparent, not real.

It is, indeed, highly probable that all the primary data which contribute to the building up of experience are afforded through the intermediation of *incoming* nerve-currents. Grouping these in a convenient but not logically exclusive manner—for the motor sensations and those of the skin include elements supplied by touch—we may say that such data are supplied first from the organs of special sense, those of sight, hearing, taste, smell, touch, the temperature senses, and the sense of direction;

secondly, from the organs concerned in bodily movements; and, thirdly, from the heart, blood-vessels, skin, lungs, glands, digestive organs, and so forth. Thus we have (1) special sensations, (2) motor sensations, and (3) visceral sensations, all of them experienced through the intervention of incoming nerve-currents which reach the higher brain-centres whose activity is accompanied by consciousness. Now, in the case of the first peck, there are, to begin with, the initiating sensations of sight; and, secondly, the motor sensations due to the performance of the act of pecking. There may be visceral sensations as well, but these do not now concern us. When we say, then, that the first peck, though it is an organic and automatic response, nevertheless affords data to consciousness, we mean that the act of pecking yields to consciousness motor sensations already combined in complex groups, and due to incoming currents from the organs concerned in this particular kind of movement.

A further statement of the matter from the physiological point of view may serve to make the conception clearer. We have seen that what is unquestionably inherited, and what is, therefore, an essential feature in all instinctive response, is motor co-ordination. A stimulus gives rise to a commotion of some sort in the cortical region of the brain, and this is accompanied by sensation, say of sight. It also gives rise to a commotion in the lower brain-centres, or in some cases those of the spinal cord, such as to cause the automatic distribution of outgoing currents along efferent nerves to certain motor organs,—those concerned, for example, in pecking or in swimming. And these outgoing currents are so nicely and delicately ordered and graded in intensity as to produce just the particular movements required. This is the inherited motor co-ordination, probably a purely organic matter of the physiological order. But when the activity is carried out thus automatically in response to the appropriate stimulus, its performance is accompanied by consciousness. This is due to complex groups of incoming currents from the parts concerned in the response carried along afferent nerves to the sensorium—probably the cortical centres of the brain. Thus are afforded to consciousness the primary experience-data, already grouped according to the nature of the organic response. This point is of some importance in psychological interpretation. The primary grouping is inherent in the data, and much of the labour of conscious correlation is thus saved. The grouped data constitute what Mr. Rutgers Marshall terms instinct-feelings. To condense the conception into a phrase, we may say that the organic genesis of the brain-changes which accompany the primary experience data is *by backstroke* (that is to say, afferent in origin). The instinctive motor co-ordination is by outstroke, through the intermediation of efferent nerves, and so far it is a purely physiological and organic matter; there is, then, an afferent backstroke from the organs concerned in the instinctive response, and by this backstroke ingoing nerve-currents are conveyed to the higher brain-centres. Here it is that there emerges the initial bit of conscious experience in the light of which subsequent responses of the same kind may be guided to finer issues. For it must be remembered that we are dealing with the very first occasion on which the instinctive response occurs. On this one occasion the accompanying consciousness arises wholly by backstroke. On subsequent occasions, under associative suggestion, revivals in consciousness of previous experience-data modify the whole process and introduce the effective guidance of consciousness.

The net result of our discussion of the matter is therefore this, that on the occasion of the first performance of an instinctive activity the co-ordination involved (and it is sometimes quite elaborate) is automatic, and cannot be regarded as under the guidance of consciousness; but that the carrying out of the activity furnishes data to consciousness in the light of which the subsequent performance of a like activity may be perfected, or modified, or checked. From this it follows that only on the occasion of its first performance does such a congenital activity present itself for our study in its instinctive purity. For on subsequent occasions it is more or less modified by the results of the experience acquired by the individual. It then possesses acquired elements in addition to those which are congenital and instinctive; and when such acquired modification is rendered stereotyped and uniform by repetition, it is, so far as thus modified, a habit. In such organisms as birds and young mammals, therefore, instincts are to be regarded as the automatic raw material which will be shaped and moulded under the guidance of consciousness into what may be called *instinct-habits*, if by this compound term we may understand activities founded on a congenital instinctive basis, but modified by acquired experience.

In the case, too, of such an instinctive procedure of the deferred type as that presented by the diving of a young moorhen, though, on the first occasion of its performance the congenital automatism predominates, yet it is difficult to believe, and is in itself improbable, that the individual experience of the young bird does not, even on the first occasion, exercise some influence on the way in which the dive is performed. If we desire to reach a true interpretation of the facts, we must realize the fact that an activity may be of mixed origin. And if we distinguish—

as we have endeavoured clearly to distinguish—between instinct as congenital and habit as acquired, we must not lose sight of the fact that there is much interaction between instinct and habit, so that the first exhibition of a deferred instinct may well be carried out in close and inextricable association with the habits which, at the period of life in question, have already been acquired.

Accepting this view, at any rate provisionally, we may now proceed to ask what is the nature of that conscious impulse which is commonly assumed to accompany the performance of an instinctive activity. In truth we do not know and can only conjecture on general grounds. Indeed, the presence of any such impulse as a psychological factor is wholly conjectural. We see a chick pecking at a grain of corn, and say that it has an instinctive impulse to respond to the stimulus in this way. We place a tiny moorhen or duckling in the water and see it swim off; and say that the touch of water on the breast calls forth an instinctive impulse to paddle. We observe that the larva of the great water-beetle leaves the pond and buries itself in damp earth, and again attribute its behaviour to the promptings of an instinctive impulse. It may be that such a psychological impulse is present in each case. It would certainly be hazardous to deny its presence. But we know very little about it; and perhaps the safest course is to look at the matter from a physiological and organic point of view, leaving the question of the possible psychological accompaniment an open one. Let us, however, first see what the physiological conditions are.

The psychology of impulse would seem to be in outline somewhat as follows. In matters of human conduct impulsive action is contrasted with the actions which are performed in distinct reference to motives. Thus, impulsive behaviour is distinguished from deliberate conduct, the

former, being, it would seem, the more deeply ingrained in
the mental nature, lying far nearer to automatism than the
latter, the deliberate act. And many of us have often a hard
struggle to hold in check, by the exercise of our better
judgment, the impulsive tendencies which are natural to us
through inheritance or the force of acquired habit. A
heightened emotional state, such as that of anger or fear,
desire or irritability, is often a predisposing condition to
impulsive action. The dipsomaniac experiences recurrent
periods when his whole being seems to crave for that which
he knows is ruining him body and soul. He passes the
open door of a public-house where he sees a man raising a
glass to his lips; the added stimulus in this critical state
is too much for him. He yields to the impulse, calls for
brandy, and gulps it down. Given a state of craving or
emotional excitability; given an opportunity for its satisfaction; the impulse, I take it, is the immediate
accompaniment of the organic conditions of the moment;
when the organic tension accompanied by the somewhat
indefinite states of consciousness we term, according to its
intensity, a need, want, or craving, is reinforced by a
definite stimulus prompting to its immediate satisfaction.
Now the impulse, if this brief sketch of its nature be
correct in outline, is essentially an internal state which
prompts us to the performance of certain actions. It is
the antecedent on which the actions themselves are consequent. The performance of the action—such as the blow
struck by an angry man—is not to be regarded as the
cause, but as the result of the impulse. And in us the
term impulse is applied to the psychological condition of
the moment; it is a state of consciousness. But it is one
that has certain organic accompaniments, and is the
outcome of physiological conditions. And since, in a
consideration of instinctive behaviour, the psychological

aspect is a matter of somewhat hazardous inference, it is advisable to fix our attention on the organic aspect. Let us therefore endeavour to apply to instinct the conclusions which seem to result from our brief sketch of the nature of impulse.

Taking once more the case of the recently hatched chick as a simple and sufficiently typical one, we may put the matter in this way. The need for food is beginning to make itself felt, and to throw the organism into a state of preparedness for the response appropriate to the satisfaction of hunger. Acting on the chick thus prepared to respond, the sight of a small, perhaps moving, object stimulates the pecking activity as an organic response, and the result of this is that the organism under the influence of the general need, supplemented by the special stimulus, is, so to speak, thrown into a state of unstable equilibrium. It is consciously or unconsciously urged to strike at the moving object. The stimulus is continued; and at length, when the instability reaches a certain pitch, the organism topples over to the peck. For the stimulus must generate a certain amount of organic instability before the organic mechanism will fall to the response. Now it is quite possible that before the organism actually falls to the response, there are outgoing currents which throw the mechanism into a state of preparedness to respond, and that there is a faint backstroke from the motor mechanism thus partially stimulated, which is accompanied by a conscious state. Let us assume that this is so, and endeavour to fill in hypothetically the conscious accompaniments of the successive stages of an instinctive response. First, there is an indefinite feeling of want or need, such as hunger, afferent in origin; then there is the felt stimulus at sight of a moving grub or worm, also obviously afferent; on this there may follow a state of consciousness due to an afferent backstroke from the incipient innervation of the organs concerned in the response; and then there succeeds the consciousness which accompanies the actual carrying out of the automatic response by which the general discomfort, and the particular effects of the stimulus, are relieved by an appropriate motor act and its consequences. This again, on our interpretation, is afferent in origin. Now impulse may perhaps be fairly regarded as the condition immediately preceding the actual response which restores stability after the preceding instability generated by a special stimulus acting upon an organism already unstable through the general effects of a want; such condition being, I repeat, afferent in origin. To put the matter more generally, we may say that such an impulse is the tendency of the organism to satisfy its immediate needs and to fulfil the conditions of its being; and that according as this tendency is checked or realized, we speak of the thwarting or the satisfaction of impulse.

It is right, however, to warn the reader that the term "impulse," like many other terms in psychology, is used in different senses by different authors. The impulse of which we speak is sometimes spoken of as blind impulse— the Trieb of German authors. It is right also to repeat that in the case of the initial performance of an instinctive activity the presence of any such *conscious* impulse is hypothetical. On the other hand, that the organism under the influence of a stimulus or complex group of stimuli is thrown into a state of unstable equilibrium, and that stability is reached through the appropriate response, seem to be legitimate inferences from the observed facts. And perhaps the safest statement that we can make with regard to the subjective accompaniment is that, if there be such an accompaniment, it may take some such form as we have above described as impulse. If we understand then by impulse an organic tendency which may have a conscious accompaniment, we shall have gone as far as seems at present justifiable in going, where instinctive behaviour is concerned.

It now only remains to say a few words concerning the relation of the acquired automatism of habit to the congenital automatism of instinct. When we say that some oft-repeated habit is carried out automatically, we mean that it is done without conscious guidance and control. The cerebral cortex with its concomitant consciousness has somehow left the impress of its control, uniformly exercised in certain specific ways, upon the automatic mechanism. How this is effected we do not know. But the fact is a familiar one. Many actions which at first require our fully conscious guidance and control pass, through frequent repetition, into the condition of automatic acts generally accompanied by consciousness as an adjunct, but sometimes performed unconsciously. They have become merely organic responses conscious or unconscious. They conform therefore to our definition of automatic acts as those which are performed without the immediate and effective intervention of those molecular changes in the cerebral cortex which are accompanied by consciousness.

Whether in the case of automatic actions of the acquired type the channels of nervous discharge in the brain still run through the cortex, or whether by a process of " short-circuiting " they are restricted to the lower brain-centres, it is impossible at present to say. If we knew with anything approaching certainty what special parts of the cortex are concerned in the essentially controlling process, it might be possible to decide between these two views. Unfortunately we do not. All that can be said, and that with as much confidence as is permissible in such a difficult matter, is that whatever parts of the cortex (or other region of the brain) were concerned in effective guidance and control are, in the automatism begotten of habit, so concerned no longer.

As in the case of the congenital automatism of instinct, so, too, in the case of the acquired automatism of habit, the stimulus or group of stimuli produces a state of instability, the restoration of stability being effected by the performance of the habitual activity. If we apply, as above suggested, the word "impulse" to the tendency of the organism to pass on the application of a specific stimulus from the relative instability of a need or want to the relative stability of satisfaction, we have in the case of acquired automatism an habitual impulse answering to the instinctive impulse. When such a tendency is in any way checked or thwarted, the preliminary state of instability would seem to be thereby increased or emphasized, and the impulsive tendency is *pari passu* augmented. A very acute thinker and able writer — Mr. Henry Rutgers Marshall—goes so far as to say that "the word 'impulse' is in general use to indicate those phases of consciousness which are produced by the *inhibition* of instinctive activities that have been stimulated by the presence of the objective condition that usually calls them out, but which for one reason or another are not at once realized." * In this I think Mr. Marshall goes too far. The impulsive tendency is indeed emphasized and augmented; but to say that it is produced by the inhibition appears to be an overstatement of the case.

In conclusion one may picture the organism starting with a certain amount of congenital automatism of the more or less definitely instinctive type, and passing on to reach a certain amount of the acquired automatism of

* *Nature*, vol. lii. p. 130.

habit. The latter state is in part a modification of the former; but it contains superadded elements as well. And it is one of the functions of that Intelligence with which we shall deal in the next chapter, to exercise a guiding influence in the establishment of the acquired automatism of habit.

CHAPTER VII.

INTELLIGENCE AND THE ACQUISITION OF HABITS.

WHEN a drill-sergeant takes in hand a number of raw recruits, he has to keep a vigilant eye on the actions of each, checking useless, misguided, or mistaken activity in this direction, eliciting more prompt and vigorous response to his commands in that direction, making the men act, not as isolated units, but as constituent members of a corporate body, and aiming throughout at that co-ordinated action on which their future efficiency will depend; so that, when they take their places in the ranks, each may be ready to perform his own part in due subordination to the combined action of the whole, without faltering and without hesitation. The men are duly organized into squads, companies, battalions, and so on; and thus we have a disciplined army with its brigades, divisions, and army corps; with its artillery, engineers, cavalry, and infantry; with its intelligence, commissariat, and medical departments, each with distinctive responsibilities, and under its own especial officers; the whole capable of the most varied and yet most orderly evolutions at the will of the commander-in-chief.

It is the function of consciousness, represented in the flesh by the cerebral cortex, to drill and organize the active forces of the animal body in a somewhat analogous manner. But when it enters upon its duties, consciousness finds that a considerable amount of the drilling has already been done. There is no need to teach the organic mechanism how certain activities are to be performed, for they are already carried out automatically. The intelligence department, with its special senses and so forth, is already organized so far as the supply of information is concerned. The commissariat department, digestive organs, heart, lungs, and the rest, is in pretty good working order, and eagerly on the look-out for supplies. Many complex activities, adaptive actions of the reflex kind and of the type we have termed instinctive, are at once performed under appropriate conditions without the guidance of consciousness. Consciousness merely looks on and makes a memorandum of what is going forward. The number and the complexity of those instinctive activities that consciousness thus finds ready to its hand varies in the different grades of animal life; being at a maximum in such forms as insects and spiders. They are more marked in birds than in mammals, and seem to be inconspicuous or difficult to trace in man. There are, however, also many more or less isolated activities, with very little initial adaptive value; and these resemble raw recruits. Such are the comparatively aimless and random limb movements of the human infant, as he lies helpless on his mother's lap. Consciousness has to combine and organize these vague efforts in directions that are useful for the purposes of animal life, and adapted to the conditions under which the forces of that life are employed; gradually to bring the effective work done by the several companies, represented by groups of muscles, into due relation to each other, and, assuming the supreme command, to carry on the battle of life at the best advantage.

Such an analogy as this must not be pressed too far. It is adduced merely for the purpose of illustration. The drill-sergeant, for example, is dealing with intelligent

L

beings, themselves capable of directing and controlling their own actions. But consciousness as drill-sergeant is dealing with automatic movements or activities, instinctive or random as the case may be, themselves incapable of self-guidance. What the analogy here serves to illustrate is this : that neither drill-sergeant, on the one hand, nor consciousness, on the other, can directly produce the activities which are dealt with. The activities must be given. All that can be done is to stimulate some to increased energy of action, and to check or repress others. And just as the drill-sergeant must vigilantly watch his men, since he is dependent on such observation for information as to the correct performance of their actions, so, too, is consciousness entirely dependent on the information received through the incoming channels of afferent nerves for the data upon which its guidance, through the exercise of augmentation and inhibition, is based. Further, just as the superior officer has to bring into due relation the evolutions which are carried out under the control of subordinates, so does consciousness correlate the data received through many groups of afferent nerves, and co-ordinate a number of varied activities into a more or less definite course of behaviour. It is true that the analogy here again to some extent fails, since the drill-sergeant and his superior officer are separate individuals, while consciousness is continuous, and is drill-sergeant and superior officer rolled into one. But though this continuity of consciousness remains unbroken, we have abundant evidence, in the course of our own experience, that, during the gradual establishment of the supreme conscious control of the bodily activities, the regulation of details of active response is step by step relegated to sub-conscious guidance, which, though constantly in touch with, requires but little attention from, the supreme centres of voluntary control. The horseman, the billiard player, the pianist, knows well that, when once skill has been attained, such further guidance as is required under the special conditions of any particular occasion may be safely left to sub-consciousness, scarcely troubling the attention at all. Habit has in large degree rendered these actions part of the acquired automatism. But consciousness, like a wise superior officer, still keeps vigilant watch. So long as the performance is satisfactory and accurate, the superior officer sees as if he saw not; but when anything goes wrong, consciousness, as superior officer, steps in more or less smartly and decisively.

Few are likely to question the importance in animal life of the acquisition of habits, including as we must under this term nearly all the varied forms of animal skill. For even when the skill is founded upon a congenital and instinctive basis, it is (except perhaps in some instinctive activities of insects and other invertebrates) improved, and guided to finer and more delicate issues, in the course of individual experience. So that we may regard the function of consciousness as twofold; first it is concerned in the establishment of habits; and, secondly, in the utilization of all the active powers, including the habits so established, in meeting the varied requirements of daily life. How, then, is the guidance of consciousness effected? Upon what principles are the acquisition of skill and the utilization of skill to be explained?

There can be no question that, from the psychological point of view, the association of impressions and ideas, some illustrations of which have already been incidentally given, is of fundamental importance. Whatever may be the position assigned to so-called " association by contiguity " in human psychology, there can be no question

as to its essential importance in the more primitive
psychology of such animals as young birds. When chicks
learn rapidly to distinguish between the caterpillars of the
cinnabar moth and those of the small white butterfly, so
that they gobble up the one without hesitation and avoid
the other without fail, they give the plainest intimation
that an association has been formed in each case
between appearance and taste. Prof. Preyer notes
that his chicks rapidly learnt to associate the sound
of tapping with the presence of food. I have already
described how one of my chicks, which had but recently
learnt to drink, standing in its tin, subsequently stopped
as it ran through the water in such a way as to lead one
to infer that wet feet had become associated with the
satisfaction of thirst. Young pheasants seemed to associate
water with the sight of a toothpick, on which I gave them
some drops. Ducklings so thoroughly associated water
with the sight of their tin that they tried to drink from it
and wash in it when it was empty, nor did they desist
for some minutes. A moorhen chick, for whose benefit we
had dug up worms with a spade, and which, standing by,
jumped on the first-turned sod and seized every wriggling
speck which caught his keen eye, would soon run from
some distance to me as soon as I took hold of the spade.
There is no need to multiply instances. The study of young
birds is an impressive lesson in association psychology;
and one daily grows more convinced of the importance of
association in the acquisition of experience of this homely
and elementary but essentially practical kind.

But it may be said that though association is unquestionably important, yet its efficiency in the guidance of
action depends upon something deeper still. Granted
that, in a chick which has first seen and then tasted a
nasty morsel, an association is formed between sight and

taste, so that on a subsequent occasion its peculiar appearance suggests its peculiar nastiness. What is the connection between the nastiness of a cinnabar caterpillar and the checking of the tendency to eat it, or between the niceness of the caterpillar of the small white butterfly, and the added energy with which it is seized? Why do taste-stimuli of one kind have the one effect, and taste-stimuli of a different kind have just the opposite effect? What are the physiological concomitants of the augmentation of response in the one case, and of the inhibition of response in the other case? I conceive that there is but one honest answer to these questions. We do not know. This and much beside must be left for the science of the future to explain. This much may, however, be said. Certain stimuli call forth disturbances, probably in the cortex of the brain, the result of which is the inhibition of activities leading to the repetition of these stimuli; certain others call forth cortical disturbances, the result of which is the augmentation of the activities which lead to their repetition. The accompaniments in consciousness of the former we call unpleasant or painful; the accompaniments in consciousness of the latter we call pleasurable. This appears to be a plain statement of the facts as we at present understand them.*

Now, there can be no question as to the strongly-marked hereditary element in such augmentation of response when the cortical disturbances have pleasurable concomitants and the inhibition of response when the cortical disturbances have unpleasant concomitants. This is, in fact, founded on the innate powers or faculties which the organism derives from its parents and more distant

---

* Compare Prof. J. Mark Baldwin's statements in his "Mental Development of the Child and the Race" (1895), p. 278 and elsewhere, concerning what he terms "biological or organic imitation."

ancestors. But if the cortical augmentation and inhibition are founded in heredity; and if this augmentation and inhibition form the basis upon which all acquisition and all control are based; what becomes of the distinction between instinctive and acquired activities? What, of that between automatic and controlled behaviour?

Let us look again at the facts which we are endeavouring to interpret. A chick sees for the first time in its life a cinnabar caterpillar, instinctively pecks at it under the influence of the visual stimulus; seizes it, and under the influence of the taste-stimulus instinctively shrinks. So far we have instinct and automatism. Presently we throw to it another similar caterpillar. Instinct and automatism alone would lead to a repetition of the previous series of events; seeing, seizing, tasting, shrinking. The oftener the experiment was performed the more smoothly would the organic mechanism work, the more definitely would the same sequence be repeated— seeing, seizing, tasting, shrinking. Is this what we actually observe? Not at all. On the second occasion the chick, under the influence of the previous experience, acts differently. Though he sees, he does not seize, but shrinks without seizing. We believe that there is a revival in memory of the nasty taste. And in this we seem justified, since we may observe that sometimes the chick on such occasions wipes the bill on the ground as he does on experiencing an unpleasant taste, though he have not touched the larva. The chick, then, does not continue to act merely from instinct and like an automaton. His behaviour is modified in the light of previous experience. What, then, has taken place in and through which this modification, born of experience, is introduced? In answering this question we disclose the essential feature of the distinction we have all along been drawing—that between congenital and acquired activities. The answer may be given in two words—*association* and the *suggestion* that arises therefrom. The chick's first experience of the cinnabar caterpillar leads to an association between the appearance of the larva and its taste; or, from the physiological point of view, to a direct connection between the several cortical disturbances. On the second occasion the taste is suggested by the sight of the cinnabar larva; or, physiologically, the disturbance associated with taste is directly called forth by the disturbance associated with sight. It is through association and suggestion that an organism is able to profit by experience, and that its behaviour ceases to be merely instinctive and automatic. And such association would seem to be a purely individual matter—founded, no doubt, on an innate basis, linking activities of the congenital type, but none the less wholly dependent upon the immediate touch of individual experience. Hence the development of consciousness as effective for the guidance of life, takes its origin in the *linkage*, through association, of sentient states. In the absence of such linkage sentience is a mere adjunct accompanying certain organic transactions in the nervous system or elsewhere.

In watching, then, the behaviour of young birds or other animals, we observe a development which is to be interpreted as the result of conscious choice and selection. For the chick to which a handful of mixed caterpillars is thrown, chooses the nice ones, and leaves the nasty untouched. This selection is dependent upon an innate power of association which needs the quickening touch of individual experience to give it actuality and definition, without which it would lie dormant as a mere potentiality. On this conscious selection and choice depends, throughout its entire range, the development of those habits which are acquired as opposed to those which are congenital; and on it depends, as we shall hereafter see, the whole of mental as contrasted with merely biological evolution.

Let us be quite clear as to what is here meant by conscious selection. By it is meant, that activities are determined by the associative effects produced in consciousness; or, in other words, that they are due to experience. The organism that profits by experience, avoiding this because it has been found unsatisfactory, and choosing that because previous trial has shown it to be good, exercises conscious selection.

The foundations of animal intelligence * rest on individual choice or selection, which in turn is dependent upon association, and the suggestion it renders possible. For how could a chick learn to avoid cinnabar caterpillars if the sight of their black and golden-ringed bodies had not become associated with their distastefulness, and that so intimately and with such a nicety of mechanism that the instinctive tendency to peck at any small object at suitable distance is arrested by the restraining impulse due to the associated taste? A single experience is often sufficient to establish an association. I noticed that one of my seven-

---

* The reader may be referred for a comparison of the "mentality of the higher animals" with that of man to Lecture xxiv. in Professor Wundt's "Lectures on Human and Animal Psychology." "The criterion of 'intelligent' associative action and of intelligent action proper [that to which I should restrict the term 'rational,' and 'intellectual'], can," he says, "only be this—that the effect of association does not go beyond the connection of particular [or at most 'generic' as distinguished from 'general'] ideas, whether directly excited by sense-impressions, or only reproduced by them, while intellectual activity in the narrower sense of the word presupposes a demonstrable formation of concepts, judgments, and inferences, or an activity of the constructive imagination" (Eng. Trans., p. 357). In Professor Wundt's opinion, in which I concur, "the animal actions which border most closely on the realm of human understanding give us no warrant for inferring the existence of true concepts, judgments, and [logical] inferences" (*ibid.* p. 359).

days-old chicks pecked repeatedly at something near the corner of the turned-up newspaper which formed the wall of the enclosure, the paper being propped against a more solid support. The speck which had caught Blackie's keen eye turned out to be the number of the page. He then transferred his attention to the corner of the paper, which he could just reach. Seizing this he pulled at it, bending the paper down, and thus formed a breach through which he escaped into the wider field of my study. I caught and put him back near the same spot. He went at once to the corner, pulled it down and escaped, but was captured, and set down on the other side of the pen. Presently, he sauntered round to the old spot, reached up to the corner of the newspaper, pulled it down, and again effected his escape. A single chance experience had sufficed to teach him, and the association held good. I parted with him in the evening of that day, so that I am unable to say how long the association lasted; but other observations lead me to believe that an association once formed is not soon obliterated. A moorhen that had learnt to avoid cinnabar caterpillars refused to touch one though three weeks had elapsed since he had seen any or had opportunity of reviving the association, and though, in the mean time, he had seen many strange worms.

It does not appear to me that we are forcing upon a technical term a meaning widely divergent from that which current usage sanctions in a familiar word, in designating as " intelligent " Blackie's repeated escape from confinement when chance had taught him how to break bounds. In what essential respect does it differ from the behaviour of Tony, my fox-terrier, who opens the gate by lifting its iron latch with his head, having, after looking out between the bars in a number of places in the railings, at length chanced to gaze out under, and at the same time inadvertently lift, the latch? He, too, after a while profited by the fortunate results of an originally fortuitous experience, and now opens the gate whenever he wants to do so. At any rate, using the word as a technical term for behaviour based on direct association, this profiting by individual experience is of the very essence of intelligence. No doubt important conditions to the intelligent over-coming of difficulties are persistency and varied effort. I have noted this again and again in the case of young birds. It was especially noticeable in jays. Every projecting bit of wire or piece of wood in their cage was pulled at from all points, and in varied ways. Every new object introduced into the cage was turned over, carried about, pulled at, hammered at, stuffed into this corner and into that, and experimented with in all possible ways. Such persistency and varied effort affords to in-telligence abundant material from which some fortunate and helpful association may arise.

Dr. Mills, in his diary of the kitten,* describes how persistent were its efforts, from the twenty-sixth to the twenty-eighth day of life, to get into some partially filled book-shelves, even when the entrance was barred up. "The history of the kitten's whole bearing towards the book-shelves has been to me," he says, "a most in-structive one. I have never witnessed such perseverance in the accomplishment of an object in any young animal —not excepting the child. It seemed that the greater obstacles the greater the efforts the kitten put forth to overcome them — behaviour that we usually consider especially human, and ever an evidence of unusual strength of character."

No doubt there are well-marked variations in this innate persistency and experimentalism, if we may so

* *Trans. Roy. Soc. Canada,* 2nd series, vol. i. sect. iv. pp. 197, 210.

call it. Not long ago I was walking on a Sunday afternoon with a gentleman who took with him five young
hounds. We came to a gate the lower bars of which
were close together, the upper bars being further apart;
and, when we had climbed over, we watched the pups.
All at first struggled to get through the lower bars, but
they were too narrow. Presently first one, then another,
and then a third, tried higher up, and scrambled through
the wider opening. The fourth persistently struggled at
the lower bars; the fifth occasionally struggled, but spent
most of his time in. whining. Here then, are three,
if not four, grades of intelligence. First, the cleverest
pup, who soon got through by trying a new place, and
showed the way; secondly, two others who soon followed
his example—the third apparently through imitation;
then the stupid but persistent pup ; and, lastly, the
one who gave it up and whined—unless, indeed, we regard
the desisting from hopeless attempts as a mark of intelligence. My friend went back and called the three successful pups after him, and they got through without
much difficulty. He then rejoined me in the field, and
the intelligent pups at once scrambled up to the wider
opening: they had learnt their lesson. But the other
two still struggled and whined; and though we remained
in the field for twenty minutes, neither .of them learnt
the trick of that gate. An intending purchaser of one of
these five pups would hardly have selected either of
these two duffers !

The point, however, which it is desirable to emphasize
is, that intelligence involves selection or choice; that
the profitable experience is chosen for repetition; and that
such conscious selection is rendered possible only through
association. It may indeed be asked, Why bring in this
word "association" so often? Why not say simply that it is by

memory that the profiting by experience is made possible ?
There can, of course, be no objection to ascribing the facts
to memory. But let it be clearly noted that the memory
is of such a kind that *this* suggests *that;* it is just the
connection by means of which *this* and *that* are linked
together, so that *this* revives *that* in memory, to which the
term " association " is applied.

What, then, we may now ask, is the relation of experience to impulse ? In reply to this question, we may
say that the congenital impulse may, through experience,
be confirmed, modified, or held in check; and that such
confirmation, modification, or inhibition gives rise to an
acquired impulsive tendency. Let us, however, look a
little more closely into the nature of this acquired impulsive tendency. It is not going too far to say that every
bit of practical experience leaves the organism something
different from what it found it. The chick that has had
experience of the nastiness of the cinnabar larva is
neither organically nor impulsively what it was before
the experience. It is an organism with different reactive
tendencies. And the difference is due to acquisition. Let
us state this in terms of the conception of impulse
which has already been formulated. Impulse, I said, is
the tendency of any organism to satisfy its needs and fulfil
the conditions of its being. Now, the chick comes into the
world with certain congenital impulses, certain tendencies
to satisfy its congenital needs and to fulfil the inherited
conditions of its being. But at the touch of experience
its needs are modified or further defined; the conditions of
its being are no longer what they were, for they too have
undergone modification or further definition. On the congenital basis has been grafted an acquired disposition.
When new stimuli come there is an impulsive tendency
to realize, not the old being, the conditions of which were

determined solely by heredity, but a new being, in which that which was due to inheritance is modified by that which has been acquired through individual experience. Thus we may say that after a little experience the impulsive tendencies are the net result of two factors—inheritance and individual acquisition.

By repetition, the results of acquisition become more and more firmly ingrained in the organic and impulsive constitution. Habit is second nature. The congenital automatism with which the animal starts gives place, under the play of repetition, to an acquired automatism. Between the earlier stereotyped congenital response on the one hand, and the later stereotyped acquired response on the other hand, lies the period of youthful plasticity. The stimuli to the first—the stereotyped congenital response— are to some extent unspecialized; the chick will peck at any object of a suitable size at an appropriate distance. But the stimuli to the second—the acquired response— are specialized, defined, or particularized. The experienced chick habitually responds in one way to looper caterpillars, and in a different way to cinnabars. The former, the congenital responses, tend to meet the general requirements of the race ; the latter, the acquired responses, are adapted to the special requirements of the individual. A congenital tendency leads the little moorhen either to assume the defensive attitude, or to run away, at the sight of any large approaching object ; acquired tendencies lead it to tolerate or welcome the approach of the familiar fox-terrier or man, but to react even more vigorously on the approach of the unfamiliar goose or sheep. It is in the period of youthful plasticity that intelligence has its most important part to play—so far as the genesis of habit is concerned—at any rate, in such organisms as young birds, whose intelligent adaptability is in marked contrast with the stereotyped stupidity (as it appears to us from its relative lack of plasticity) of the ordinary hen. And even with human beings there is at least some truth in the sigh with which the philosopher regarded the bright and active Eton and Harrow boys at Lords', when he remembered that, ere many years had passed, they would become mere bishops and members of parliament. But there always remains, it must be noted, over and beyond the period of youthful plasticity, a greater or less balance of intelligence for further adaptation throughout adult life. The higher the mental grade of the organism, and the more varied the conditions of that life, the greater the balance of intelligence that remains—only, however, to grow less and less as maturity verges on senility.

It is on the relation of intelligence to repetition, and hence to that acquired habit which becomes second nature, that we have to fix our attention. For those activities which are frequently repeated, become ingrained in the organic nature as more or less fixed habits * of response ; and the more firmly the habit is ingrained, the more imperious is the impulse to the performance of the habit. Just in so far as the individually acquired nature gains strength and permanence does the need for its realization under the appropriate conditions of stimulation increase in force and insistency. The craving which accompanies the thwarting of habitual activities increases in strength *pari passu* with the growth of acquired automatism. The organism which to begin with was a creature of congenital impulse becomes more and more the creature of acquired impulse. It is a new being, but one with needs yet more imperious than those with which it was congenitally endowed.

* These are the acquired instincts of Prof. Wundt, "Lectures on Human and Animal Psychology," Trans., p. 397.

It is, however, a practical problem of no little difficulty to determine in particular instances whether a given adaptive activity is an instinct or a habit; whether it is congenital in its definiteness, or has acquired this definiteness by intelligent selection and recurrent repetition. The observations which have been described in preceding chapters had for one of their objects, the determination of this point for some of the activities of bird life. Let us now take a particular case—for such a case is both more instructive and more interesting than mere generalities— by which the difficulty in question may be further illustrated.

In 1874 Darwin drew attention, in the columns of *Nature*,* to the fact that primrose flowers were cut off, and a piece of the calyx, between one- and two-tenths of an inch in length, was removed. He attributed the destruction to birds, who would thus obtain the nectar contained in the flower, but asked for further information.

Many letters appeared in response to Darwin's appeal. Among them one by Major E. R. Festing, who said,† "A month ago I saw a caged hen bullfinch that would treat any quantity of primroses which were given her in precisely the way described by Mr. Darwin. She gave one snip only to each flower, not again touching the remains of it, which fell to the floor of the cage." And other evidence pointed to the bullfinch as the bird which possessed this habit.

Darwin returns to the subject in a subsequent number,‡ and writes as follows: "It is clear that the ovules are the chief attraction; but the birds, in removing by pressure the ovules, could not fail to squeeze out the nectar at the open end, as occurred when I squeezed similar bits between

* Vol. ix. p. 482. † *Nature*, vol. x. p. 6.
‡ Ibid., vol. x. p. 24.

my fingers. The birds thus got a dainty morsel, namely,
young ovules with sweet sauce." And then, in reference
to the instinctive character of the action, he continues,
"In my former letter I remarked that if the habit of
cutting off the flowers proved to be a widely extended
one, we should have to consider it as inherited or
instinctive; as it is not likely that each bird should discover, during its individual lifetime, the exact spot where
the nectar, and, as I must now add, the ovules, lie concealed, or should learn to bite off the flower so skilfully
at the proper point. That the habit is instinctive, Prof.
Frankland has given me interesting evidence. When
he read my letter he happened to have in the room a
bunch of cowslip flowers and a caged bullfinch, to whom
he immediately gave some of the flowers, and afterwards
many primrose flowers. The latter were cut off in exactly
the same manner, and quite as neatly, as by the wild
birds near here. I know that this is the case by having
examined the cut-off portions. Prof. Frankland informs
me that his bird pressed the cut-off portions of the calyx in
its beak, and gradually worked them out on one side, and
then dropped them. Thus the ovules were removed and
the nectar necessarily squeezed out. Now, the caged
bullfinch was caught in 1872, near, but not in, the Isle
of Wight, soon after it had left the nest, by which time
the primroses would have been out of flower; and since
then, as I hear from Prof. Frankland, it had never seen a
primrose or a cowslip flower. Nevertheless, so soon as
this bird, now nearly two years old, saw these flowers,
some machinery in the brain was set into action, which
instantly told it in an unerring manner how and where to
bite off and press the flowers so as to gain the hidden prize."

This appeared to be a final solution of the matter.
But the observations of a subsequent correspondent

tended to throw doubt on the instinctive nature of the bird's procedure. " I have a bullfinch," she says,* " which was hatched last summer after primroses were over. They were, therefore, quite new to him when I offered him the first I could get this season. He pulled it to pieces quite indiscriminately, biting stalk, flower, or calyx quite indifferently, and the same with a few more which were given to him at the same time. But since then he has often had a few at a time, perhaps twenty or thirty in all, and he now almost always bites out the lower part of the calyx as described by Mr. Darwin in *Nature*. Sometimes he bites a little too high up, but almost instantly tries again with better success. When that part is eaten, he attacks the stalk rather than the corolla.

" Last spring I offered primroses to four bullfinches belonging to friends. Not one seemed to pull the flower to pieces according to any method. Two of them I saw only once. Another (an old bird, and somewhat shy), after being supplied with the flowers for several days, seemed as unskilful in picking out the titbit as he was at first. The fourth was a young bird. His mistress was called away before she had heard what was the peculiarity for which I was watching. A few days later she told me she had given him primroses in the mean time, and had noticed that he ate only the green part. [This was *not* the case with the first I offered him.] In those few days he had learnt the art of primrose-eating, not, indeed, quite perfectly, but wonderfully well considering how little practice he had had.—C. A. M."

It will be seen, then, that it is by no means so easy as might at first sight be supposed, to determine whether an habitual activity is truly instinctive or is due to the play of individual selective intelligence.

* *Nature*, vol. xiii. p. 427.

There is a point of considerable importance to which attention may here be drawn. Assuming that the habit of the bullfinch is due to intelligence, let us carefully note the *rôle* that it plays. It is essentially selective. The bullfinch, to begin with, pulls the primroses to pieces with what may be termed an exuberance of activity. But in the midst of it all, just one particular snip at the tube of the flower is found to provide the ovules and the sweet sauce. All the rest is then neglected, and the one effectual snip selected for repetition.* The *rôle* of intelligence, therefore, is not to furnish a new activity which shall be adapted to what we, the onlookers, call the end in view, but to select from a number of relatively indeterminate activities that one which experience proves to be effectual.

It has again and again been pointed out that the origin of variations and their selection in the struggle for existence, are different problems, however intimately they may be associated in the process of evolution. The fitter variations must be given ere they can survive. So now it must be pointed out that the origin of activities some of which may be adaptive is a different problem from that of the intelligent selection of those which are adaptive. The more adaptive activities must be given ere they can be selected from among those which are less adaptive.

Herein, then, lies the utility of the restlessness, the exuberant activity, the varied playfulness, the prying curiosity, the inquisitiveness, the meddlesome mischievousness, the vigorous and healthy experimentalism of the young. These afford the raw material upon which intelligence exercises its power of selection. Observers of human life have not failed to contrast this youthful

* Prof. Mark Baldwin has developed this point in his interpretation of the psychology of the child. See his " Mental Development in the Child and the Race," chap. v.; and *American Naturalist*, July, 1896, p. 548.

expansiveness ready to try all, dare all, and do all, with the narrower and more restricted, if more concentrated, efforts of those in whom the stern lessons of experience have checked so much that is picturesquely impossible. And this exuberant expansiveness of youth is a biological and psychological fact of profound significance.

One or two examples in further illustration of habits which may be fairly regarded as acquired may now be given. Mr. J. Southwell * has described how sparrows at first pulled to pieces yellow crocuses to get at the nectar, but afterwards simply bruised the perianth tube sufficiently to extract the sweet fluid; and he suggests that this habit—begotten, be it noted, of intelligent restriction—is acquired, and not inherited.

In the *Zoologist* † for January, 1896, Dr. Lowe describes a curious habit of the blackcap which he observed in Tenerife. The birds visit the flowers of *Hibiscus rosa-sinensis* and tear out pieces from the two upper segments of the calyx, thus causing a drop of sweet fluid to exude. This acts as a "bait," attracting numerous insects on which the birds feed. A similar habit has been observed in the Grand Canary in the case of a tit (*Parus tenerifæ*), which perforates the calyx of a shrubby species of *Abutilon*. "The object of this proceeding seems to be to afford a ready means by which ants may arrive at the nectary." These, "after consuming the nectar, are found in a semi-torpid state, making no attempt to escape on being disturbed. They thus fall an easy prey to the tits, which visit all the flowers at short intervals during the day, and clear off all the ants. Another bird closely resembling the willow wren also makes periodic visits to the *Abutilon* flowers for the purpose of feeding on the ants," but was not observed to take any part in lacerating the calyx.

* *Nature*, vol. x. p. 7.   † Vol. xx. pp. 1–10.

How far, if at all, these habits are instinctive, we do not know. The plants which the birds treat in this way are, Dr. Lowe says,[*] all exotics, so that the habit has in all probability been acquired since their introduction into the Canary Islands. It would seem to be the result of intelligence, and handed on through imitation.

Another change of habit, probably of intelligent origin, is afforded by the oft-quoted case of the kea (*Nestor notabilis*) of Middle Island, New Zealand. It belongs to the family of the brush-tongued parrots, and, according to Mr. Taylor White,[†] lived on the mountains above the forest-line, feeding upon the lichen on the stones. If this was the case, it would seem to be a modification of the normal habits of the family, which usually feed on nectar, insects, fruits, and berries. About 1868 it was observed to attack living sheep. Those which, having missed a shearing, had long wool died suddenly, the only apparent cause of death being a wound far down the back. This was found to be due to the kea, which was, according to Mr. White, attracted to the sheep by the resemblance of the wool to lichens, the spot chosen being due to the fact that it there escaped the efforts of the sheep to dislodge it. The bird's object was to obtain blood; but it may subsequently have found the kidney fat which lay beneath. Whether this curious change of habit is tending to become hereditary and instinctive we do not know. Imitation would presumably be sufficient to account for the handing on of the habit. But the bird is being destroyed by the owners of sheep, and will probably ere long become extinct.

Mr. Joseph Willcox records a curious habit of the crow

---

[*] *Zoologist*, vol. xix. 1895. Cp. Wallace's "Darwinism," p. 75.

[†] *Proc. Acad. Nat. Sci. Philadelphia*, 1877. Abstracted January, 1878; noted in *Nature*, vol. xiii. p. 589.

blackbird of Florida (*Quiscalus purpureus*). Standing on the brink of a river, he "noticed a commotion among a congregation of these birds, which were anxiously looking into the water. A large bass was pursuing its favourite food, the small fry, and the latter, in their frantic efforts to escape, jumped out of the water, and many of them fell on the land. The blackbirds, evidently experts at the game, immediately pounced upon the small fish and swallowed them before they could get back into the water."

Intelligence, like Mr. Micawber, is always keenly on the look-out for something to turn up, and, when it does turn up, profits by the experience thus gained. If a crow-blackbird, for example, standing by the water-side, saw first a commotion in the water, and then young fry leaping out on the sand, and found the latter pleasant to the taste, he would probably haunt the water's edge next day, and, should he see a commotion in the stream near the bank at some distance off, would hurry thither in the expectation of finding a dish of whitebait. All of this is rendered possible by that association of impressions and ideas without which intelligence would not exist. And then his neighbours and friends, seeing him enjoying a good meal, will soon be self-invited guests at the repast.

That the imitation implied in the last sentence is an important factor in the development of habits, there can be no question. Although the psychological and physiological conditions of imitation are by no means thoroughly understood, it will be well to devote the next chapter to the consideration of this factor.

CHAPTER VIII.

IMITATION.

THAT imitation, or what we are accustomed to regard as such, is an important factor in animal life, especially among gregarious animals, is scarcely open to question. But the biological and psychological conditions are not easy to understand. Some forms of imitation are often spoken of as instinctive; but some are voluntary, and under the guidance of intelligence. It is to the latter that the term " imitation," in its usual acceptation, would seem to be properly applicable. And the exact nature of the connection between this conscious and voluntary imitation and the involuntary instinctive process to which we apply the same term, requires careful consideration. Let us first look at some of the facts which illustrate imitation of the latter and apparently instinctive type.

If one of a group of chicks learn by casual experience, such as I have before described, to drink from a tin of water, others will run up and peck at the water, and will themselves drink.* A hen teaches her little ones to pick up grain or other food by pecking on the ground and dropping suitable materials before them, the chicks seeming to imitate her actions. One may make chicks and young pheasants peck by simulating the action of a hen with a pencil-point or pair of fine forceps. According to

* Dr. Mills records a similar observation on puppies (*Trans. Roy. Soc. Canada*, sect. iv. (1894), p. 43.

Mr. Peal's statement, before quoted, the Assamese find that young jungle pheasants will perish if their pecking responses are not thus stimulated; and Prof. Claypole tells me that this is also the case with ostriches hatched in an incubator. A little pheasant and guinea-fowl followed two ducklings, one wild, the other tame, and seemed to wait upon their bills, to peck where they pecked, and to be guided by their actions. It is certainly much easier to bring up young birds if older birds are setting an example of eating and drinking; and instinctive actions, such as scratching the ground, are performed earlier if imitation be not excluded. I have observed that if a group of chicks have learnt to avoid cinnabar caterpillars, and if then one or two from another group are introduced and begin to pick up the caterpillars, the others will sometimes again seize them, though they would otherwise have taken no notice of them. One of the chicks, coming upon a dead bee, gave the danger or alarm note; another at some little distance at once made the same sound. A number of similar cases might be given. But what impresses the observer, as he watches the early development of a brood of young birds, is the presence of an imitative tendency which is exemplified in many little ways not easy to describe in detail.

What generalization, then, can be drawn from this somewhat indefinite group of facts ? What is their relation to instinctive procedure in general ? Instinctive procedure, we must remember, is congenital behaviour of a more or less definite kind, involving the inherited co-ordination of motor activities due to outgoing nerve-currents, and initiated by an external stimulus under organic conditions of internal origin. Now, it would seem that where the external stimulus is afforded by the behaviour of another organism, and the responsive behaviour it initiates

is similar to that which affords the stimulus, such responsive behaviour may be described as imitative. A chick
sounds the danger note; this is the stimulus under which
another chick sounds a similar note, and we say that the
one imitates the other. Such an action may be described
as imitative in its effects, but not imitative in its purpose.
It is objectively, but not subjectively imitative. Only from
the observer's standpoint does such instinctive behaviour
differ from other modes of instinctive procedure. It is for
him that the instinctive response falls under the head of
imitation. We seem justified in asserting that, from the
biological point of view, any stimulus or group, of stimuli,
may give rise to a congenital response of any kind. In
the case of an imitative action, the stimulus is afforded by
the performance by another * of an action similar in
character to that which constitutes the response. From
the observer's point of view, this is noteworthy, and, from
the point of view of biological interpretation, important.
But from the performer's point of view, if one may so say,
it is in line with all other cases of instinctive activity.
A stimulus, visual, auditory, or other, is followed automatically by a co-ordinated response, and there is no
similarity between either the stimulus or the states of
consciousness accompanying it, on the one hand, and the
response, or its conscious concomitants, on the other
hand.† Such, it would seem, is the nature of instinctive

---

* This seems to be part of the accepted implications of the word
"imitation." Prof. Mark Baldwin uses the term with an extended signification, so as to include, under the head of imitation, repetition of an action
by the same individual. From the observer's point of view, it is, of course,
open to us to call the repeated act one that is imitative of the previous act of
which it is a repetition; but if we do so we must abandon the accepted
usage, according to which "imitation" is applied to the repetition by one
individual of the behaviour of another individual. There appears to be no
sufficient reason for such a complete change of accepted usage.

† Prof. Mark Baldwin has suggested that imitation should be defined as
a response which tends to reproduce its own stimulus—a "circular activity,"

imitation, or that congenitally automatic behaviour which, from the observer's standpoint, is imitative.

Passing reference may here be made to those instinctive actions for which mimicry is now a recognized biological term. Certain distasteful butterflies, for example, are mimicked by others, which are believed to have escaped destruction because of their mimetic resemblance to the others. There is no intentional imitation. The mimicry is of purely objective significance. And not only in form, but also in their instinctive behaviour, are many of these insects, and perhaps some birds, mimetic of others. Such behaviour is, from the purely objective point of view, imitative. But since there does not seem to be any good ground for supposing that the mimetic behaviour is called forth by the stimulus of such behaviour in the models, it does not fall under the head of the instinctive imitation we are considering. By using the term "mimetic" in its biological signification,* we may mark off these cases of mimicry in behaviour from true examples of instinctive imitation—that is to say, instinctive behaviour called forth by similar behaviour in others.

Now, as we have already seen, instinctive procedure forms part—and a not unimportant part—of the raw material on which intelligence exercises its influence, fashioning and moulding it, and guiding the activities concerned to finer issues in individual adaptation. The

as he describes it. But the instinctive imitations of young animals do not necessarily tend to reproduce their own stimuli. A chick, seeing its companions run away or crouch, will do so itself; and this we should describe as an imitative action, but (save for the observer) there is here no reproduction of the initiating stimulus (see "Mental Development of the Child and the Race," *passim*).

* Mr. C. A. Witchell, for example, in treating of the song of birds, uses the term "mimicry" as equivalent to "imitation," which is confusing to the biologist, for whom "mimicry" as a technical term has acquired a restricted signification.

first performance of an instinctive activity, whether imitative or not, affords the data to consciousness for the perfecting or the modification of the activity and the formation of instinct habits—that is to say, acquired modifications of congenital responses. Given, therefore, a congenital and instinctive imitation, intelligence may utilize it as the basis of an imitative action of the conscious type. To such conscious or intentional imitation we may now turn.

When a child consciously and of set purpose tries to imitate another child or an older person, his action is in all cases founded on a certain amount of preliminary experience. Let us suppose that he is imitating the action of another in tracing with a pencil a simple curve. This is impossible unless he have already acquired some data in the light of which control over his arm and finger movements may be exercised. His object is to apply this control in such a way as to reproduce the movements of the other so as to obtain the same results. He must have some data to work with. Either instinctive imitation has afforded such data, or acquired experience of the use of his limbs and fingers has taught him that, to do this thing which another is doing, and so reach similar results, he must guide his movements in certain definite ways. Given such preliminary data, further progress would seem to be a matter of trial and error, the repressing of such movements as lead to failure, the emphasizing and repeating of such movements as lead to success. Failure is accompanied by more or less painful dissatisfaction; success, by more or less pleasurable satisfaction. Thus, step by step, further control is gained until the imitative action is sufficiently perfect.

It would be convenient to distinguish between two allied, but at the same time somewhat different, processes; and for our present purpose, though the distinction of terms cannot, perhaps, be conveniently maintained, we will describe the reproduction of another's action as imitation, and the reproduction of the objective results of the action, copying. In the case of the curve, the child first imitates the action—holds the pencil and moves the fingers in certain definite ways. But as soon as a passable result is reached, it is on this, and not on the movements, that he fixes his attention. His object is no longer to imitate the action so much as to reproduce the copy. Copying, though often based upon imitation, as we are using the words, may thus be distinguished therefrom. And just as instinctive imitation is in line with, and similar in character to, all other instinctive activity, so is copying in line with, and similar in character to, all other intelligent acquisition. Certain actions are performed, and according as their results afford satisfaction or dissatisfaction, they are enforced or suppressed. At the same time, just as instinctive imitation is marked off from other modes of instinctive activity by the fact that it gives rise *in the observer* to a visual or other impression similar to that which initiated the response, so too is copying to be distinguished from other modes of intelligent activity by the fact that (both from the observer's and the performer's point of view) its results reproduce the stimulus * which initiated the appropriate activity. And it is on these results that, in copying, the attention is chiefly fixed.

A further example will bring this out more clearly. In the reproduction by the normal child of the sounds its companions utter, there is far more of copying than of intentional imitation, as we have used these words. The

---

* This reproduction of stimulus is made a cardinal feature in Prof. Mark Baldwin's treatment of imitation in his "Mental Development in the Child and the Race."

child probably inherits a congenital power of articulation, which may fairly be termed instinctive, since articulation involves a relatively definite co-ordination which is absent in the case of merely inarticulate sounds. His own articulations afford auditory stimuli which, by association, become linked with the effects in consciousness of those motor processes by which they are produced. He obtains certain results from his own activities, and hears also the results of the activities of others. Thus the data are afforded for copying these results, and the child gradually learns to reproduce articulate sounds, and incidentally and unconsciously to imitate certain motor activities. I say "incidentally and unconsciously," because the action of the vocal cords is hidden from his sight, and the learning to produce certain sounds cannot, in the normal child, be in any important degree the result of imitating the lip-movements of others. And it is instructive to note that the acquired articulation of deaf mutes *is* mainly a matter of imitation, and not of copying, since the sounds produced are inaudible to the producer, and thus afford no data for copying. The normal child, in learning to articulate like its companions, thus copies certain sounds, and unconsciously imitates certain actions—though, from the observer's point of view, the actions are, no doubt, imitative.

As has before been said, the distinction in the use of the terms "imitation" and "copying"—often used interchangeably—could not, perhaps, be conveniently maintained. The distinction is here used as a temporary one to emphasize the difference between reproducing an action or movement, and reproducing a given result of such activity. Sometimes the attention is chiefly fixed on the one, sometimes on the other. Both are commonly called imitation; when, for example, we say that a child imitates the tones of another's voice. Both are commonly called copying; as when we say that monkeys copy their masters. The context, as a rule, sufficiently indicates which process predominates—whether the attention of the imitator is chiefly fixed on the curve to be reproduced, or on the movements necessary to reproduce it; on a sound to be made, or the actions necessary to make it.

We have already seen that intelligent procedure is the result of certain processes in the cerebral cortex or elsewhere, which have pleasurable or unpleasant concomitants in consciousness. The actions which bring pleasure are repeated and strengthened; those which are unpleasant are checked or inhibited. What, then, are the special and peculiar conditions of intelligent imitation? Wherein lies the distinguishing feature of the incentives in consciousness to the voluntary copying, either of movements or their results? A child hears certain articulate sounds produced by his companions, and hears also certain articulate sounds which he himself utters. What is the incentive to imitation? The only answer to this question which seems admissible is that the resemblance of the sounds he utters to the sounds he hears *is itself a source of pleasurable satisfaction;* and that, within certain limits, the closer the resemblance the greater the satisfaction. The tendency to imitate is based upon an innate and constitutional bias to get pleasure out of such resemblances; to gain satisfaction by reproducing what others are producing. If there be no such innate proclivity, it is difficult to see whence the incentive to imitation can be derived. At a later stage in the process of development, emulation is, no doubt, an important factor, and there arises a desire not only to imitate but to improve upon the copy.

And here it may be well to remind the reader of the distinction which has already been drawn between what is instinctive and what is innate. Both have their foundations in heredity. But we have restricted the term instinctive to the congenitally responsive behaviour evoked by an external stimulus under given internal conditions. We have treated the instinctive activity from the frankly objective and biological point of view, and have regarded the instinctive response as prior to experience. That which is innate, on the other hand, is the inherited tendency to deal with these data in certain ways. Acquisition is impossible if there be not an innate power of association, and if there be not innate susceptibilities to pleasure and pain. The instinctive response as such is independent of association, and independent of the pleasurable or unpleasant effects of that response. That which is instinctive is the basis of definite congenital and organic responses; that which is innate is the basis of acquisition, rendered more or less definite in experience, and leading up to habit. Instinctive imitation is thus an organic response independent of experience; intelligent imitation is due to conscious guidance, the result of experience, and based upon the innate satisfaction which accompanies the act of reproductive imitation.

Let us now pass on to consider the place of intelligent imitation—what we may perhaps fairly term imitation proper—in the animal kingdom. Its very ubiquity makes it difficult to exemplify in a way that shall be adequately convincing. The abnormal arrests our attention more readily than the normal, and hence the cases of imitation usually cited are generally of this class. In the song of birds, for example, imitation is probably a most important factor, but it is chiefly the imitation of another species that arrests our attention. Thus the mocking-bird's feats of imitation are as familiar as an oft-told tale. Mr. L. M. Loomis told Mr. F. M. Chapman of one in South Carolina

which during ten minutes' singing imitated the notes of
no less than thirty-two different species of birds found in
the same locality. Mr. Chapman adds that this was a
phenomenal performance, and one he had never heard
approached, for, in his experience, many mocking-birds
have no notes but their own, and good mockers are
exceptional.* It would be interesting to gain further
information of the conditions under which good mockers
are developed. Is the sequence of imitative strains always
similar in the same individual? Or does he recombine
them in new order? There would seem to be here a field
for careful experiment and observation.

Our common English jay has the reputation of being
a consummate imitator, sometimes of strange sounds.
Montagu says that the low song of one individual was
interspersed with sounds imitative of the bleating of a
lamb, the mewing of a cat, the note of the kite or buzzard,
the hooting of an owl, and the neighing of a horse!
Bewick describes how a jay imitated the sound of a saw
so well as to cause much surprise, the day being Sunday.
And a correspondent in the *Magazine of Natural History*
—he may have been of Irish extraction!—says that one
imitated the goldfinch's song " most inimitably " (!), and
also the neighing of a horse.†

One more example among wild birds must suffice. Mr.
Warde Fowler, in his " Summer Studies of Birds and
Books,"‡ gives a quotation from the diary in which he noted
the performance in Switzerland of a marsh warbler. " I
am now writing," he says, " in a cool spot between the
allotments and the Aar, and listening to the marsh-warbler,

---

* "Birds of Eastern North America," p. 378.

† These cases are taken from Yarrell, "British Birds," 2nd edit. vol. ii.
p. 122.

‡ Pages 80, 81.

whose song is as wonderful as ever. Sometimes a grating outburst like that of a sedge-warbler; sometimes a long-drawn sweet note like a nightingale's. Then I have within the last few minutes certainly heard the chaffinch imitated, and even the nuthatch's metallic note. But a low pleasing soliloquy also goes on at intervals. Ah! there is the great tit; now the white wagtail, and I am beginning to get bewildered. This bird creeps about a good deal in the bushes, but now and then appears on a topmost shoot, and sits there singing with his bill wide open, and a red-yellow 'gape' showing very plainly. Now and then he flies into a tree over my head. Ah! there is the call of the redstart, and surely this is the skylark's song; and there is the chaffinch again, if ever I heard a chaffinch." *

Mere mention of the specially taught imitations of the parrot, magpie, raven, jackdaw, starling, and other birds must suffice. In all these birds there would seem to be an innate proclivity to copy the sounds they constantly hear, though it varies a good deal in different individuals. A short description of the teaching of bullfinches will serve to illustrate the most favourable conditions for imitation in this case.

"In Germany," † says Bechstein, "those young bull-finches that are to be taught to sing particular tunes must be taken from the nest when the feathers of the tail begin to grow, and must be fed only on rape seed soaked in water, and mixed with white bread. Although they do not warble before they can feed themselves, it is not necessary to wait for this to begin their instruction, for it will succeed better, if we may say so, when infused with their food, since experience proves that they learn those airs more quickly,

---

* Mr. C. A. Witchell has given a great deal of evidence on the subject of imitation among wild birds in chap ix. of his "Evolution of Bird Song," p. 159.

† Quoted in Yarrell's "British Birds," 2nd edit. vol. i. pp. 577, 578.

and remember them better, which they have been taught just after eating. . . . Nine months of regular and continued instruction are necessary before the bird acquires what amateurs call firmness; for if the instruction cease before this is obtained, they would destroy the air by suppressing or displacing the different parts, and they often forget it entirely at their first moulting. In general it is a good plan to separate them from the other birds even after they are perfect, because, owing to their great quickness in learning, they would spoil the air entirely by introducing wrong passages; they must be helped to continue the song when they stop, and the lesson must always be repeated while they are moulting, otherwise they will become mere chatterers. Different degrees of capacity are shown here, as well as in other animals. One young bullfinch learns with ease and quickness, another with difficulty and slowly : the former will repeat, without hesitation, several parts of a song; the latter will hardly be able to repeat one part, after nine months' uninterrupted teaching. But it has been remarked that those birds which learn with most difficulty remember the songs which they have once well learned better and longer, and rarely forget them, even when moulting. . . . Many birds, when young, will learn some strains of airs whistled or played to them regularly every day; but it is only those whose memory is capable of retaining them that will abandon their natural song, and adopt fluently and repeat without hesitation the air that has been taught them. Thus a young goldfinch learns, it is true, some part of the melody played to a bullfinch, but it will never be able to render it as perfectly as this bird." *

We have now given at sufficient length some evidence of imitation in the song or other utterances of birds.

* For imitation in birds and also in mammals, see Romanes' "Mental Evolution in Animals," pp. 222, 223.

How far does it extend? Mr. C. A. Witchell, who has paid much attention to the subject, is unhesitatingly of opinion that though the call-notes, alarm notes, and other such utterances are instinctive, yet the song itself is traditional and the result of imitation. With regard to the former point, I have no doubt whatever, from my own observations, that the notes of young chicks, guinea-fowl, peewits, partridges, pheasants, and moorhens are instinctively definite; as are probably those of the young flycatcher and young jay, though in these cases the birds were brought to me when a few days old. Nor can there be any question that the call-note and the warning note of the hen are also truly instinctive, though deferred. Mr. H. J. Charbonnier, a careful observer, tells me that a young magpie, which was brought to him as a nestling a fortnight old, always chattered and croaked in true magpie language, and was never heard to imitate other birds. Another magpie, however, picked up the note of the sparrow, and generally talked " sparrow," though it would sometimes introduce a few lower notes of its own proper tongue.

With regard to the latter point, there is undoubtedly a good deal of evidence in favour of the contention which Mr. Witchell espouses. One of the oldest observations is as follows. The Hon. Daines Barrington * placed three young linnets with three different foster-parents, the skylark, the woodlark, and the titlark or meadow-pipit, and each adopted, through imitation, the song of its foster-parent. Nor did they abandon this for their own true song when they were placed among songsters of their own species. Mr. Witchell † quotes from a letter of Mr. W. A. P. Hughes, who informed him that " a young bird (finch) reared by

---

* *Phil. Trans.*, 1773, p. 264.
† " Evolution of Bird Song," pp. 172, 173.

hand, and not allowed to hear another bird, never learns a perfect song, but sings a series of disconnected notes, without any similitude to the parents' song. Young bull-finches or greenfinches bred from the egg under canaries learned their foster-parents' songs, and had none of the harsh notes of their actual parents; while young green-finches taken from the nest when fledged, and then reared by hand, always had some of their respective parents' notes, although learning another song under a tutor. A goldfinch-canary mule with a pure goldfinch song, when two years old, learned the song of a linnet, and sang both songs alternately and mixed. The time when the young bird really picks up the song is in the nest, and before it can feed itself. I have seen the featherless little birds singing; that is, I have seen their throats going, and heard their squeaky note, as though they were practising." Mr. Hudson says [*] "that young oven-birds (*Furnarius*), when only partially fledged, are constantly heard apparently practising their duets in the intervals when the parents are absent. On the hypothesis of tradition, it is just because the young bird has predominant opportunities of hearing its parents' notes that it sings the parent song. On the other hand, Dr. A. G. Butler,[†] though he obtained evidence of imitation in abundance, was led, from many observations, to conclude that the tendency to imitate the song proper to the species is stronger than the tendency to imitate alien song, and that where foreign notes were caught up, they were introduced into and added by the bird to its own strains. I was assured many years ago by a bird-fancier in London, that he had reared young nestlings, such as thrushes and linnets, amid the strains of many caged birds singing with varied power, and that the

[*] " Naturalist in La Plata," p. 257.
[†] *Zoologist*, 1892, p. 30.

thrushes always, and the linnets for the most part, sang true, imitating the song of their own kind. Couch, in his "Illustrations of Instinct," * says that he knew a goldfinch, which had never heard the song of its own species, nevertheless singing this song, though tentatively and imperfectly. And speaking of the Dartford warbler, Colonel Montagu says † that young males brought up from the nest "begin to sing with the appearance of their first mature feathers, and continue in song all the month of October, sometimes with scarcely an intermission for several hours together. The notes are entirely native, consisting of considerable variety, delivered in a hurried manner, and in a much lower tone than I have ever heard the old birds in their natural haunts."

It is clear that further evidence based on observation under test conditions is needed. But if we may not yet unreservedly accept the view that the song of birds is wholly a matter of imitation, with little or no congenital tendency to sing true to type, yet it is an established fact that imitation is an important factor.

If the question be now asked,—Of what service can it be to the individual or the race to possess such an innate tendency to imitate song, and, as Mr. Witchell contends, to incorporate alien strains?—the answer does not appear to be altogether adequate or complete. According to Mr. Wallace, song is primarily for purposes of recognition. According to Darwin it is a means to sexual selection. Since most song-birds pair, we may perhaps surmise that the slight variety reached through the incorporation of alien strains is a means of recognition not only specific, but also individual, in its character. The hen bird, on this view, not only recognizes her mate as one of her

---

* P. 13, quoted in Romanes' "Mental Evolution in Animals," p. 222.
† Quoted in Yarrell's "British Birds," vol. i. p. 344.

own species, but as her own special mate. And if we admit sexual selection—a matter to be more fully discussed in a future chapter—we may perhaps suppose that such modifications of song evoke in different degrees the emotional state that accompanies the act of pairing. For those who believe that the hen birds select those who most strongly stir the sexual emotion, we have here the diverse modifications of song which may thus have differential effects. Such may be the advantages of imitation in the particular field of bird-song.

But should not the question be made broader and more general? Should we not ask, What is the organic value of the imitative tendency as evinced in many ways in the life of birds or other creatures? I cannot but think that in a number of cases it would make all the difference between survival and destruction. Mr. Tegetmeier states * "that if pigeons are reared exclusively with small grain, as wheat or barley, they will starve before eating beans. But when they are thus starving, if a bean-eating pigeon is put among them, they follow its example, and thereafter adopt the habit. So fowls sometimes refuse to eat maize, but on seeing others eat it, they do the same, and become excessively fond of it." Is it not clear that such imitation as Mr. Tegetmeier here describes might be a means of saving those who acted on it from starvation and death? Young water-fowl that, seeing their parents dive, did the same, would stand a far better chance of survival than those who stayed at the surface. One can well understand how natural selection would foster the imitative tendency, and working on congenital variations might eventually render the imitative behaviour a truly instinctive activity.

It has certainly in many cases produced a predisposition to imitate the actions of their own kind rather than

* Quoted in Mr. A. R. Wallace's " Darwinism," p. 75.

those of another species.   When chicks and ducklings are
brought up together, they keep to some extent separate,
and there is little imitation on the part of either of the
habits of the other species.   Spalding noted that chicks
showed no signs of imitating the peculiar habits of young
turkeys in the matter of catching flies.   It would seem,
indeed, that imitation serves to initiate or to emphasize
those activities to the performance of which there is already
a congenital bias.   Thus a blackbird which had been in cap-
tivity for two years in a large aviary, and had never been
mated or troubled with family cares, seeing some recently
introduced young thrushes fed by their parents through
the bars, began himself to feed them in a similar manner.*
Here an activity to which there is a congenital bias was
called into play through the suggestive touch of imitation.

If, then, the young have a tendency to imitate the actions
of their parents; if, too, among the members of gregarious
species, there is much imitation;—it is clear that we have
here a conservative factor in animal life of no slight
importance.   Just as imitation is of great value in
bringing the human child to the level of the adults who
form the family and social environment, so too does the
less fully conscious imitation of the lower animals serve to
bring the young bird or other creature into line with the
members of its own species.

I have several times observed that, in broods of chicks
brought up under experimental conditions by themselves,
and without opportunities of imitating older birds, there
are one or two more active, vigorous, intelligent, and
mischievous birds.   They are the leaders of the brood;
the others are their imitators.   Their presence raises the
general level of intelligent activity.   Remove them, and
the others show a less active, less inquisitive, less

* *Nature*, vol. xlviii. p. 369.   Letter signed "E. Boscher."

adventurous life, if one may so put it. They seem to lack initiative. From which one may infer that imitation affords to some extent a means of levelling up the less intelligent to the standard of the more intelligent; and of supplying a stimulus to the development of habits which would otherwise be lacking.

Under normal conditions, however, the conservative tendency of imitation, bringing the newly born members of the animal community into line with the average behaviour of the species is probably its most important office. Mr. W. H. Hudson, in his "Naturalist in La Plata," speaks of fear in birds as being "the result of experience and *tradition*." * And I have, in another work,† adopted this term. "I am inclined to regard imitation and tradition," I there said, "especially in animals which live in flocks, packs, or herds, as of very great importance. By tradition I mean this: that the animal is born into a group of animals which perform a number of activities in certain ways, and that through the imitative tendency it falls into these ways, which are thus handed on or carried down through tradition." We should distinguish this process by which habits are handed on from generation to generation, as clearly and sharply as possible from transmission through heredity. Hence I regard Prof. Mark Baldwin's subsequently proposed term "social heredity" ‡ as unfortunate. It is, as Prof. Ritchie has well pointed out in discussing human civilization, just because the effects produced are independent of heredity, that they demand special attention. Since, therefore, Prof. Baldwin can advance no claim to priority in drawing attention to the facts either for men or animals,

* Page 93.
† "Introduction to Comparative Psychology," pp. 170, 210.
‡ "Mental Development in the Child and the Race," chap. xii.

and since his term is in itself unsatisfactory, there seems no valid reason for adopting it.

Mr. Hudson's term "tradition" is quite in keeping with both etymology and popular usage, and serves to emphasize the fact that the phenomena are not due to heredity. By tradition in this sense, then, the habits of a given species may be handed on from generation to generation; and though inherited in the sense in which we speak of the inheritance of property, and it is thus that Mr. Ritchie uses the phrase "social inheritance," they do not necessarily become hereditary in the biological sense of the term. When the mongrel pup, whose development Dr. Wesley Mills watched and describes, was introduced to the society of other dogs, its progress was, he tells us, extraordinarily rapid. It was subject to the influence of canine tradition, and reacted at once to this influence. The young bird or mammal, especially in the case of gregarious species, is born into a community where certain behaviour is constantly exhibited before its eyes. Through imitation it falls in with the traditional habits, and itself serves as one of the models for those that come after. There can be no question that this tradition is of great importance in animal life. And it is clear that, if this be so, it is necessary, in any study of habit and instinct, to be on our guard, that we may distinguish clearly between heredity and tradition. What we are apt to regard as hereditary instincts may in some cases be shown to be traditional habits. And often we are unable to say, in the present condition of our knowledge, whether the performance of certain activities is due to heredity or to tradition; whether they are instinctive or due to imitation. Here, as elsewhere in this field of study, there is need of further observation under experimental conditions. The young must be brought up apart from their parents or other members of their kind. If they still exhibit the activities in question, such as the love-antics of many birds in the pairing season, there is probably an instinctive basis, and we may fairly conclude that the performance is handed on in all its definiteness through hereditary transmission. If they fail to exhibit the activities, other conditions being as far as possible normal, the probabilities are that the performance is traditional and due to imitation.

But though we must thus carefully distinguish between what is congenital and instinctive on the one hand, and what is acquired through imitation and handed on by tradition on the other hand, we must not forget that, in animal life, as it presents itself to our observation and interpretation, the two factors often combine to form what we have termed instinct-habits. Instinctive procedure is modified and moulded under the guiding touch of acquired experience. And there are probably many activities, such as the flight, and perhaps the song, of birds, which are founded on an instinctive basis, which are quickened through imitation, and which reach completion by much practice and that constant repetition under the guidance of individual experience which leads onwards to perfected habit.

CHAPTER IX.

THE EMOTIONS IN THEIR RELATION TO INSTINCT.

In attempting to deal with the relation of emotion to habit and instinct, we must devote our attention chiefly to the objective aspect: to the outward manifestations and the organic conditions of emotional states. The inner or subjective aspect must always be largely conjectural, involving as it does a difficult and admittedly hazardous application of the adage, "Put yourself in his place." We see an animal habitually act in a more or less definite way under certain given circumstances, and we interpret the facts as arising out of, or accompanied by, what is termed an emotion. My fox-terrier, for example, whenever he meets a particular black poodle, at once begins to dance round him and bark—he is usually a remarkably silent dog—while his coat above the backbone bristles up. One interprets this as the expression of an emotional state. But on trying to determine the exact nature of the state, we find it by no means easy so far to put ourselves into the fox-terrier's place as to enable us even to guess, with anything approaching accuracy, what his emotional feelings are like. The poodle, I may say, takes very little notice of Tony's demonstration, and even the fox-terrier himself does not appear to mean serious business. Quite different, at any rate, is his demeanour when there is a probability, or even the bare possibility, of a fight. He moves slowly, with head held a little low; his back is yet more thoroughly roughened; his attention is absolutely fixed on his antagonist, whose every movement he watches with the keenness with which a fencer watches his adversary; while all his muscles are ready for prompt and immediate action. If the emotional state in both cases is anger, it is anger with a difference. I do not attempt to define the difference beyond saying that there is an element of practical business in the one case which seems to be absent in the other; and this still leaves the matter tolerably indefinite.

If we may judge from our own experience, there are presumably, in addition to these actions and attitudes, to the bracing up of the muscles and general readiness and alertness, all of which constitute a group of *motor effects*, another and not unimportant group of *visceral effects*. These seem to be specially characteristic of the class of emotions with which we are dealing. The cold sweat, the dry mouth, the catch of the breath, the grip of the heart, the abdominal sinking, the blood-tingle or blood-stagnation,—these and their like, in varied modes and degrees, characterize the emotions of fear, dread, anger, and so forth, when they rise to any pitch of intensity, and contribute largely to their sharpness and piquancy. In so far as muscles are brought into play in connection with the effects of this type, they are for the most part the involuntary muscles. It will be convenient, therefore, though perhaps not strictly accurate, to distinguish this group of visceral effects, which may be regarded as part of the private and individual business of the body, from the other group of motor effects through which the organism has to deal with that which evokes the emotion.

Now, remembering that we have here under consideration only what Prof. W. James terms the coarser emotions, the lower emotions of animal life, and are not at present concerned with the more subtle emotions, the higher emotions and sentiments, intellectual, moral, æsthetic, and so forth—remembering this, I say, let us see how the facts may be interpreted.

The view that has been until recently almost universally accepted may be put briefly thus: When Tony sees the butcher's cur, he at once experiences an emotion, and the result of the emotion is that he acts in certain definite ways, and that his heart, his respiration, his salivary glands, and so forth, are more or less affected. The emotion, on this view, produces these effects; it is the middle term of a series of events. From the physiological point of view, this middle term is a commotion of some kind in the cortex of the brain; it results from the stimuli which give rise to the sight of the cur; it produces a number of nerve-currents running down the appropriate nerves so as to cause on the one hand certain motor effects, and on the other hand certain visceral effects. The commotion in the brain is what the dog feels as an emotion; and it precedes any expression of the emotion in the activities of his body.

Hints more or less definite of a different interpretation may be found in the literature of the emotions prior to 1884. In that year Prof. William James published a paper in *Mind,** in which he boldly contended, and backed up his contention with well-directed arguments, that the motor and visceral effects are not generated by the emotion, but are themselves its source and origin. The series of events, on Prof. James's view, may be put briefly as follows (subject to certain modifications to be noticed presently): The sight of the butcher's cur gives rise to a commotion in the lower

* *Mind*, 1884, vol. ix. p. 188. Prof. Lange, of Copenhagen, published independently in the same year a similar theory of the emotions.

centres of Tony's brain, and the effects of this commotion
are distributed by outgoing nerves to muscles, glands, and
so forth, giving rise to motor effects and visceral effects;
from the muscles and glands there are then transmitted
to the brain impulses which set up a second commotion in
the cortical region, and it is this second commotion that
gives rise in Tony's consciousness to the emotional state.
Such in crude outline is Prof. James's contention. We
may express it in a word by saying that the emotion is
generated by a *back-stroke* from the motor organs and
viscera concerned in the so-called "expression." It may
be well, however, to quote Prof. James's own words.

"Our natural way of thinking about these coarser
emotions," he says, "is that the mental perception of
some fact excites the mental affection called the emotion,
and that this latter state of mind gives rise to the bodily
expression. My theory, on the contrary, is that *the bodily
changes follow directly the perception of the exciting fact,
and that our feeling of the same changes as they occur* is *the
emotion.* Common sense says, we lose our fortune, are
sorry, and weep; we meet a bear, are frightened, and run;
we are insulted by a rival, are angry, and strike. The
hypothesis here to be defended says that this order of
sequence is incorrect; that the one mental state is not
immediately induced by the other; that the bodily manifestations must first be interposed between; and that the
more rational statement is that we feel sorry because we
cry, angry because we strike, afraid because we tremble,
and not that we cry, strike, or tremble because we are
sorry, angry, or fearful, as the case may be. Without
the bodily states following on the perception, the latter
would be purely cognitive in form, pale, colourless, desti-
tute of emotional warmth. We might then see the bear
and judge it best to run, receive the insult and deem it

right to strike, but we should not actually feel afraid or angry."

No doubt Prof. James has here stated his case with almost paradoxical emphasis, so as to bring out the antithesis between his own view and that which is commonly held. As a slyly humorous critic observed at a scientific meeting when Prof. James's view was under discussion, "One might as well say that a man was ill because he took the doctor's medicine instead of taking the stuff because he was ill." And, indeed, there is one important qualification which should be introduced,* and which serves to make the conception somewhat less repugnant to common sense. Tony has had some practical experience of the ways and behaviour of the butcher's cur and other dogs of that type. Let us grant that the primary genesis of the emotion they evoke was by backstroke; let us grant that it was due to a secondary brain-commotion produced by motor and visceral action; let us grant, in a word, that Prof. James's theory holds good for the *first* experience of the emotion in question. What, however, about the second and all subsequent experiences? Association will have stepped in and exercised its modifying influence. We have seen that a chick which seizes a juicy worm gains thereby a bit of experience in the light of which worms become the more alluring, since the sight of them at once calls up through association a re-presentation of this juiciness, a sort of anticipatory savour soon to be reinforced by the actual taste of the worm. In the case of an emotion, on the backstroke hypothesis, the same kind of effect will be produced by association. After the first experience through which the secondary brain-commotion had its

---

* In the *Psychological Review* for September, 1894—in which references to some of the leading criticisms of his theory are given—Prof. James himself insists on the effects of association (see p. 518).

primary genesis, the sight of the cur on all subsequent occasions will at once call up a re-presentation of the emotional state, a sort of anticipatory foretaste of that which may soon be reinforced by a repetition of the actual motor and visceral commotion. No doubt the anticipatory and re-presentative stage of the emotion will be faint and colourless as compared with the presentative effects of the reinforcing backstroke, just as the anticipatory taste which precedes the first mouthful of a ripe peach is faint as compared with the taste of the fruit in the mouth : but it must not be neglected ; it serves to distinguish the second, and all subsequent emotional experiences of like kind, from the first, in which alone we have the unmodified facts of primary genesis. Thus our analysis brings us down once more to the distinction between what is congenital and what is acquired through experience, and in this way the study of emotional states is seen to be in close touch with our special subject, habit and instinct.

"In speaking of the instincts," says Prof. James in the opening paragraph of his chapter on the emotions,* "it has been impossible to keep them separate from the emotional excitements which go with them. Objects of rage, love, fear, etc., not only prompt a man to outward deeds, but provoke characteristic alterations in his attitude and visage, and affect his breathing, circulation, and other organic functions in specific ways. When the outward deeds are inhibited, these latter emotional expressions still remain, and we read the anger in the face, though the blow may not be struck, and the fear betrays itself in voice and colour, though one may suppress all other signs. Instinctive reactions and emotional expressions thus shade imperceptibly into each other. Every object that excites an instinct excites an emotion as well. Emotions, however, fall short of instincts,

* "Principles of Psychology," vol. ii. p. 442.

in that the emotional reaction usually terminates in the subject's own body, whilst the instinctive reaction is apt to go further and enter into practical relations with the exciting object."

Although I cannot endorse the whole of Prof. James's treatment, I quote this passage as indicating the close alliance that exists between emotion and instinct. In it the visceral elements are duly emphasized. Mr. H. Rutgers Marshall lays the main stress, it would seem, on the motor elements; and in his treatment, the close connection between instinct and emotion is carried well-nigh to the point of identification. "Instinct," he says,* "is, strictly speaking, a term to be applied to tendencies observed objectively in ourselves and others, and not to the mental states which are co-ordinate with these tendencies. The compound word *instinct-feelings* I shall use to indicate the mental states that correspond to instinctive activities. Emotions, then, may not improbably be found to be complex co-ordinated instinct-feelings. . . . It seems proper to define emotions as relatively fixed psychoses (or mental states), corresponding to fixed co-ordination of instinctive activities which arise on the appearance of definite objects." Again, and more recently, Mr. Marshall says,† "I have suggested that we use the term 'instinct-feelings' to indicate the conscious coincidents of the animal activities we call instinctive; and I have endeavoured to show that when these instinct actions are relatively fixed and forceful, then their co-incident 'instinct-feelings' gain names, and form the class of psychic states known as the emotions." Here, then, the emotion is regarded as the subjective aspect of that which, in its objective aspect, is an instinctive activity.

* "Pain, Pleasure, and Æsthetics," pp. 63-65.
† *Nature,* vol. lii. p. 130.

Without citing further authorities, let us now note how the emotional theory under consideration stands. It must be regarded as a theory of primary genesis ; this is essential. All effects due to association through experience must be resolutely excluded. Not that, in practical experience, the part played by association is unimportant. It is, so far as adult experience is concerned, profoundly important. But it is without bearing on the question of origin, and that is the question under consideration. As a matter of primary genesis, then, the theory before us affirms that an emotion, such as that of fear, when, for example, a chick which has been left undisturbed for forty-eight hours shrinks from your hand if you be rough, is due *not directly, but indirectly,* to the sight of the advancing fingers. It does not fear and then shrink ; it shrinks instinctively, and then for the first time experiences the emotion of fear. The emotion, thus indirectly produced at sight of the hand, was held by Prof. James in his earlier presentation to be due to the joint effects of both motor and visceral reaction, but in his later writings he assigns to visceral action the chief part. " Visceral factors," he says,[*] " seem to be the most essential ones of all." We shall have presently to decide, as far as possible, between the relative claims of the visceral and the motor factors. For the present we may leave the question open, and inquire how far the theory of indirect origin is in accord with the conclusions we have already reached.

It has been shown that soon after birth a chick will peck at small objects which catch its eye ; that a young duck or moorhen will swim directly it is placed in water ; that such activities as scratching, preening the down, sand-dusting, bathing, scratching the ground, are distinctly and unmistakably congenital. These activities and their like

[*] *Psychological Review*, September, 1894, p. 512 ; see also p. 529.

O

have all the appearance of being organic and automatic responses to the requisite stimuli under appropriate conditions, external and internal; and the general conclusion we have reached is that, so far as they are concerned, what is unquestionably inherited is motor co-ordination. On the other hand, there seems to be no inherited knowledge of what is good to eat, and what is not; of what is harmful, like a bee, and what is harmless, like a moth; of a natural enemy, such as a cat or hawk, and a harmless creature, such as a sheep or goose. All this experience is a matter of individually acquired association. Let us put the matter from the physiological and organic point of view. All instinctive activity involves the due ordering and co-ordination of outgoing nerve impulses, starting from the central nervous system, probably the lower brain-centres. This is inherited. The growth of experience involves the bringing into relation, probably in the higher brain-centres, of the effects of incoming impulses; those, for example, from the eye, and from the organs of taste. This correlation of sensory data is seemingly not inherited; association-links have to be forged by each individual through acquisition. Now, apart from all the more special arguments in favour of motor impressions being due to incoming impulses (and not to a consciousness of outgoing impulses from the brain), there is this general consideration to which due weight should be given. These impressions are indubitably correlated with impressions of sight, taste, touch, hearing, and so forth, and take their place in the development of experience, alongside those of the special senses. And it will certainly be a gain to physiological interpretation if motor impressions (that is, the elements in consciousness due to movements of our own limbs and bodies) be proved by the joint labours of physiologists and psychologists to be of like nature to the impressions of the special senses with which they enter into such intimate association. The data of experience should surely be co-ordinate data ; and such they are on the theory that the motor elements in consciousness are due to incoming impulses. But the value of the emotions is in affording data for the elaboration of experience. Hence the presumption is in favour of their being, in primary genesis, due to incoming impulses from visceral actions, as well as motor activities.

To put the matter briefly, instinctive activities appear to be due to automatic co-ordinations of outgoing impulses, while acquired experience seems to be due to the correlation of incoming data. Acquired experience is thus, so far as motor elements are concerned, due to the effects of back-stroke. But the emotions take their place in the development of acquired experience ; hence it may be fairly inferred that the visceral contributions of the emotional states are also by back-stroke. If this be so, and not otherwise, we may say that all the data of sense-experience are of peripheral origin, some due to incoming impulses from the special senses, some to incoming impulses from the motor organs, and some to incoming impulses from the viscera and involuntary muscles. And with this conclusion my observations and inferences on habit and instinct are in full accord.

Let us now return for a short space to the emotional reactions of the fox-terrier. On Professor James's view, as I interpret it, the emotional state, whatever may be its exact nature, is the subjective accompaniment of the whole complex group of activities, plus the whole complex group of visceral actions, plus representative elements of like nature ; in a word, of the whole bodily condition of the dog at the time, together with all that this bodily condition suggests through association. What is in the focus of Tony's consciousness is the black poodle in the one case, and that low-bred butcher's cur in the other. That which we call the emotion fills in, I take it, the background of his consciousness, and is generated by a multitude of activity-feelings due to innumerable physiological impulses raining in upon his sensorium from I know not how many muscles, muscle-sheaths, tendons, and articular surfaces, together with visceral impulses raining in from I know not how many glands, involuntary muscles, and organs of the body. Thus, omitting further reference to the re-presentative elements of like nature to the presentative elements, I interpret Professor James's theory.

Now what is the relation of all this to habit and instinct? Tony's demeanour towards these two dogs is, without question, habitual. Whenever he meets them he goes through the same actions, and behaves in a similar way. But the behaviour towards these particular dogs is, I suppose, the result of experience. What the precise experience was which led the black poodle to call forth one set of activities, and the butcher's cur another, one need not pretend to know. It can scarcely be supposed that Tony came into the world with a congenital tendency to react to poodles and curs of those special types in those special ways, though cases of so-called hereditary antipathy, such as that of Dr. Huggins's dog Kepler * to butchers

---

* The facts of this case are briefly as follows. Dr. Huggins possessed an English mastiff, Kepler, which was brought to him when it was six weeks old, from the stable in which it was born. The first time Dr. Huggins took the dog out he started back in alarm at the first butcher's shop he had ever seen; and throughout his life he manifested the strongest and strangest antipathy to butchers and all that pertained to them. On inquiry, Dr. Huggins ascertained that in the father, grandfather, and two half-brothers of Kepler's the same curious antipathy was innate. Of these, Paris, a half-brother, on one occasion, at Hastings, sprang at a gentleman who came into a hotel where his master was staying. The owner caught the dog, and apologized, saying that he had never known him to behave thus before, except

(however it be interpreted), suggest that the stimulus to reaction is sometimes already defined in hereditary transmission. As we have seen in other cases of habits of congenital origin, while the response is congenitally definite, that which evokes the response is to a large extent determined by individual experience. This, however, does not detract from the congenital nature of the responsive activity itself. And, surely, all must have observed a hundred times that dogs have a tendency to behave in just these ways. No one with any experience of dogs can have failed to observe both these types of reaction. They are characteristic of canine nature. They are reactive tendencies, which it needs only the touch of experience to particularize, and to direct on suitable objects.

What, then, is inherited in such cases ? Must not the reply be—a bodily organization, with congenital powers of response in certain ways, under certain conditions ? And will not this apply, not only to the co-ordinated outgoing impulses which give rise to motor activity, but to the outgoing impulses which take effect in visceral action ? You may safely assert that your dog will react in this or that fashion to other dogs in virtue of the innate tendencies of his nature ; but you cannot say what dog will call forth this demeanour or that ; or, if you can do so, it is on different grounds : it is the result of your knowledge of his individual character, or past experience.

It will be evident from this brief discussion of Tony's emotions that there is an element of complexity and difficulty introduced through the combination of what is congenital and what is acquired. And this is perhaps still more the case with the emotional reactions of adult

to a butcher. The man at once said that this was his business. It may be urged, however, that the so-called hereditary antipathy would probably be more correctly described as a congenital reaction to certain olfactory stimuli.

human beings, in whom a far wider range of experience and all sorts of intellectual and æsthetic factors are introduced by their extended knowledge and thought. It is therefore clearly of importance to eliminate, as far as possible, the element of acquired experience, and to study such responses as appear to have a pleasurable or an emotional accompaniment in their instinctive purity. This I have endeavoured to do in the observations on young birds to which we must now return. Let us take pleasurable accompaniments first.

The young moorhen I had in Yorkshire when he was set free from his basket in the morning and taken to the little beck, executed a pretty and characteristic dance, stretching up his head, flapping his skinny wings, and leaping up and down with springy action. There can be little question that this morning dance, this engaging discharge of pent-up energy, was accompanied by a pleasurable state which, on Professor James's view, took its origin in primary genesis from complex physiological impulses carried inwards to the sensorium from all parts of the body directly or indirectly participating in the activity. Having performed his dance, if the day was warm, and especially if the sun shone brightly, he would wade into the running water and take his bath. He ducked his head under, threw water over his shoulders, fluttered his feathers, waved his arm-like wings, and vigorously wagged his black tail. One could not resist the conclusion that he obviously enjoyed his dip; the whole set of actions (which, by the way, are instinctive in the narrower sense, and were performed in all their perfection for the first time on the morning of the forty-second day of life) seem to generate a pleasurable state to which it would be hard for us, not being moorhens, to give a name. He would then stand in the sun, and with a contented cheeping note, preen his feathers, wringing the water from them, shaking himself with obvious pleasure, now rubbing his head across his breast and sides; now stretching out his neck and bending his head to get at the parts close under the throat. All these actions were, it would seem, suffused with pleasurable enjoyment. Then he would walk about or wade in the stream, picking up odds and ends and testing them in his bill, all the while nodding his head and flicking his tail in a way that itself is indicative of pleasure. When, before his companion died from the effects of a long journey, the two were wandering about my small garden, they would occasionally approach each other bending forwards, and standing low with bent legs and heads thrown back, would open their red beaks, swear in harsh and angry tones, and hold the nearly naked wings high up over the back in a peculiar and highly characteristic way. An emotional state was expressed in the most unmistakable manner.

Let us assume that all these activities are instinctive in the broader sense, if not in the narrower; and they appear for the most part to be instinctive, even in the narrower acceptation of the term. They are thus congenital in their nature. And let us fix our attention on the very first performance of one of the complex activities,—say the instinctive activities concerned in taking a bath which seem to be called forth by running water. Granting this to be the requisite stimulus, let us try and interpret the performance, assuming, for the purposes of discussion, that the pleasurable state is the subjective aspect of the motor activities; the visceral effects taking only a subordinate share in the calling forth of pleasurable feelings.

It will be necessary first to say somewhat—as little as is consistent with clearness—concerning the nature of pleasure and its antithesis pain. First of all let us exclude from our present consideration that form of pain which accompanies some organic lesion. A cut, a prick, a sprain, a toothache, a tearing of the tissues, an inflammatory process—any one of these, or their like, requires, it may be urged, a consideration quite independent of that which deals with the pleasure or discomfort that accompanies the normal performance of certain activities. Leaving pain of this kind on one side, as possibly requiring a different explanation, I accept the interpretation of those who regard pleasure and its antithesis as qualities, rather than separate elements, of consciousness. To put the matter picturesquely, in the absence of pleasure and its antithesis, there would be in consciousness a picture in neutral tints—one which would neither attract nor repel. Pleasure and its opposite give the picture colour, and make it either attractive or repellent. Pleasures and pains on this view are, as Mr. Marshall puts it, qualities either of which, under the proper conditions, may belong to any element in consciousness.

Now for the bearing of this on the view that an emotion is predominantly or solely due to motor elements supplied by the performance of such an instinctive activity as the moorhen's early morning dance. It may be suggested that the motor elements provide the neutral-tint picture, while the distinctively emotional character of the states of consciousness is due to the colouring of the picture in tones of pleasure and pain. On this view the primary basis of an emotional state is afforded by the pleasurable or painful tone which suffuses the whole background of consciousness during the performance of certain instinctive or habitual activities, and accompanies the multitudinous motor elements, thus crowding in upon consciousness.

From the standpoint of introspection the pleasurable or painful accompaniment of activity-feelings is apparently something clearly distinguishable from an emotional state. If I read aright the testimony of my own consciousness I often experience pleasurable or painful activity-feelings without emotion, and sometimes have a strong emotion in which there seems to be no recognizable contribution, presentative or re-presentative, from the activity-feelings.

It would seem then, if there be any truth in the considerations just hinted at rather than developed, that what is specially characteristic of emotion, as such, does not take its origin in the motor elements; and it becomes probable that it is the visceral elements which afford the differentiæ of emotion. If so, it is not the instinct-feeling in its motor aspect—what we may term the activity-feeling —that is concerned in the primary genesis of an emotion, but rather the concurrent and associated set of visceral actions. Let us see, therefore, whether observations on the active and emotional life of young birds throw any light upon this problem. Take the case of a young frightened moorhen. On land he runs away, and perhaps crouches in the rushes ; in the water he dives, and comes up quietly under the bank and there stays still. The activities involved in running and diving are very different ; must not the activity-feelings be very different too ? And yet we must surely suppose them to have a common emotional element. Again, when a moorhen catches sight of a worm and runs hard to secure it, the activity-feelings must, as such, one would suppose, be very similar to those experienced when the moorhen runs vigorously away from a goose. And yet in the one case he is frightened, and in the other case he is not. Here similar activity-feelings are associated with wholly different emotional states.

Frightened chicks scatter and crouch ; but many birds seem to show more markedly than the chick a crouching response and a running-away response. As I have noticed on Inch Michrie, in the Forth near Edinburgh, young fledgeling terns crouch as you approach, and will even let you stoop and pick them up. But if once disturbed out of their crouching attitude, they scuttle off through the long grass tussocks. So, too, with young peewits. Mr. A. S. Eve, of Marlborough College, tells me how, walking across the downs, a brown mass caught his eye. At first it seemed a piece of dung, even as he stooped over it; but slight motion, as of breathing, made him regard it as a toad, and he picked it up. Instantly two long legs kicked violently, while a stretched neck and open beak gave rise to loud squealing! The concealment of head and legs, and the colouring of the young bird completely deceived him; and the sudden transition to motion and noise nearly made him drop the bird from his hand. The protective nature of the instinctive activity is here well seen. But what we have to note is that there must have been in the little pee-wit's consciousness a rapid transition from the activity-feelings of crouching to those of running away. And there seems to be a continuity of emotional state that is not dependent on any similarity of instinctive activity.

A similar diversity of response, as exemplified in rails, is thus graphically described by Canon Atkinson.* "A gentlemen's dog catches a land-rail and brings it to his master, unhurt of course, as is the well-trained dog's way, but to all appearance perfectly dead. The dog lays the bird down at his master's feet, and he turns it over with his toe. It simply moves as it is moved, all its limbs limp. Continuing to regard it, however, the man sees an eye opened, and he takes it up. The 'artful dodger' is quite dead again in a moment, head hanging and dangling, limbs loose, and no sign of life anywhere. It is put

* " Forty Years in a Moorland Parish," p. 335.

in its captor's pocket, and not liking the confinement
begins to struggle. When taken out it is just as lifeless
as before; but being put down on the ground and left
undisturbed—the gentleman having stepped to one side,
but continuing to watch—it lifts its head in a minute or
so, and seeing all apparently serene, it starts up on a
sudden and 'cuts its lucky' with singular speed.

"In the case of the water-rail which came under my
own observation, it was picked up on a snowy day by the
most intimate of the friends of my youth and early manhood.
He assumed that it was dazed with cold, and perhaps what
we Yorkshire folks call 'hungered' as well. So he brought
it home with him, and laid it on a footstool in front of the
dining-room fire. Five minutes passed—ten were gone—
and still the lifeless bird lay as it was put down, dead to all
seeming; only not stiff, as it ought to have been if dead of
cold as well as hunger. A few minutes later, my friend,
who was very still, but yet with an eye to the bird, saw it—
not lift its head, like the land-rail, and take a view, but—
start off in a moment with no previous intimation of its
purpose, and begin to career about the room with incredible
rapidity. It never attempted to fly. Any other captive
bird in its position would have made for the window at
once, and beaten itself half to pieces against the glass.
Not so the rail. With it, in its helter-skelter and most
erratic course, it was anywhere rather than the window or
the fire. Round the room, across the room, under the
sofa, under the table, from corner to corner, and from side
to side, steering itself perfectly, notwithstanding legs of
chairs, legs of tables, the sofa-feet, footstools, or what not,
on and on it careered; and it was not without some
patience and many attempts that it was eventually
secured."

Now here again, the activity-feelings associated with

"shamming dead," must be as different as can well be imagined from those associated with scuttling off at full speed. And yet one would suppose that there is much community in the emotion experienced; just as there is in the case of a schoolboy who first hides from the bully whose approach he fears, and then runs off as fast as his legs can carry him. Speaking from personal recollection of the latter case, I am disposed to refer this community of emotional tone to a painful affection of the heart and breathing, a dryness of the mouth, and a terrible sinking in the pit of the stomach with all sorts of unpleasantly, creepy feelings in the skin and tissues generally. And I expect the land-rail feels uncommonly queer in his gizzard, both when he "shams dead" and when he scuttles away. But of course, not being a land-rail, I cannot affect to speak with any certainty as to his emotions.

One more case in point may be given. The Duke of Argyll once disturbed, on a Scotch loch, a dun-diver or female of the red-breasted merganser (*Mergus serratus*), with her brood of ducklings, and gave chase in a boat. But the little birds, not more than a fortnight old, eluded their pursuers by swimming and diving. "At last * one of the brood made for the shore . . . we pursued it as quickly as we could, but when the little bird gained the shore, our boat was still about twenty yards off. Long drought had left a broad margin of small flat stones and mud between the water and the usual bank. I saw the little bird run up a couple of yards from the water, and then suddenly disappear. Knowing what was likely to be enacted, I kept my eye fixed on the spot, and when the boat was run upon the beach, I proceeded to find and pick up the chick. But on reaching the place of disappearance, no signs of the young merganser was to be seen. The closest scrutiny,

* *Contemporary Review,* July, 1874.

with the certain knowledge that it was there, failed to enable me to detect it. Proceeding cautiously forwards, I soon became convinced that I had already overshot the mark; and on turning round, it was only to see the bird rise like an apparition from the stones, and dashing past the stranded boat regain the lake—where, having recovered its wind, it instantly dived and disappeared."

Now, here there are no less than four different activities, swimming, diving, crouching, running, and yet, accompanying them all, as we can scarcely doubt, a common emotional state. To which, in an older bird, will be added a fifth, escape by flight. Again I venture to suggest that the little duckling had all the while a terrible sinking in its little gizzard, and that in such cases similarity of visceral elements may give community of emotional character to conscious backgrounds of diverse nature so far as activity-feelings by themselves are concerned. The fact that the same activity-feelings may accompany very different emotional states, when a bird runs, flies, or swims with eagerness towards food or a mate, and when he uses the same motor-activities in escaping from a dangerous enemy; and the fact that the same or closely allied emotional states may be accompanied by very different activities, when a bird in fear runs, swims, dives, flies, utters its alarm note, or crouches in silence; these two facts, taken in conjunction, lead me to go even farther than Prof. James, and to suggest that the visceral back-stroke is, genetically, not only by far the most essential feature in the emotional state, but that it is what differentiates the emotional state, as such, from the pleasure or pain which may accompany the performance of bodily activities.

One may well believe, however, that these visceral elements have, in the course of evolution, become closely associated with the performance of definite instinctive activities so that they arise whenever these activities are evoked. Nay, more; so close is the association that the same stimulus evokes not only the instinctive response but also the visceral reaction which is the primary genetic basis of the emotion as such. This is obviously in line with our whole interpretation of the phenomena. Our interpretation of instinct is that a stimulus gives rise to a co-ordinated group of outgoing nerve-currents to the motor organs concerned in the congenital response; that this is purely organic; but that the automatic performance of the activity gives origin to a group of ingoing currents which evoke activity-feelings and afford primary data to consciousness. Our interpretation of emotion in its primary genesis is that a stimulus gives rise to a co-ordinated group of outgoing nerve-currents to the viscera, heart, lungs, digestive organs, skin, and so forth; that this, too, is purely organic; but that the automatic reaction of these visceral organs gives origin to a group of ingoing currents which evoke emotional states and afford the primary emotional data to consciousness. Our present point is that the same stimulus may give rise at the same time both to the co-ordinated motor group and to the co-ordinated visceral group; both to instinctive reaction and to the visceral reaction essential to emotion. The two are in fact in such cases inseparably connected in origin, though they are distinguishable both physiologically and in their effects in consciousness. The result of their common origin is that instinctive data and emotional data are simultaneously presented to consciousness, and that their association in consciousness is of the closest possible nature. With the growth of experience this constant association is yet further strengthened, and the motor and visceral effects are yet further consolidated, so that each tends to supplement and reinforce the other.

And the value of the emotions in the evolution process is tolerably obvious. The prolonged visceral back-stroke in fear or anger, for example, leads to continuous exertion in flight or fight; a continuous exertion that is all the more pronounced if visceral and motor groups are closely linked by the bonds of association. Even the general collapse of extreme dread or terror may be seen to have its protective value in the case of birds or other animals that, like the rails above described, are said to sham dead—in which, that is to say, the collapse has been organized through natural selection into an instinctive response of stillness and limpness.*

In fine the general conclusions that we reach as to the relation of emotion to instinct are somewhat as follows. Instinctive activities are primarily automatic responses of the organism to certain external stimuli under certain internal conditions; the performance of these activities affords to consciousness by back-stroke certain motor data which are correlated with the data provided by the special senses. But there are other automatic responses of the organism, or effects in the organism, which are more or less closely bound up with some at least of the instinctive activities. These are visceral effects. They, too, like the co-ordinated activities, are due to outgoing impulses from the lower brain centres. They, too, afford to consciousness certain data, which are correlated with the other data of experience; and these data, visceral in origin, are, if not the sole, at any rate the distinguishing constituents of what we term the coarser emotions (for under this term exceedingly complex states of consciousness are included, comprising many diverse data sensory and motor as well

---

* Dr. Wesley Mills has discussed the conditions of the so-called death-feigning response in the "Trans. Roy. Soc. Canada," Sect. iv., 1887, p. 181, *et seqq.*

as visceral); these visceral data, I submit, are what give
to the states of consciousness their distinctive emotional
character. What therefore is congenital in emotion is
of like nature with that which is congenital in the
activities termed instinctive, namely, an organized group
of outgoing impulses. What we have termed "activity-
feelings" are the conscious effects of the back-stroke from
the motor-activities, more or less tinged no doubt with
pleasure or pain. What I regard as distinctively
emotional is the conscious effect of the back-stroke from
the visceral actions, more or less tinged again with
pleasure or pain. This back-stroke, whether from motor-
activity or visceral action, is a matter of primary genesis.
In subsequent experience, memory through association,
affords re-presentative echoes of primary presentations,
and these, together with modifications introduced by
individual acquisition, serve to render extraordinarily
complex the emotional states of adult animals, and still
more the emotional states of adult human beings, in
whom conceptual thought, with all that it involves and
brings with it, has been developed.

It must not be supposed, then, that, in tracing the
genetic connection that exists between instinct-feelings
(motor in origin) and emotional back-stroke (visceral in
origin), I am contending that what is commonly termed
an emotional state is just this and nothing more. That
would be absurd. The whole state of consciousness to
which the term emotion may be conveniently applied,
because it contains the emotional factor, is by no means
so simple as this. What we commonly describe as an
emotion is, indeed, a highly complex state of consciousness
involving a great number of diverse elements; elements
due to the special senses, sight, hearing, and so forth,
through which we are aware of the presence of the object

exciting the emotion; elements due to motor-sensations and impressions concerned in the active response, gesture, and expression; elements due to visceral action derived from glands, heart, lungs, digestive organs, and so forth; and a number of elements of a re-presentative kind called up by association and due to previous experience. For the practical observer and interpreter of human or animal life, the emotion is the net result of the experience which includes all these diverse elements. The psychologist has a special purpose in view. He analyses the complex bit of experience, being desirous of ascertaining just where in the midst of this complex whole the characteristically emotional quality has its seat, and just how it had its origin in primary genesis. And he reaches the conclusion, if our discussion be adequate, that the characteristic quality of emotion as congenital is to be found in the visceral factor, and endeavours to explain its mode of origin in the genetic development of experience.

P

CHAPTER X.

SOME HABITS AND INSTINCTS OF THE PAIRING SEASON.

IF, in accordance with the conclusion reached in the last chapter, the characteristic and differentiating quality of such emotions as fear and anger is to be regarded as due, in primary genesis, to visceral changes affecting the brain through afferent nerves; the expression of the emotions in characteristic actions and attitudes must be held to be more or less closely associated with the emotions which they indicate. And this association may well be so close and intimate as to lead to the coalescence of the motor and visceral elements into an apparently uniform and homogeneous state of consciousness. An analogy from the phenomena of vision will make this clearer. When we look out across a stretch of country and see a distant object, such as a church spire, the impression of the object, as directly seen at that distance, seems to be homogeneous and simple. But, setting aside any act of judgment by which the matter may be complicated, analysis shows that, in addition to visual sensations due to the stimulation of the retina, there are also motor sensations due to the movements and relative positions of the two eyes and to accommodation within the eyeballs. And it is these motor sensations which give to vision its distance element. But so closely do the retinal and motor elements coalesce in visual impressions, owing to their constant and uniform association, that their diversity of origin is not recognizable without careful and patient analysis. So, too, in those emotional states which have a constant and uniform motor expression in action or attitude, the visceral and motor sensations coalesce to give rise to an apparently homogeneous state of consciousness. And the contributions to consciousness due to "expression" can only be dissociated from the emotion itself by the application of psychological analysis.

From the point of view of heredity, we may say that in these cases there is such congenital organization of structure in the central nervous system, that co-ordinated outgoing or efferent impulses are distributed both to viscera and to the organs concerned in expression. This distribution of nervous impulses is part of the congenital automatism. On the other hand, at the moment of primary experience, opportunities are afforded for the correlation of the afferent or incoming impulses from the diverse viscera and organs which have thus been called into activity. And this correlation is a matter of individual acquisition.

We must now proceed to notice that though the emotion itself, as such, is, so to speak, a private and individual matter, having an import that is wholly subjective, its expression is not thus restricted. It is an indication to others of the emotional state of the organism. When the cobra raises its head and expands its hood, this is an advertisement of its deadly powers, and of its emotional state being such that it is ready to call these powers into play. That this kind of activity is congenital and instinctive is shown by the fact that young snakes (Vivora de la Cruz), taken before birth from their just-killed mother, threatened to strike, and made the burring noise with the tail characteristic of its kind.*

* Mr. W. Larden in *Nature*, vol. xlii. p. 115.

There can be no question as to the advantage that must accrue to the organism from a close association between an emotional state which, whatever else it may imply, means business, and such action and attitude as may indicate this fact to a possible enemy. The dog that will chase a fleeing cat will change his demeanour, and not unfrequently leave her alone, if she turns and threatens to scratch his eyes. At the same time it does not by any means follow that the emotional state at the back of a given mode of expression is necessarily at all times the same. A snake may well threaten to strike in fear as well as in anger. The stag that lowers his antlers to do battle with a rival may be tingling with sexual excitement; while the stag at bay that turns and lowers his antlers to the advancing hounds is driven thereto by an emotional state akin to despair. So long as the "expression" indicates an emotional condition which shows that the animal means business, is thoroughly in earnest, and is ready to put forth its powers to the utmost —that is enough from the biological point of view. And it matters not a jot whether the emotional condition be one of general irritability or excitement, one of anger or fear, or sometimes one and sometimes another. Hence we may fairly conclude that the same "expression" may be associated with different emotional states, and may be more stereotyped and uniform than the accompaniment in consciousness.

The action and attitude, then, to which we apply the term emotional expression is, biologically, of suggestive value. It has been developed and organized as an expression suggestive to others. Like the warning colours of certain insects and other animals, it is an indication of certain qualities, and of a preparedness to make them felt. Their suggestive value depends largely on association in those for whose guidance they are used. And among animals of the same kind, or animals of about equal strength, they are apt to call forth answering expressions of like nature. The young cockerel or the young moorhen that begins to show fight, immediately throws his companion into a corresponding attitude. When animals live in flocks or herds, the sudden flight of any one individual startles all the others into a like procedure. I have elsewhere confessed * that as a boy I sometimes visited a farmyard for the vicious purpose of shooting little pigs with a catapult. The shot, taking effect upon some luckless pigling, was followed by a squeak and a rush, in which not only my particular quarry, but the whole litter participated. Each little pig experienced certain suggested feelings of alarm or fright, and at the same time seeing his brothers running, imitated their action. Thus the sight of another pig scuttling off on the one hand, and a feeling of fright on the other hand, would become linked by association; and in this way participation in common actions would beget a community in emotional experience, and would lay the foundations of suggestive influence.

The sounds and cries of animals are expressive of emotional states, and have a distinctly and often definitely suggestive value. Allusion has already been made to the notes of young birds; to their emotional accompaniments, so far as we can interpret the matter; to their suggestive value, at least in some cases; and to their congenital nature. No one can have watched with attention—attention of ear as well as eye—the behaviour of a hen with her brood of chicks, without noticing the different effects of the call note and the warning cry.

Let us take, as a starting-point for somewhat more detailed consideration, the song of birds. The fact that

* "Introduction to Comparative Psychology," p. 321.

this is heard for the most part in the pairing season indicates its association with the mating instinct and the emotional condition appropriate to the season of courtship. In this season life is at high tide; there is an unusual expenditure of energy; and some of this energy finds vent in the joyous stream of song. If this be not an expression of emotion, we must give up all attempts at subjective—or, as Clifford termed it, ejective— interpretation of observable activities. But if, as we have been led to infer, expression is for external reference, and has suggestive value, the conclusion is irresistible that the male bird sings for his mate, and that the biological value of song is to call forth an answering emotion on his part.

We here open up the question of sexual selection, which is associated with the revered name of Charles Darwin; and it may be well to state his views on this subject in his own words. "Most male birds," he says in his summary,* "are highly pugnacious during the breeding season, and some possess weapons adapted for fighting with their rivals. But the most pugnacious and the best-armed males rarely or never depend for success solely on their power to drive away or kill their rivals, but have special means for charming the female. With some it is the power of song or of giving forth strange cries, or instrumental music, and the males in consequence differ from the females in their vocal organs, or in the structure of certain feathers. From the curiously diversified means for producing various sounds, we gain a high idea of the importance of this means of courtship. Many birds endeavour to charm the females by love-dances or antics, performed on the ground or in the air, and

---

* "Descent of Man," vol. ii. part ii. chap. xvi. pp. 250-256. 2nd edit., 1888.

sometimes at prepared places. But ornaments of many kinds, the most brilliant tints, combs and wattles, beautiful plumes, elongated feathers, top-knots, and so forth, are by far the commonest means. In some cases mere novelty appears to have acted as a charm. The ornaments of the males must be highly important to them, for they have been acquired in not a few cases at the cost of increased danger from enemies, and even at some loss of power in fighting with their rivals. The males of very many species do not assume their ornamental dress until they arrive at maturity, or they assume it only during the breeding season, or the tints then become more vivid. Certain ornamental appendages become enlarged, turgid, and brightly coloured during the act of courtship. The males display their charms with elaborate care, and to the best effect; and this is done in the presence of the females. The court-ship is sometimes a prolonged affair, and many males and females congregate at an appointed place. To suppose that the females do not appreciate the beauty of the males, is to admit that their splendid decorations, all their pomp and display, are useless; and this is incredible. . . .

"If it be admitted that the females prefer, or are unconsciously excited by, the more beautiful males, then the males would slowly but surely be rendered more and more attractive through sexual selection."

Such are the essential features of the theory of sexual selection. Like the theory of natural selection, with which it has obvious points of relation, but, as we shall see, important points of difference, it attempts to account for the selection of given variations in colour, plumage, and vocal or other activity, and does not profess to give any account of the mode of origin of these variations. It contends that, given the variations, sexual selection will guide them to special developments.

Those, of whom Mr. Alfred Russell Wallace is chief, who are not prepared to admit sexual selection by preferential mating as a factor in organic evolution, assert that there is no sufficient evidence of choice on the part of the female bird. Mr. Wallace attributes the origin of plumes, brilliance, and specialized activities to exuberant vitality; he regards their suppression in the hen * as due to natural selection through the elimination of conspicuous hens during the important period of incubation; and he develops a theory suggested by Mr. Alfred Tylor,† that the diversified coloration follows the chief lines of structure, and changes at points, such as the joints, where function changes. " Why, in allied species, the development of accessory plumes has taken different forms," he admits, ‡ " we are unable to say, except that it may be due to individual variability, which has served as the starting-point for so much of what seems to us strange in form or fantastic in colour, both in the animal and vegetable world."

So far as coloration and special adornments are concerned, it would seem that, on Mr. Wallace's view, they are of utilitarian value for the end of recognition. " Each ornament," he says, " is a recognition mark, and therefore essential to both the first production and subsequent well-being of every species." But recognition marks are, if we grant their utilitarian value, of essential importance in connection with mating. The sight of such ornaments would therefore become associated with

---

* Generally in the hen. When the female is brightly coloured and the male dull in hue, he is said to undertake the duties of incubation.

† "Coloration in Animals and Plants."

‡ "Darwinism," p. 293.

the mating impulse and the emotional states which accompany sexual union. May we not, therefore, fairly suppose that adornment is of suggestive value, and itself tends to call forth the sexual emotions? And, if so, may we not further suppose that deficiency of such adornment would evoke less strongly the sexual impulse, and would, therefore, place the male in which such ornament was lacking at a disadvantage in securing a mate?

Let us grant that the song of birds is primarily the outcome of exuberant activity, and also that it is probably a means of recognition. The recognition is presumably not only specific, but individual, for the bird probably not only recognizes the song as that of one of her own species, but recognizes the individual notes of her own mate. If, then, song is an expression of emotional condition, and if it calls forth an answering emotion in the hen, it would seem to be, to say the least of it, not improbable that the bird which in this way excites the most emotion is more likely to be accepted as a mate than others which excite less emotion and call forth in a less degree the sexual instinct.

The question has been unduly complicated and placed in a false light through the introduction of the unnecessary supposition that the hen bird must possess a standard or ideal of æsthetic value, and that she selects that singer which comes nearest to her conception of what a songster should be. One might as well suppose that a chick selected those worms which most nearly approached the ideal of succulence that it had conceived. The chick selects the worm that excites the strongest impulse to pick it up and eat it. So, too, the hen selects that mate which by his song or otherwise excites in greatest degree the mating impulse; and there is no more need to suppose

the existence of an æsthetic standard in this case than
there is to hypothecate a gustatory ideal in the case
of the chick that eats a juicy worm. Stripped of all its
unnecessary æsthetic surplusage, the hypothesis of sexual
selection suggests that the accepted mate is the one that
most strongly evokes the pairing instinct.

That the sexual impulse, and certain specialized
activities which are associated with it, is instinctive,
and truly congenital though deferred, stands in no need
of demonstration. It affords, however, a good illustration
of that co-operation between internal organic factors and
an external exciting cause which is characteristic probably
of all, and certainly of the most highly developed, instincts.
We have seen that, in other matters, congenital instinctive
tendency affords an unspecialized basis on which are
founded habits in the formation of which individual choice
has likewise played its part. It is difficult to accept the
view that individual choice has played no part where the
sexual instincts are concerned. But supposing that it
has played its part—and this is essential to the contention of those who accept sexual selection—the effects
will be wrought into the congenital tissue of the race if,
and only if, there are certain individuals which, through
failure to elicit the pairing response, die unmated. Is
preferential mating, supposing it to occur, carried to such
a degree that some individuals fail to secure a mate?
That is the question. If so, sexual selection is a factor
in race-progress; if not, though it may occur in nature,
it is inoperative as a means of evolutionary development.
The whole question, in itself a difficult one, is further
complicated by the fact that the males which are possessed of the most exuberant vitality, and are therefore
by hypothesis rendered the most acceptable through
emotional suggestion, are likely to compete with other

males of less exuberant vitality by direct combat. Such competition, by which the weakest are excluded from mating through no choice on the part of the female, falls under the head of natural selection, and not of sexual selection, if by that term we understand preferential mating.

This serves to bring out the difference, before adverted to, between natural selection through elimination and conscious selection through choice. The two processes begin at different ends of the scale of efficiency. Natural selection begins by eliminating the weakest, and so works up the scale from its lower end until none but the fittest survive; there is no conscious choice in the matter. Sexual selection by preferential mating begins by selecting the most successful in stimulating the pairing instinct, and so works down the scale until none but the hopelessly unattractive remain unmated. The process is determined by conscious choice. It is in and through such choice that consciousness has been a factor in evolution. The relations of the two processes will, however, be more fully considered in a later chapter.

It forms no part of my present purpose to discuss in detail the theory of sexual selection. Only in so far as the conceptions which it involves bear upon problems of habit and instinct does the theory concern us here. The song of birds is an instinctive or an habitual activity, which appears to be the expression of an emotional state coincident in time, in the majority of song-birds, with the season of courtship. Emotional expression is, in other cases, of suggestive value. It is, therefore, not improbable that song arouses in the hen an answering emotional state; and it is said that hen-canaries mate with the best singer. If the number of male birds is in excess of that necessary to satisfy the pairing requirements of the hens (and this will apply both to polygamous and monogamous species), some must fail to find a mate. But whether the odd males are weeded out through natural selection (being, if we accept the somewhat extravagant suggestion of M. Stolzmann,* overweighted with, or rendered conspicuous by, adornment for that very purpose), or whether they are rejected through failure to elicit the appropriate emotional response, we do not know.

Perhaps the most definite direct evidence of the exercise of choice on the part of the female is that which Darwin cites from Audubon.† This observer, who spent a lifetime among the birds of the United States, " does not doubt that the female deliberately chooses her mate. Thus, speaking of a woodpecker, he says that the hen is followed by half a dozen gay suitors, who continue performing strange antics, 'until a marked preference is shown for one.' The female of the red-winged starling (*Agelaius phœniceus*) is likewise pursued by several males, 'until, becoming fatigued, she alights, receives their addresses, and soon makes a choice.' He describes also how several male nightjars repeatedly plunge through the air with astonishing rapidity, suddenly turning, and thus making a singular noise ; ' but no sooner has the female made her choice, than the other males are driven away.'

---

* *Proc. Zool. Soc.*, 1885, p. 421. I say "somewhat extravagant," because it would appear that natural selection by weeding out the more adorned and leaving only the less adorned to breed would, in the absence of preferential mating, have left us little or no adornment to discuss. Again, we must ask M. Stolzmann this question : By what process of elimination under natural selection have the advantageous adornments been produced ? Upholders of sexual selection have not failed to realize the disadvantageousness of secondary sexual characters, but have assumed that the disadvantages are outweighed by the superior acceptability, as mates, of their possessors.

† "Descent of Man," vol. ii. part ii. chap. xiv. pp. 128–129, 2nd edit., 1888. The citations from Audubon, " Ornithological Biography," vol. i. pp. 191, 349 ; vol. ii. pp. 42, 275.

With one of the vultures (*Cathartes aura*) of the United States, parties of eight, ten, or more males and females assemble on fallen logs, ' exhibiting the strongest desire to please mutually,' and, after many caresses, each male leads off his partner on the wing." These cases appear to have been carefully observed. Still, there is unquestionably need of more direct evidence.

Mr. William Brewster, of Cambridge, Massachusetts, has communicated, and kindly allows me to quote, the following observations, which bear upon the point we are considering :—

" The case of apparent sexual selection which I mentioned to you the other evening came to my notice in the spring of 1877, when I was collecting birds at St. Mary's, Georgia. Finding a pair of summer tanagers (*Piranga rubra*) in an isolated grove of pines, I shot the male. Visiting the place a day or two afterwards, I found that the female had another mate, which I also killed. This was repeated, until, in about a week, I had secured in all either four or five males—I cannot now remember which. These males, when arranged in the order in which they had been killed, formed a graded series, of which the first was an unusually richly coloured bird, the last an exceptionally dull one, the others representing various intermediate shades or stages of coloration. I was confident then—and I fully believe now—that all these males were successively mated to one and the same female ; but my only evidence of this was that I never saw more than one female in this immediate locality, and that on the different occasions she looked and acted like the same bird."

" I have written," adds Mr. Brewster, " to Mr. Maynard, inquiring about a similar experience which I think he once had with some red-winged blackbirds."

Mr. Maynard's reply was as follows: "About the date you say (*i.e.* 1868 or 1869) I shot three male redwings in one meadow (at Newtonville, Mass.), all over one nest. The first was in high plumage, the second less so, the third quite young, and I left with the female a young bird of the previous year, judging by the absence of red on the wing."

We have taken the song of birds as an example of activities which are associated with a state of emotional exaltation. There are, however, as has incidentally appeared, other forms of activity, such as so-called love-antics, aerial evolutions, dances, and many modes of active display, often correlated with the possession of special external adornments, of which one or two typical cases may be given, since they further open up the question of the nature and origin of habit and instinct.

"How many evenings," writes Mr. F. Chapman, in his "Birds of Eastern North America," * "have I tempted the malaria germs of Jersey lowlands to watch the woodcock (*Philohela minor*) perform his strange sky-dance! He begins on the ground, with a formal periodic *peent*, *peent*, an incongruous preparation for the wild rush that follows. It is repeated several times before he springs from the ground, and on whistling wings sweeps out on the first loop of a spiral which may take him three hundred feet from the ground. Faster and faster he goes, louder and shriller sounds his wing-song; then, after a moment's pause, with darting headlong flight, he pitches in zigzags to the earth, uttering, as he falls, a clear twittering whistle. He generally returns to near the place from which he arose, and the *peent* is at once resumed as a preliminary to another round in the sky."

Mr. Ernest E. Thomson describes † how the American

* P. 153.
† Quoted by F. M. Chapman, "Birds of Eastern North America," p. 198.

harrier or marsh hawk (*Circus hudsonius*) endeavours to win the admiration of the hen bird by a number of extraordinary aerial evolutions.   Sometimes he soars to a great height, then falls straight downwards nearly to the ground, turning several somersaults during the descent, and uttering at the same time a reiterated screeching."

Let us now turn to the dance.   In an article on "The Lives and Loves of North American Birds," * in which Mr. John Worth notices and interprets Major Charles Bendire's "Life-histories of North American Birds," there is a graphic description of the dance as it is performed by prairie chickens, or sharp-tailed grouse.   The birds in companies of from six to twenty individuals assemble on some hillock or knoll, fifty to a hundred feet across, the "floor" being worn and beaten smooth by years of tramping.   After remaining for a while inactive, "one of the cocks," we are told, "lowers his head, spreads out his wings nearly horizontally, and his tail perpendicularly, distends his air-sacs and erects his feathers, then rushes across the floor, taking the shortest of steps, but stamping his feet so hard and so rapidly, that the sound is like that of the kettle-drum ; and at the same time he utters a kind of bubbling crow, which seems to rise from his air-sacs, beats the air with his wings, and vibrates his tail so that he produces a loud rustling noise, and thus becomes a really astonishing spectacle.   Soon after he commences all the cocks join in, rattling, stamping, drumming, crowing, and dancing furiously; louder and louder the noise, faster and faster the dance becomes, until at last they madly whirl about, leaping over each other in their excitement."

Our second example shall be taken from Mr. W. H. Hudson's delightful chapter on "Music and Dancing in

* *Nineteenth Century,* April, 1893, vol. xxxiii. p. 594.

Nature." *　" The finest of the Platan rails," he says, " is
the ypecaha, a beautiful active bird about the size of a
fowl.　A number of the rails have their assembling-place
on a small area of smooth, level ground just above the
water, and hemmed in by dense rush beds.　First one bird
among the rushes emits a powerful cry, thrice repeated ;
and this is a note of invitation, quickly responded to by
other birds from all sides as they hurriedly repair to the
usual place.　In a few moments they appear to the
number of a dozen or twenty, bursting from the rushes
and running into the open space, and instantly beginning
the performance.　This is a tremendous screaming concert.
The screams they utter have a certain resemblance to the
human voice, exerted to its utmost pitch and expressive of
extreme terror, frenzy, and despair.　A long piercing
shriek, astonishing for its vehemence and power, is succeeded by a lower note, as if in the first the creature
had well-nigh exhausted itself ; this double scream is
repeated several times, and followed by other sounds,
resembling, as they rise and fall, half-smothered cries of
pain and moans of anguish.　Suddenly the unearthly
shrieks are renewed in all their power.　While screaming
the birds rush from side to side, as if possessed with mad-
ness, the wings spread and vibrating, the long beak wide open
and raised vertically.　This exhibition lasts three or four
minutes, after which the assembly peacefully breaks up."

Mr. Hudson also describes a somewhat similar performance of the wattled, wing-spurred, and long-toed jacana,
a performance which seems specially designed to bring out
the concealed beauty of the silky, greenish-golden wing-
quills ; and he has an inimitable paragraph on the strange
visits and dances of the spur-winged plovers.　Here the
male bird leaving his mate pays a call on a neighbouring

* " Naturalist in La Plata," p. 266.

couple, who receive him graciously, tread with him a measured dance accompanied by resonant drumming notes, and then bow him out, with their beaks bent to the ground. He returns to his mate, with whom he will himself receive a visitor later on.

This keen and sympathetic observer of animal life is not prepared to accept, and even rejects with some scorn, the idea that the activities he so well describes have any connection with preferential mating. " What relation," he asks, " that we can see or imagine, to the passion of love and the business of courtship have these dancing and vocal performances in nine cases out of ten ? " One may not unreasonably suppose, however, that the state of emotional exaltation shown by such exuberant activity bears *some* relation to the pairing impulse, which seems in many cases to reach its maximum intensity at the same time of year. But whether this relation, supposing it to exist, be such as to lead to preferential mating, is undoubtedly a question which is open to discussion, and stands in need of further evidence from direct observation, which is by no means easy to obtain. Let us, for the purposes of discussion, rule out preferential mating as inoperative, and ask how the nature and origin of the activities in question can be otherwise explained. " The explanation I have to offer," says Mr. Hudson, " lies very much on the surface, and is very simple indeed, and, like that of Dr. Wallace with regard to colour and ornaments, covers the whole of the facts. We see that the inferior animals, when the conditions of life are favourable, are subject to periodical fits of gladness, affecting them powerfully and standing out in vivid contrast to their ordinary temper. . . . Birds are more subject to this universal joyous instinct than mammals, and there are times when some species are constantly overflowing with it. . . . If all

Q

men, at some exceedingly remote period of their history, *had agreed to express* the common glad impulse, which they now express in such an infinite variety of ways or do not express at all, by dancing a minuet, and minuet-dancing *had at last come to be instinctive,* and taken to spontaneously by children at an early period, man's case would be like that of the inferior animals." *

Now, in this explanation there are in effect three distinct propositions : (1) The origin of the activities is to be found in periodic joyousness and emotional exaltation. (2) The particular nature of the expression is determined by common agreement. (3) The instinctive element of the performance is due to inheritance by direct transmission without elimination or selection.

To the first of these propositions no exception need be taken. Even those who may hesitate to accept the view of Mr. Wallace and Prof. Geddes, that plumes and other structural adornments are due to a surplus of growth-power combined with that expenditure of protoplasmic energy, and consequent development of waste products, which characterizes the male as compared with the more conservative and tissue-saving female,—even those who hesitate to accept these views as applied to extravagance of structural adornment, may be willing to accept fulness and richness of vitality as a sufficient cause for fulness and richness of motor activity as expressed in aerial evolution, dance, and song. Granting, therefore, that the first of the three propositions may be accepted, at least provisionally, as affording an explanation of the origin of varied and multiform activities, the next question that arises is, What has guided these activities into certain definite channels of dance or display or screaming concert? One hardly knows whether to take quite seriously Mr. Hudson's suggestion—

* "The Naturalist in La Plata," pp. 279-282. The italics are mine.

placed in our second proposition—that the definiteness is
due to an agreement so to express the overflowing joyousness begotten of vitality in full flood. But, if we do not
take the suggestion seriously, how is the definiteness to be
accounted for ? In the case of plumes and symmetrical
markings, no matter how splendid or how delicate, we can,
perhaps, in our ignorance, fall back on "laws of growth"
and a tendency to symmetrical synthesis. But the jacana
dance, or the performances of the prairie hen, can hardly
be attributed to any such inherent "laws" or "tendencies."
To what, then, can the definiteness be due ?

Presumably, the most true and modest, if not the most
satisfactory and comfortable, answer to this question is
that we do not know. But there can be no harm in a little
guessing, so long as our guesses are not regarded as
more than suggestive. It is possible that imitation, and
what Mr. Hudson has himself so well described under
the head of tradition, may be regarded as a means, if not
of developing, at least of maintaining, the definiteness of
performance. The young birds are born into a society in
which certain habits of dance, song, or other modes of
activity, are already organized. By that sub-conscious and
half-aware imitation which seems to be a trait of animal
life (a sort of extended sheep-through-the-gap-ishness), they
fall into the habits of their elders, as their elders did before
them when they too were young and plastic. Their ways
are moulded to those of the community in the heart of
which they are reared. They have neither the wit nor
the will to modify the family traditions by new-fangled
innovations. And if they had, and proceeded to exercise
their originality, they would, by so doing, place themselves
outside the social life, and would probably die unmated.
Moreover, it is not improbable that a certain amount of
natural selection through elimination would accompany

the traditional process. Any individual which, through lack of vigour or other more positive defect, was excluded from, or exhausted by, the dance or other performance, would so far drop out of the social life and run less chance of taking his share in the special business of pairing, not in virtue of any preferential mating, but just because, while others were stimulated by the performance to sexual activity, the weaklings were exhausted and excluded from the full life of the community. Song-birds matched against each other have been known to sing till they dropped exhausted to death. The extravagant and prolonged antics and dances may well be a means of eliminating the weakly and leaving the strongest and toughest dancers in full sexual vigour to perpetuate, not only their strength and toughness, but also any congenital tendency they may possess towards the specialized performance of the definite activity. The period of dancing and display is also a period of pugnacity, and those whose vital power is lowered by the strain of the one will be those who are worsted in the combats arising out of the other. So that out of the traditional dance there may arise a process of natural selection, whereby the most vigorous males, those with the greatest amount of reserve power for the development of plumage and for effective mating, and with the greatest congenital tendency to follow the traditions of the community, would survive to transmit their vigour as displayed in certain definite ways.

And if we may admit, on the part of the females, whether they participate in the dance or not, a heightening of the sexual emotion at the period of predominant activity, we may further suppose that there is at least this much of preferential mating as well—that the hens accept most readily the attentions of those through whose antics this heightened sexual impulse has been aroused.

Observation, and that of a peculiarly difficult and delicate nature, can alone decide whether there is such elimination and such selection as is here suggested.

I am not sure that I have represented Mr. Hudson's views correctly in saying that, as stated in the third proposition, the instinctive element of the performance is due to inheritance by direct transmission without elimination or selection. The essential question, however, is this: Are we sure that the performances are instinctive? May not such essentially social procedures be handed on by tradition without becoming ingrained in the congenital nature? We shall have occasion to see in the last chapter that in human progress a greatly developed form of tradition takes the place of heredity, and that evolution is in large degree transferred from the organism to his environment. May not tradition, in bird life and in the animal world, suffice for the handing on of some habitual activities? This is another question which ignorance prevents our answering with any certainty. No doubt we have been wont to assume that these habitual activities are instinctive and congenitally definite. But of decisive and conclusive proof, there is in many cases little enough.

In the case of bird-song there is some evidence, though not so much as could be wished. We have already discussed it in the chapter on Imitation, and there saw that, according to some observers, the singing of birds is, unlike their call-notes and sounds of alarm, wholly traditional and entirely due to imitation. This view could not, however, be unreservedly accepted without more conclusive evidence. There may be congenital elements forming an instinctive basis, requiring perhaps under normal conditions the appropriate auditory stimulus provided by the song of their own species, in the absence of which there may be failure to sing at all, or imitation of alien strains

Further observations under varied test conditions are needed to decide the question one way or the other.

With regard to the truly instinctive nature of the activities of the dance, of antics, of strange performances, and of aerial evolutions there is not much evidence. We cannot say with any certainty whether they have been wrought into the congenital tissue of bird life, or are acquired habits transmitted through the influence of tradition, like so many of the social customs of mankind. Might it not be possible to bring up broods of prairie hens under conditions which should exclude the conservative influence of tradition? If they went through all the antics of the dance under such circumstances, this would be definite evidence of the truly instinctive nature of the performance.

It is now time to summarize. There are certain activities observable among birds during the pairing season. These are certainly habitual, and in some cases instinctive. Whether they are instinctive in all cases we do not yet know. They may be kept definite through the influence of tradition. Even under tradition they may, if they chance to be correlated with exceptional vigour, be rendered instinctive through natural selection by the elimination of those who fail in vigour. They may also be rendered instinctive through sexual selection by preferential mating if it can be shown conclusively that choice is exercised, and that some are thereby excluded from mating. They may, again, be rendered instinctive through the hereditary transmission of acquired activity, in which case the definiteness of the performance must presumably be due to some form of intelligent selection. If they be regarded as expressions of sexual emotion, such expression may probably have suggestive value, and serve to evoke an answering emotion. In this case the act of pairing would be correlated with the expression of sexual emotion through certain specialized activities; and those individuals which were not expressive, together with those which were insensible to the suggestive influence of expression, would be less ready to mate and to transmit the specialized modes of expression. In all these matters further and fuller evidence from direct observation is to be desired.

CHAPTER XI.

NEST-BUILDING, INCUBATION, AND MIGRATION.

THE activities which were considered in the last chapter are characteristic of a period of high vitality, and one of emotional expressiveness and susceptibility. Whether we accept or reject sexual selection by preferential mating as a factor in the evolution of these specialized activities, it is a matter of observable fact that these activities are coincident in time with the pairing impulse. And it is probable that any selection, which may have been instrumental in their development, has been in some way associated with the mating instinct. If struggle or competition has occurred, it has centred round the processes essential to the propagation of the race; and the specialized activities of song, dance, or aërial evolutions may be regarded as expressions of the emotional state which accompanies and characterizes the pairing season, and may be held to possess, at least in some cases, a suggestive value.

There are, however, other activities characteristic of the same period in which the element of suggestion cannot be regarded as of much importance. Nest-building, the instinct of incubation, the maternal offices—these do not depend in any appreciable degree upon a suggestive element. Their direct biological value is, perhaps, more apparent than that of song or dance or strange antics, since they are more obviously of utility. To a consideration of some of the activities of this type we will now turn.

Is nest-building an instinctive activity, or is it a habit

rendered definite through intelligent imitation? Is the habit transmitted through organic inheritance, or handed on through the influence of tradition? Mr. Wallace has advocated the latter view—at least, so far as specific definiteness is concerned. On his view, if I rightly interpret it, a bird may inherit an indefinite tendency to exercise its energies in building; but how it builds depends upon the tradition of its species. Exclude imitation, and they no longer built a typical nest. Thus chaffinches taken to New Zealand, and turned loose there, built nests which bore "some resemblance to those of the hang-birds (*Icteridæ*), with the exception that the cavity is at the top. Clearly these New Zealand chaffinches," says Mr. Dixon,* to whom we owe the observation, "were at a loss for a design when fabricating their nest. They had no standard to work by, no nests of their own kind to copy, no older birds to give them any instruction, and the result is the abnormal structure."

Mr. Wallace quotes this under the heading of "variations of the habits of animals." It would be well to restrict the term "variations" to departures of congenital origin, and to apply the term "modifications" † to those departures which are individually acquired. According to those, who are unable to accept the inheritance of acquired characters, of whom Mr. Wallace is one, the two modes of departure from the activities normal to the species are of very different value. Modifications, since they are acquired, are not on this view inherited, and can play no part in the development of instinct; while variations are those departures which by natural selection can be rendered definite and stereotyped as instincts. This,

---

* *Nature*, vol. xxxi. p. 553. Quoted in "Darwinism," p. 76.

† Prof. Mark Baldwin adopts this usage in his paper on "A New Factor in Evolution," in the *American Naturalist* for July, 1896.

of course, is not intended as a criticism of Mr. Wallace's
views concerning nest-building, since he does not regard
the habit as founded on a definitely instinctive basis.   It
is a suggestion towards increased exactness in our technical
nomenclature which may be found generally useful.

No doubt nest-building is subject both to variation of
congenital origin and to modification through experience.
Mr. Blackwall, in the first volume of the *Zoological Journal,*
says, " It is evident that birds of the same species possess
the constructive powers in very different degrees of perfection, for, though the style of the architecture is usually
adhered to, the nests of some individuals are finished in
a manner greatly superior to those of others ; " and he
quotes a case in which a yellow bunting failed to build at
all, depositing its eggs on the bare ground, in which situa-
tion she sat upon them till they were hatched.*   Such
differences are probably due to variation.   On the other
hand, modification may often occur.   Bolton, in the preface
to his " Harmonia Ruralis," says, " I observed a pair of
goldfinches beginning to make their nest in my garden on
May 10, 1792 ; they had formed the groundwork with
moss, grass, etc., as usual, but on my scattering small
parcels of wool in different parts of the garden, they in
a great measure left off the use of their own stuff, and
employed the wool.   Afterwards I gave them cotton, on
which they rejected the wool, and proceeded with the
cotton ; the third day I supplied them with fine down,
on which they forsook both the others, and finished their
work with the last article.   The nest, when completed,
was somewhat larger than is usually made by this bird,
but retained the pretty roundness of figure and neatness
of workmanship which is proper to the goldfinch." †   Very

* See Yarrell, " British Birds," vol. i. p. 491.
† Ibid., vol. i. p. 541.

frequently birds, as Mr. Headley says, in his interesting book on "The Structure and Life of Birds," * "adapt themselves to new situations. The swallow and the house-martin have availed themselves of barns and houses. The palm-swift in Jamaica, till 1854, always built in palms. But in Spanish Town, when two cocoanut-palms were blown down, they drove out the swallows from the piazza of the House of Assembly and built between the angles formed by the beams and joists. In America the tailor-bird now uses thread and worsted for its nest, instead of wool and horsehair, and wool and horsehair may originally have been substitutes for vegetable fibres and grasses. In Calcutta an unconventional crow once made its nest of soda-water bottle wires, which it picked up in a back yard. In districts liable to floods, moorhens often build in trees. In New Zealand the paradise ducks, which usually build on the ground near rivers, have been known, where disturbed, to build on the tops of high trees, and to bring down their young on their backs to the water." But all this, as Mr. Headley points out, does not show that birds have not a nest-building instinct of congenital definiteness. It only shows that, as we have had occasion to note in many other cases, their instinct is modifiable by intelligence and experience. The habit may well be built upon an instinctive basis, and receive its final touches through individual experience.

Mr. Jenner Weir, writing to Darwin in 1868, says † : "The more I reflect on Mr. Wallace's theory, that birds learn to make their nests because they have themselves been reared in one,‡ the less inclined do I feel to agree

* Pages 334, 335.

† Quoted in Romanes' "Mental Evolution in Animals," p. 226.

‡ This was Mr. Wallace's earlier view ; his later view introduces tradition in a broader sense.

with him. . . . . It is usual with canary fanciers to take out
the nest constructed by the parent birds, and to place a
felt nest in its place, and when the young are hatched and
old enough to be handled, to place a second clean nest,
also of felt, in the box, removing the other. This is done
to prevent acari. But I never knew that canaries so reared
failed to make a nest when the breeding time arrived. I
have, on the other hand, marvelled to see how like a wild
bird's the nests are constructed. It is customary to supply
them with a small set of materials, such as moss and hair.
They use the moss for the foundation, and line with the
finer materials, just as a wild goldfinch would do, although,
making it in a box, the hair alone would be sufficient for
the purpose. I feel convinced nest-building is a true
instinct."

This view of Mr. Jenner Weir's is based, it will be seen,
on personal observation which is well to the point. Here
is another piece of direct evidence. Mr. John S. Budgett,
a careful observer, placed in 1890 a greenfinch's egg under
a canary, and this in due course was hatched, the young
bird proving to be a hen. In the following autumn he
bought a caged bird, a cock, probably of the same year,
and in the succeeding spring turned them out into an
aviary with furse and box bushes in it. Materials of
suitable kind were supplied—twigs, roots, dried grass,
moss, feathers, sheep's-wool, and horsehair. The hen
soon began to build her nest, while the cock did not
seem to take the slightest interest in her proceedings. Mr.
Budgett never saw him with a twig in his mouth. In
a few days she had finished her nest, and Mr. Budgett
having sought and found several wild greenfinches' nests,
made careful comparisons. Taking them as a whole, he
says, the aviary nest was like the wild ones in every
particular, made of wool, roots and moss, lined with

horsehair. A second nest which the aviary greenfinch built was also perfectly typical.

In the same year Mr. Budgett reared from a few weeks old a young hen bullfinch, and kept it in a cage till the next spring, when he bought a cock, probably an old bird, and turned them together into the aviary. The hen soon began to build, and finished her nest in about four days; but she used neither roots nor twigs, of which there was a plentiful supply. The nest was composed of nothing but dried grass, with a little wool and hair. She laid therein five eggs, two of which hatched, but the little birds soon died. She then began another nest, this time a typical bullfinch's nest of fine twigs and roots lined with horsehair. Here five eggs were again laid, all of which were hatched, and three reared. She also built a third nest, which was perfectly typical of her species.

Further evidence of this kind is much to be desired. But this, as far as it goes, appears to be decisive. Some birds build their nests true to type, without opportunities or with but the slenderest opportunities of imitation or instruction. It appears to me that the evidence before us justifies the conclusion that nest-building in definite ways is an instinctive activity; * but that it is modifiable by individual experience. Whether the modifications are inherited we do not know. It may be well to note how largely the performance of this activity is due to internal impulse, the external stimulus, being perhaps afforded by the sight of the requisite materials.

It is also advisable to draw attention to the complexity and delicacy of the activities involved in nest-building. There is necessarily a good deal of careful selection of the appropriate materials; and these materials are used in

---

* The nest-building of the sticklebacks, both three-spined and ten-spined, is without doubt truly instinctive.

special and often very elaborate ways. One has only to
examine such a common nest as that of the chaffinch to
be profoundly impressed with the skill and, if one may so
put it, the delicacy of touch of which it affords such unmistakable evidence. The nests of the golden-crested
wren, the blue-tit, the sand-martin, the reed-warbler,
which is made so deep that the eggs do not roll out
though the supporting reeds be waved by the wind almost
to the surface of the water—each so different and yet each
in its way so admirable—tell the same tale; as do such
foreign nests as those of the Baltimore oriole, a pensile
structure of grasses, bark, and various plant-fibres, firmly
and beautifully interwoven, or those of the tailor-bird,
daintily stitched with fibre, or hair, or bits of thread. If
further and fuller investigation and inquiry establish the
truly instinctive nature of nest-building, we must not
fail to realize the delicate complexity of the congenital
activities concerned. And then we must ask the question :—
Can all the niceties of the congenital process be attributed
to natural selection? If not, Can it be regarded as evidence
of the inheritance of acquired habit? I find it somewhat
difficult to picture to myself the eliminative steps by which
the definiteness of nest-building in any given species became congenital under natural selection. But I find it
almost equally difficult to make clear to myself how the
uniformity of type could result from the inheritance of
intelligently acquired habit. Intelligence is so individual
a faculty, enabling the organism to adjust his life to his
own special surroundings, that it is difficult to see how, out
of the somewhat divergent individualism to which intelligence tends, there could come that stereotyped uniformity which the nests of any given species present·
Imitation would no doubt tend to uniformity, but here,
again, it is difficult to see why a bird should imitate the

nests of its own species, and not the equally good, or perhaps, better nests of an allied species. The subject is full of difficulties whichever way it be regarded. And if we ask by what steps the Baltimore oriole has come to build his hanging nest in just that particular fashion, we can only reply, evasively, that with all our advances in biological knowledge a child can still ask questions which its elders find it hard to answer.

The laying of eggs in the nest when it is built is undoubtedly a habit of congenital origin; and problems of interest and some difficulty arise out of a study of the colour and markings of these eggs. These problems are not directly connected with habit and instinct, and they do not therefore call for consideration here. But the strange and abnormal habits of the cuckoo demand some notice.

The cuckoo (*Cuculus canorus*) is in several respects an anomalous bird. "He is a 'vagrom man,' as Dogberry would say: a vulgarian, a disreputable parasite. Yet he is in some ways an interesting creature, and the world has," Mr. Cornish,* reminds us, "always a fondness for interesting scamps." In the matter of food, he will eat hairy caterpillars which are rejected by most birds. There appears to be a great preponderance of males, the proportion being variously estimated at from twenty, to five to one. Mating is indiscriminate; and polyandry prevails. The hen bird lays a largish number of eggs, some say at relatively long intervals of several days. According to the careful observations of Dr. Rey, however, the hen cuckoo lays an egg every other day, from the middle of May till the middle of July, and, at times, lays one every day for short periods. They are remarkably small for the size of the bird, and are somewhat variable both in this respect and in that of coloration. They are

* "Wild England of To-day," p. 108.

not laid in a nest constructed by the cuckoo herself, but are dropped in alien nests, being carried thither in the bill. Sometimes an egg is turned out at the same time, but whether purposely or by accident, it is hard to say. Although there are instances on record of cuckoos feeding their young—or in any case feeding young birds of their own kind—and even of incubating eggs in an alien nest,[*] yet, in the vast majority of cases, the foster-parents on whom the egg is foisted hatch out and bring up the naked, blind, broadshouldered, hollow-backed, changeling which heaves out of the nest, rather perhaps from sheer size and awkward random activity than of set purpose—the nest-lings that of right belong there. Henry Jenner describes in the "Transactions of the Royal Society for 1788," how two cuckoos were hatched out in a hedge-sparrow's nest, together with one hedge-sparrow—an egg remaining un-hatched. In a few hours a contest began between the two cuckoos, one of which at last succeeded in ejecting the other, together with the young hedge-sparrow, and the unhatched egg. Long doubted, but occasionally re-described from observation, this summary ejection has recently been not only watched but sketched from life by Mrs. Hugh Blackburn.[†] The young outlaw, having thus rid himself of his rivals, grows apace, and is fed, through what would seem to be a strange modification of maternal instinct, by the foster-parents with indefatigable zeal. Miss Hayward describes and figures [‡] a little whitethroat feeding a young cuckoo of four or five times her own size. Finally, contrary to what is held by many ornithologists

[*] See Morris' "British Birds," vol. ii. (1852), pp. 56 and 59.
[†] "Birds from Moidart and Elsewhere."
[‡] "Bird Notes." Cf. the figure of the long-tailed cuckoo of New Zealand and its host, the grey warbler, in Buller's "Manual of the Birds of New Zealand," p. 39.

to be the usual rule, the old birds are the first to migrate, leaving their young to follow as best they may.

The hosts selected—if indeed the word is appropriate —by the cuckoo are numerous, and of different sizes, from that little scrap of a fellow, the blue tit, on the one hand, to the magpie, the jay, and the lesser grebe on the other hand. No less than forty-three several hosts are recorded for England alone, and if continental records be included, the list includes eighty-seven species belonging to eleven different families—the warblers and finches being the most abundant,* and the hedge-sparrow, one of the first birds to build a nest easily discovered either by boy or cuckoo, among the commonest of all. It is said by some ornithologists that the egg is dropped by the parent bird in nests where its colour will assimilate with that of the eggs proper to the nest; and it has been suggested by some that this may be due to intelligent selection on the part of the cuckoo, and by others that cuckoos act instinctively; that is to say, there is said to be an instinctive tendency in cuckoos which lay eggs of a given type to drop them into appropriate nests. This is the view taken by Dr. Rey, of Leipzig, who contends that cuckoos instinctively deposit their eggs, the colour of which for any particular bird is, he believes, constant, in the nests of the species by which they were reared. Each species of host thus rears a particular kind of cuckoo. He says that the eggs deposited among the variable eggs of the red-backed shrike are themselves variable; while those deposited in the nest of the wren, among her uniform eggs, have great uniformity of colour. On the other hand, Dr. J. A. Norton, of Bristol, who has paid much attention to the matter, which is one of direct observation, and who has kindly furnished me with some interesting notes on the whole question of cuckoo

* See Mr. Edward Bidwell, Norf. and Nor. Nat. Hist. Soc., vol. iii. p. 536.

habit, informs me that though he has observed good cases of matching—for example, a bluish egg in a hedge-sparrow's nest, and a reddish one in that of a spotted flycatcher—yet such cases are in his experience exceptional. To my question: "Is colour assimilation the rule?" he replies, "Emphatically, no."

It is clear, then, that different observers are not agreed as to the facts. It is possible that the habit in England is different from that on the Continent; but further observations are needed to establish any such difference. In any case Dr. Norton regards it as probable that the cuckoo, having laid an egg on the ground, carries it in her bill, and drops it into the first nest that she comes across. There is little or no intelligence displayed in the whole business. Dr. Norton informs me of a case in which the cuckoo had deposited her egg in an old disused nest, and of others in which the eggs had been dropped into nests in holes from which the young cuckoo was too large to escape. It would seem very doubtful whether intelligence has played any decisive part in the establishment of the cuckoo instinct. We must remember that there are three associated facts or groups of facts. First, the relatively small size of the eggs, about one-third that of the eggs of the American cuckoo; secondly, the deposition of these eggs in alien nests; and thirdly, the ejection of other nestlings by the young changeling whose broad shoulders and hollow back seem specially adapted to this purpose. Now, the first and third of these—the small size of the eggs, and the ejection of other nestlings—cannot be regarded as due to intelligence, but may fairly be attributed to natural selection. The parent bird would be unable to carry large eggs in her bill, and these would be left on the ground, and would remain unhatched, thus giving rise to a steady process of elimination of large eggs. And the young cuckoo who did not eject his foster brothers would run no little risk of elimination by starvation, especially when the foster parents were small and unable to bring supplies of food to satisfy his capacious appetite as well as the needs of their own offspring—though here, indeed, it might fairly be contended that his larger size and greedy voracity would itself doom the others to starvation. The eliminative steps in the establishment of the central habit of depositing the eggs in an alien nest are not so easy to explain even conjecturally. Darwin's account of the process needs modification in any case. He suggested that the habit began by the occasional laying of eggs in alien nests. But it would seem that the cuckoo lays her egg on the ground and then carries it to a nest in her bill. For such a habit the occasional laying of an egg in an alien nest would be no preparation. It would seem more probable that it began by laying eggs on the ground when the hen was forced to deposit them unprepared. And the habit of polyandrous intercourse, correlated with the preponderant number of males, may have been in some way associated with the gradual loss of the instinct of nidification. Guess as we may, however, it must be confessed that, if the instinct be due to natural selection, little is known of the stages of development. But, on the other hand, it is not less difficult to see how the strange instinct of the cuckoo could have arisen as the result of intelligently acquired habit, in a bird of somewhat remarkably low intelligence. The theory of individual acquisition, transmitted from parent to offspring, even if unaccompanied by the bio-logical difficulties involved in any form of such trans-mission, seems to involve not merely the intelligent utilization of the results of experience, but the exercise of truly rational powers of what appears to us a peculiarly depraved order.

Although the American cuckoo, a bird closely allied to our European species, does not appear to be parasitic in its habits; there is a group of birds belonging to a quite different family, that of the *Icteridæ,* which have similar habits. These are the cowbirds, concerning which Major Charles Bendire has collected all the available information in the "Report of the United States National Museum for 1893."* From his account the following *resumé* of the facts is derived.

Like our cuckoo, the cowbirds are polyandrous, the males generally outnumbering the females in the proportion of about three to one. The common cowbird of North America (*Moluthrus ater*) lays from eight to twelve eggs in a season, probably at intervals of several days. There is a large amount of variation in the size and markings of the eggs; but how far they assimilate with those among which they are laid we are not told. Major Bendire gives a list of no less than eighty-nine species in the nests of which the eggs of this cowbird have been found, sometimes four or five in one nest. It is not unusual to find some of the eggs of the species imposed upon thrown out of the nest to make room for those of the parasite, nor to find minute punctures in the shells of some of the remaining eggs. This is possibly done on purpose by the cowbird with her beak to prevent the eggs from hatching; but Major Bendire is inclined to attribute this puncturing to the sharp claws of the parent bird while sitting on the nest and depositing her own egg; for the parasitical bird seems to lay in the nest and not to carry the egg there in her bill. Hatching is usually accomplished in from ten to eleven days, generally in advance of those of the foster parent, and the growth of the young interloper is remarkably rapid. At the end of a few days the rightful

* Pages 587-624.

offspring are either smothered or crowded out of the nest by their stronger foster brother; or, failing this, starved, when he absorbs the entire attention of the foster parents. It is ludicrous, says Major Bendire, to see a fat, fully fledged young cowbird following a pair of chipping sparrows, or some small warbler, clamouring incessantly for food and uttering its begging call of *seerr-seerr* most persistently, only keeping quiet while its gaping bill is filled with some suitable morsel; and stranger still to note how devoted the diminutive nurses are to their foster child.

A smaller species or variety (*Moluthrus ater*, var. *obscurus*) has similar habits; as has also the bronzed or red-eyed cowbird of Mexico and central America (*Callothrus robustus*).

The observations of Mr. W. H. Hudson on the Argentine cowbirds (*Moluthrus bonariensis*), show that they frequently waste their eggs by dropping them on the ground, and occasionally lay in old forsaken nests. They also destroy many of the eggs in the nests they visit by pecking holes in the shells, parasitical eggs and others being indiscriminately treated in this way. The harder shell of their own eggs gives them, however, a better chance of being preserved; for, although this cowbird never distinguishes its own eggs, of which it destroys a great many, from those among which it is laid, yet a larger proportion of them escape. The hard shell may therefore fairly be regarded as a result of the process of natural selection. Furthermore, the short period of incubation,— about eleven days as compared with the fourteen to sixteen of the small birds on which it is parasitic,—gives it an advantage which may also be ascribed to natural selection. After a few days, as in the case of its North American congeners, the foster child is found to be the sole survivor of the nestlings; and, as is commonly found in the eggs of parasitical species, there is an extraordinary diversity in the colour, form, and disposition of markings. The embryos and young birds show a remarkable vitality. Mr. Hudson found three eggs which had been built in by the superposition of a new nest on the older one in which they were laid. Their shells were encrusted with dirt and glued together with broken egg-matter spilt over them. Nevertheless one contained a living embryo ready to be hatched, very lively and hungry when he took it in his hand. The young quits the nest as soon as it is able, trying to follow the old bird, and placing itself in the most conspicuous place—such as the summit of a stalk or weed—there demands food with frequent and importunate cries. Thus, one nurse, a little flycatcher, as the only means of standing above its foster-child, had acquired the habit of perching on the back of its charge to feed it.

Of the other cowbirds of the Argentine, one, the bay-wing (*Molothrus badius*), either builds its own nest, a neat and well-built structure, in the fork of a branch, or seizes that of a Leñatero (*Anumbius acuticaudatus*), and in it, or on it, constructs its own. Several females often lay in the same nest; but whether the birds pair or practice the promiscuous intercourse common to the genus, Mr. Hudson was unable to discover.

Very curious are the habits of the other Argentine species, the screaming cowbird (*Moluthrus rufoaxillaris*). For long they eluded even Mr. Hudson's acute powers of observation. But eventually he was fortunate enough to ascertain that it is parasitic on its cousin, the baywing. Both the eggs and young of the two species are so similar as to be indistinguishable. The baywing brings up both its own and its cousin's brood, and it is only after some weeks that the difference between the young of the two species becomes manifest. It is wonderful, says Mr. Hudson, that the screaming cowbird should lay only in the nests of the baywing; but the most mysterious thing is that the common Argentine species indiscriminately parasitical on a host of species, never, to his knowledge, drops an egg in the nest of the baywing unless it be forsaken.

It is clear that, though the interesting parasitic habits of the cowbirds throw side lights upon the parasitism of the European cuckoo, and though some of their features may fairly be ascribed to natural selection, yet they leave the origin of parasitism itself unsolved. We have to fall back on conjecture. Mr. Hudson is inclined to believe that the Argentine cowbird lost the nest-making habit by acquiring that semi-parasitical habit, common to so many South American birds, of breeding in the large covered nests of the oven birds (*Dendrocolaptidæ*), and he adduces evidence that this piratical habit does tend to eradicate the nest-making instinct. He further suggests that a diminution in the number of birds that build domed nests would involve the cowbird in a struggle for nests in which it would probably be defeated; and supposes that the origin of the parasitical instinct may have been in the occasional habit common to so many species, of two or more females laying together, as with the baywings. The young of those birds that most often abandoned their eggs to the care of another would inherit a weakened natural instinct; the whole race would, by intercrossing, degenerate, and could only be saved from final extinction by some individuals occasionally dropping their eggs in the nests of other species.

Little need be said concerning the instinct of incubation in its normal development. It is partly based on physiological grounds; and may fairly be claimed by upholders of natural selection as explicable on their principles.

Passing on, therefore, to the instincts associated with the consummation and natural result of the maternal act, the hatching out of the young, what seems most remarkable is that under the new conditions the bird becomes in many respects a new being. Compare the hen with her first newly hatched brood with what she was some three weeks before. Her maternity tinges all her behaviour ; she is not what she was, or rather she is that and vastly more besides. Untaught, she is a mother to the backbone ; and she has developed a new language in which to communicate with her chicks—that is, if the word "language" be used somewhat loosely for a set of definite sounds of emotionally suggestive value. The facts are so familiar, and the explanation on natural selection principles so adequate, that it is unnecessary to dwell on them. It will be better to select a specialized instinct of this period for more careful consideration.

It is well known that the peewit lapwing or plover will apparently simulate the actions of a wounded bird, with the object, as it would seem, of drawing intruders away from her nest and eggs or young. The Canadian ruffed grouse, and the willow ptarmigan, tumble along, seemingly well-nigh helpless, and lead off dog or man. Dr. W. L. Ralph,[*] writing of the American ground dove, a pretty little pigeon of the Southern States, says : "When one is driven from a nest containing eggs it will drop to the ground as if shot, and will then flutter around as if wounded, to try to draw the person disturbing it away from the nest, but, whether it succeeds or not, it will soon fly off. When a nest contains young, however, the bird will become almost frantic, until it appears to be nearly exhausted." Here it is the female bird that exhibits such careful tactics. But sometimes the male shows a like solicitude. "In 1883," says Mr. C. A.

[*] *Nineteenth Century,* April, 1893, p. 598.

Allen, " I met with a brood of young plumed partridges in Oregon. The male, who had charge of them, performed the usual tactics of feigning lameness, and tried his very best to draw my attention from the young, and, seeing I paid no attention to him, showed a great deal of distress. The young scattered promptly in all directions, and the majority were most effectually hidden in an instant."[*]

One more example may be given. It is from Mr. C. J. Cornish's pleasant book, " Wild England of To-day."

" Moving towards the lake [in Richmond Park], we flushed," he says,[†] " a pair of wild drakes from a shallow ditch, and almost at the same moment a lame duck shuffled distressfully from the same spot, and moved off slowly, with apparent difficulty, in a direction parallel to the lake. The counterfeit was so remarkable that, had we not caught a glimpse of a small black object dashing into the marsh which lay a few feet from the drain, on the opposite side from the course taken by the duck, no suspicion as to the reality of her disablement would have occurred. Meanwhile, the old bird invited pursuit, lying down, as if unable to move further ; and, resolved to see the end of so finished and courageous a piece of acting, we accepted the invitation and gave chase. For twenty yards or more the bird shuffled and stumbled through the rhododendron bushes, until she made for the lake side, where the ground was more open. Then, running fast, with her head up and discarding all pretence of lameness, for another twenty yards, she took wing and flew slowly just before us, at about three feet from the ground, until she reached the limit of the enclosure, when, uttering a derisive quack, she rose quickly above the trees and flew out over the lake. Anxious to see the sequel to this

---

[*] *Nineteenth Century*, April, 1893, p. 596.
[†] *Op. cit.*, pp. 116, 117.

beautiful instance of maternal affection, we hurried back to the little marsh where the ducklings were probably hidden, and, sheltered under a rhododendron bush, awaited the return of the wild duck to her brood. In a few minutes she reappeared, flying swiftly in circles among the trees, and, after satisfying herself that the danger was past, she alighted among some wild currant bushes about thirty yards from the marsh. There she stood for a moment, still and listening, with head erect, and, seeing nothing to alarm her, ran bustling down to the drain. After realizing that no harm had overtaken her brood on the spot where they had been surprised, she climbed the bank and tripped lightly into the marsh, when, in answer to her low quack, we soon heard the piping voices of the ducklings, which till then had remained motionless and invisible in the few yards of grass and rushes near. In a few seconds the whole family were united, and we had the pleasure of seeing the old bird swim past at the head of an active fleet of eleven black and yellow ducklings, making for the centre of the marsh."

Such tactics, be it noted, are not restricted to one or two species. They are common, no doubt with diversities of detail, to such different birds as grouse, pigeons, lapwings, rails, avocets, pipits, ducks, buntings, and warblers. How are we to account for them?

The first question to ask is, whether the habit is truly congenital and instinctive. We may readily admit that the probabilities are decidedly in favour of its instinctive nature; but of this there is, so far as I am aware, no definite and conclusive proof. And it is particularly unfortunate that we are here left at the mercy of probability. For if the habit be truly congenital and instinctive, it forms a very pretty subject for transmissionists and natural selectionists to quarrel over. If ever there was a habit, the transmissionist may exclaim, which bears the marks of its intelligent, and therefore acquired origin, this of feigning wounded is assuredly one of them! What habit, the natural selectionist may ask, is more obviously useful to the species? Is not this just the kind of activity which natural selection, if it be a factor at all, must fix upon and perpetuate through the elimination of short-comers? Those who adopted this habit would certainly thereby enable their offspring to escape destruction by enemies; and these would survive to perpetuate the habit.

Let us look at the natural selection view first, and consider the relation which on this hypothesis the habit in question bears to intelligence. For the selectionist intelligence, *in its practical application*, is an absolutely and distinctively individual factor. This is well brought out in Prof. Weismann's essay on the musical faculty. Briefly put, the case is this: natural selection may increase in a series of generations the innate store of intelligent faculty; but the application of that faculty remains a matter of individual experience. It matters not whether, as the result of such individual experience, the faculty is applied in precisely the same way for a hundred generations; it matters not that the individuals so applying their faculty are the sole survivors among a host of failures; it matters not how much elimination there is of those who have less intelligence or of those who apply it differently; the application of the faculty in this particular way cannot on selectionist principles be rendered hereditary and instinctive. In the matter of human faculty Prof. Weismann and his followers have not failed to insist on these facts, if facts they be. They say that, no matter how assiduously a man has from boyhood devoted his intellectual powers to the study of mathematics, he can hand on to his son no inherited increment of faculty. If the son, after all, does display exceptional ability, it is due, they say, to a congenital tendency quite independent of individual acquisition. What is he but another chip of the same old mathematical block ?

Now, let us not attempt to hide or slur over the conclusion which is the inevitable outcome of these contentions, supposing them well founded. *Under no circumstances*, if natural selection be all-sufficient, *can an intelligent act become hereditary and instinctive*. Intelligence and instinct are antithetical; the former can never pass into the latter or take any direct share in its evolution. If, then, natural selection have any effect in rendering instinctive such a habit as we are now considering, it must be working on a congenital tendency, independent of, but proceeding towards the same end as, intelligence. The simulation of the actions of a wounded bird, if it be due to the play of intelligence, cannot, on selectionist principles, become instinctive. And if such apparent simulation be really an instinctive activity, and be due to natural selection, it is on congenital variations, not on intelligent modifications of active response, that natural selection has been operative; while the fact that congenital variation on the one hand, and intelligent choice on the other, coincide in direction and tend to the same result, is seemingly fortuitous—is a coincidence and nothing more. But if it can justly be so regarded, it is scarcely a matter for surprise that the transmissionist finds this doctrine of coincidence somewhat hard of acceptance as compared with the hypothesis, which he himself adopts, of vital and genetic connection between the one and the other, the acquired intelligence of one generation becoming, or at least tending to become, the inherited instinct of the next.

The coincidence, if it may be so called, loses much of its force, however, when we consider that intelligent acquisition by the individual, on the one hand, and the natural selection of congenital variations, on the other hand, are both working, in their different spheres, towards the same end—that of adaptation. This is their common goal; but they endeavour to reach it by different routes. Well, then, suppose they do reach the goal, the one by intelligent adaptation, the other by organic adaptation, is this to be wondered at? Is it a coincidence in any proper sense of the term? Surely not. If two men start for the same place, the one by sea and the other by land, we should not regard it as a coincidence if both got there. If acquired adaptation and congenital adaptation reach the same end by different methods, this is due to the fact that the result *is* adaptive, and is what nature in either case is really all the while aiming at. Natural selection, too, in any such cases, is permitting the survival of those who, whether by the application of purely individual intelligence, or by congenital variations of an adaptive tendency, or both, are, as a matter of fact, adapted to their environments; and we need not be astonished if the disentangling of the factors is a task of no little difficulty.

But there is one more point of view. Is the hypothesis that the activity is founded on intelligence quite so satisfactory as at first sight it appears? It must be remembered that the very appropriateness of many instinctive activities, and their adaptation to the needs of the species, lead one to suppose, at first, that they are based on intelligent, nay, even on rational considerations. And yet closer and more searching study shows this view to be untenable. One might well suppose, for example, that the hen undertook the labours of incubation because she knew that the result would be a brood of chicks. But when we come to inquire on what grounds she could possibly reach such a conclusion, it is difficult to give a reply

which can even claim plausibility. To say that hens
have learnt to incubate because a careful study of their
neighbours' acts has led them to perceive that there
results a brood of chickens, is not only in itself extravagant, but leaves the question of the primary origin
of the habit unanswered. We are bandied about from
neighbour to neighbour, and find at the end of the process
we are just where we began. Natural selection here steps
in, and tells us that we are on a false track. Intelligence
has taken no more part in the development of the habit of
incubation than it has in the habit of laying the eggs to
be incubated.

Now obviously the case is not quite the same with the
instinct, if such it be, of enticing intruders from the nest.
Those who cheerfully read into the bird's mind the fully
developed consciousness of civilized man will perhaps say
that the lapwing reasons thus : " If I pretend to be wounded
and flutter round, I shall draw upon myself the intruder's
attention and lead him to suppose that I shall be easily
caught; and if I thus entice him away, my little ones
will be saved, and my end gained." Thus, it may be
said, might the bird argue. I have no hesitation in saying
that such a chain of reasoning on the part of lapwing
or duck is a sheer impossibility. Apart from the fact
that she has probably no experience of being wounded or
of the effects of wounds on others, the whole process is
essentially one of human ratiocination, and quite beyond
the capacity of the wisest of birds ; while there is further
supposed a histrionic power, and a realization of the
effect on others of her display, which many a human actor
might well covet.

But is not intelligence, it will be said, perhaps displayed
in a simpler and more believable form ? May not the bird,
without any exercise of abstract reasoning, have found by

experience that the trick is effectual? All one can say is that it would be experience perilously acquired. Granting what I find it rather hard to grant, that the bird has the wit to try the trick; a little over-acting, a little too much lameness of wing, and she is herself seized and killed; a little under-acting, and the trick fails, and the little ones are killed. Does it not seem probable that such experience would be dearly bought; that failure would mean either death to the parent or death to the offspring? Is it not clear that natural selection is thus introduced in any case? And may not the selectionist pertinently ask: Why, if natural selection be thus introduced as a factor, halt midway between two hypotheses? Why not take the further step—one by which all the difficulties attending the mode of intelligent origination are avoided—of allowing that natural selection exercises, throughout, its influence on congenital variations and not on acquired modifications of faculty?

While admitting the logical cogency of this argument, I cannot but think that, were the biological difficulties attending the fact of transmission removed, such an instinct as is shown by the lapwing or wild duck would be best explained by a co-operation in some way of intelligence and natural selection. I shall have a suggestion to make on this head at a later stage of our inquiry, according to which modification may be a factor in race-progress without direct transmission. The result of the foregoing discussion is, I take it, that though the instinct in question does not afford so strong a case in favour of the inheritance of acquired characters as at first sight it would seem to do, yet its development, in complete independence of intelligent guidance by the natural selection of fortuitous variations, puts no inconsiderable strain on the theory of the all-sufficiency of natural selection. As matters stand, however, the question must be left open. Like many other cases of instinct, this affords no decisive evidence, and must be relegated to a suspense account.

We may now pass on to consider, or rather to touch upon, what is the most difficult and perplexing of all the problems which are suggested by bird-life—the migratory habit—of which Professor Newton says that it is "perhaps the greatest mystery which the whole animal kingdom presents." *

What can one say that is the least fresh and helpful concerning migration? Little enough. I shall therefore merely give a brief reminder of the facts, an indication of the essential problems from our own special standpoint, some allusion to the theories which have been suggested, and a confession of ignorance.

The leading facts are sufficiently familiar. A number of our English birds, like the swallow, the cuckoo, and the nightingale, after nesting with us in the summer, depart southwards in the autumn, and return in the ensuing spring. Others, like the redwing and the fieldfare, come to us in the autumn and depart northwards in the spring to nest and rear their young. Yet others, birds of passage like the sanderling and phalarope, make England merely a resting-place on their southward or northward journey. Even the birds that are with us the year through, like the redbreast and song thrush, receive accessions or suffer diminution of numbers through migration. In the northern hemisphere, whenever, as is commonly the case, the alternate migrations are northward and southward, the nesting-place is in the northern part of the area over which the bird migrates. The distances traversed are great. "The sanderling nests in Iceland or on the shores of the Arctic Ocean, and in winter it has been seen as far south

* "Dictionary of Birds," p. 549.

as Cape Colony. The nestlings of the knot have been found in Grinnell Land in latitude 82° 33′ N., and the bird is known to winter as far south as Australia and New Zealand. The turnstone is a great traveller, nesting in Greenland or on the coasts of Scandinavia, and wintering in Australia, New Zealand, South America, or Africa. The distances travelled amount sometimes to over 7000 miles. . . . The American golden plovers breed in Arctic regions, from Alaska to Greenland, above the limits of forest growth, and when autumn comes they pass through Nova Scotia, strike boldly out to sea, and, generally leaving the Bermudas well to the west, sail on over the ocean till they reach the West Indies. Even then, it is said, they will sometimes pass the first islands they reach, and pass on to more distant ones. From Nova Scotia to Hayti, the nearest West India Island available, is 1700 miles." [*] So universal is the migration impulse, that Professor Newton is of opinion that " every bird of the northern hemisphere is to a greater or less degree migratory in some part or other of its range." [†] The outward and the homeward routes are not in all cases, perhaps not generally, the same ; and yet there would seem to be little doubt that the birds return to the particular spot from which they started some six months before. In some species the birds fly in enormous flocks ; in others the flight is less gregarious and more scattered. Much has been written on the subject of " migration routes," and it may be taken as proved that in some species these are determined by the direction of valleys, the trend of coast-lines, and so forth. But any discussion of such routes is quite beyond our present purpose. Often the birds fly at great heights ; they have

[*] " The Structure and Life of Birds," by F. W. Headley, pp. 352 and 357, 358.

[†] " Dictionary of Birds," p. 552.

been seen crossing the image of the moon in astronomical telescopes, under conditions from which it is inferred that they were flying at an elevation of from one to three miles. In dark and cloudy nights their cries may be heard by any one who has ears to hear; and it is said that in some species special cries are developed at this time only.

Such are the elementary and familiar facts with regard to migration. The essential problems are :—Is the habit truly instinctive, even in its details? How did it originate? What is the nature of the impulse prompting the bird to migrate? What are the conditions under which it is called forth? And how do the birds find their way?

If not instinctive, the habit must be attributed to tradition in the sense before defined. On this view the migratory host is always led by older birds who have themselves been led by their predecessors, and so on ever since the habit originated. This seems to be the hypothesis adopted by Prof. Palmen, who ascribes the due performance of the migration flight to experience. On this view the congenital factor is a vague and indefinite innate impulse recurrent at certain seasons. The course taken is seemingly a matter of "follow my leader." But if, as Temminck stated, and as Herr Gätke, with his fifty years' practical experience in Heligoland, is convinced from a vast mass of accumulated observations, the young birds in a great number of species invariably *precede* the old by some weeks (the reverse being the case with cuckoos), the hypothesis of tradition is, for these species, seemingly out of court, and the mystery of migration deepens. "That a chiffchaff, whose daily occupation for months has been to pick grubs from the trees, and who has never left his favourite wood, should suddenly, some evening, be seized with an uncontrollable impulse to start for North Africa, is surely," says Mr. Headley,* " a matter for wonder. Still more astounding is it that the young birds, with defective strength and no experience, should start on the great pilgrimage alone, instead of waiting for the old birds to guide them. And in spring, too, when you see the first swallow, it is a startling thought that the small bird whom you see practising his short swallow-flights, started perhaps only some ten days before on his northward voyage from Natal."

As to suggestions with regard to the origin of the instinct—the congenital tendency of a definite and determinate nature—that of Mr. A. R. Wallace, quoted by Professor Newton,† is as follows: "It appears to me probable that here, as in so many other cases, ' survival of the fittest ' will be found to have had a powerful influence. Let us suppose that in any species of migratory bird, breeding can, as a rule, be only safely accomplished in a given area; and further, that during a great part of the rest of the year sufficient food cannot be obtained in that area. It will follow that those birds which do not leave the breeding area at the proper season will suffer, and ultimately become extinct, which will also be the fate of those who do not leave the feeding area at the proper time. Now if we suppose that the two areas were (for some remote ancestor of the existing species) coincident, but by geological and climatic changes gradually diverged from each other, we can easily understand how the habit of incipient and partial migration at the proper seasons would at last become hereditary, and so fixed as to be what we term an instinct. It will probably be found that every gradation still exists in many parts of the world, from a complete coincidence to a complete separation of the breeding and the subsistence areas; and when the natural history of a

---

* " The Structure and Life of Birds," p. 351.

† " Dictionary of Birds," p. 556, quoted from *Nature,* vol. x. p. 459.

sufficient number of species is thoroughly worked out, we
may find every link between species which never leave a
restricted area in which they breed and live the whole year
round, to those other cases in which the two areas are
absolutely separated."

Here the divergence of the subsistence area from the
breeding area may be regarded as an expression of the facts
which have to be in some way accounted for; while the
hypothesis of natural selection, as applied to the particular
case, takes the form of the barest corollary from the theory
in general. Those who migrated to and fro survived; those
who failed to do so were eliminated. *Voilà tout!* Unfortunately it remains a corollary unverified and unverifiable.

Mr. Headley quotes * from Mr. Henry Seebohm the
cases of the Petchora pipit and the Arctic willow wren
which "both winter in the Malay Archipelago. They
have extended their breeding grounds from Siberia to
Eastern Europe. But though they have moved their
summer residence so far west, in winter they still return
to their old haunts in the Malay Archipelago, though
Africa is more accessible, and, we might imagine, equally
suitable." Here we see an extension of range going on
under our very eyes, and that in the breeding area which
is generally regarded as the more stable and fixed. I do
not know whether in these cases the young migrate in
advance of the older birds. But in any case it is difficult
to say whether this extended range is now instinctive, and,
if so, whether it is due to inheritance of the results of
acquired experience, or whether natural selection has been
the determining cause. In a word, the instinct of migration does not help in the least to solve the general problem
of the mode of origin of instincts.

The determining conditions of the impulse prompting

* "The Structure and Life of Birds," pp. 371, 372.

to migration are presumably in part external and in part internal. When we say that the external factor is probably due to changes of climate and food supply, while the internal factor is probably largely due to changes in the reproductive system, we have said well nigh all that is to be said—and that is little enough. In any case, the birds are marvellously true to time, especially such sea birds as the puffin, from which we may perhaps conclude that the internal factor is the main determinant, since both climatic changes and food supply are variable from year to year.

With regard to the question of direction, the sense whose organ is the semicircular canals, which are well developed in birds, has been invoked as a source of guidance. But it must be remembered that this organ, like others of the special senses, while it affords data to experience, finds in that experience its *raison d'être*. By themselves, as their action is at present understood, they could afford no foundation for the directed flight of the swallow from England to Natal, if this be truly instinctive. The semicircular canals might enable the bird to continue over wide seas a line once adopted; but unless there is in addition some sense of orientation (some equivalent in the bird's organization to the mariner's compass) it is difficult to see how they could afford instinctive guidance.

The outcome of any consideration of the whole question is a profound sense of ignorance. So great is that ignorance, that it is difficult even to speculate. Were I pressed to hazard a guess, I should be inclined to surmise that, notwithstanding the observations of Herr Gätke, while the migratory impulse is innate, and perhaps there is an instinctive tendency to start in a given direction, yet the element of traditional guidance may be effectual, in the migration stream as a whole, in some way that we have hitherto been unable to observe.

CHAPTER XII.

THE RELATION OF ORGANIC TO MENTAL EVOLUTION.

THROUGHOUT our considerations of the phenomena of habit and instinct, and of the relation of that which is congenital to that which is acquired, we have had to deal with organic activities which are associated with conscious states. It has been assumed that organic evolution has carried with it mental evolution. We have now to discuss the relation of the one to the other. Problems of great difficulty surround the subject, some of which must be resolutely ignored. We will not, for example, attempt to inquire what is the nature of the association between the organic processes in brain or ganglion and the conscious processes which are their concomitants; nor touch on the vexed question of dualism and monism. That consciousness does accompany brain action, and that, at some stage of organic evolution, this consciousness does become an effective factor in the developmental process, will be assumed.

Two phases of organic development must be distinguished; first, that in which consciousness is either absent or inoperative; and secondly, that in which consciousness is a co-operating factor. The first may be termed the merely organic phase; the second, the conscious-organic phase. The latter may again be subdivided into two phases; first, that in which mental evolution is subordinate to organic evolution; and secondly, that in which mental evolution is predominant.

It is probable that, throughout the vegetable kingdom, evolution is in the merely organic phase. If there be consciousness associated with the life of plants, there is no evidence of its being a factor in the process of development. It is not what we have before termed effective consciousness. The lowest animals fall under the same category; but where the line is to be drawn in the animal kingdom, between those in which consciousness, if present, is inoperative, and those in which it is effective, who can say with any certainty? The first requisite is to find some criterion which shall be available for the purpose of distinguishing the cases in which consciousness is operative from those in which it is inoperative. Such a criterion is the exercise of choice. But we must be careful, in our application of the criterion, to grasp what is essential to an act of choice. Invariable reaction in one way to one kind of stimulus and in another way to another kind of stimulus is regarded by M. Binet[*] as evidence of choice. "If we hold to what observation directly teaches us," he says, "the choice may be said to consist in the following acts: When an animalcule perceives certain kinds of substances, and particularly those substances which serve it as customary food, it invariably goes through the same movement, which consists of an act of prehension; but when the substance touched, seen, or collided with, as the case may be, is of another kind, the micro-organism does not go through this act." I cannot agree that this is either satisfactory or sufficient. Many inorganic substances, those on the sensitive film of a photographic plate, for example, do as much as this. If, in accordance with Pfeffer's interesting observations, the spermatozoids of a fern are attracted by malic acid and malates, crowding into a tube which contains this substance, there is here no conclusive

[*] "The Psychic Life Micro-Organisms." Eng. Trans. pp. 62, 63.

evidence of choice. They are so constituted as invariably to react in this way in presence of this material. There may be here nothing more than merely organic response. Or if, in accordance with a well-known observation of Romanes, a sea anemone in a turmoil of water and air-bubbles reacts to the slight mechanical stimulus of a solid body, there is even here no conclusive evidence of choice; one cannot even regard it as indicating the presence of choice in its physiological aspect. A sensitive plate, again, does as much as this. Amidst the turmoil of the larger ethereal vibrations termed red light, and of the yet larger waves of heat which break upon its surface, it remains unaffected; but it reacts to the relatively slight stimulus afforded by a minute ray of the smaller ethereal vibrations we term violet light. Nor does his interpretation of this observation accord with Romanes' own criterion,[*] which is in itself perfectly satisfactory and involves true choice. " The criterion of mind which I propose," says Romanes,[†] " is as follows: Does the organism learn to make new adjustments, or to modify old ones, in accordance with the results of its own individual experience? If it does so, the fact cannot be merely due to reflex action, for it is impossible that heredity can have provided in advance for innovations upon or alterations of its machinery during the lifetime of the particular individual." I do not quite understand the point of the last part of this quotation. The power of choosing and of exercising control so as to make the choice effectual, is surely hereditary in the higher animals; and, if so, surely heredity *does* provide[‡] in advance for innovations upon

---

[*] " Mental Evolution in Animals," p. 48.

[†] *Op. cit.*, pp. 20, 21.

[‡] Prof. Mark Baldwin has criticized Romanes' statement in very similar terms in " Mental Development of the Child and the Race," p. 220.

and alterations of its machinery during the lifetime of the individual. How otherwise could an animal have any power of individual acquisition? But while heredity provides a power of individual acquisition, it does not provide in advance for particular innovations or modifications. A store of innate power, and definite susceptibilities to pleasure and pain, are inherited; individual experience utilizes this innate power to mould its instinctive and other activities into new habits under the guidance of pleasure and pain. And this absence of provision in advance for particular modifications is probably what Romanes meant. Apart from this, he seems to have quite clearly indicated a valid criterion of the effective presence of consciousness—namely, the observable, profiting by experience. It is just because a chick, having tasted a nasty grub, refuses to touch it or its like for the future, that we may feel confident he exercises real choice in the matter. Invariable response under similar conditions, as in the case of the spermatozoids in the presence of malic acid, is no evidence of choice; but an alteration or modification of response in the light of individual experience does afford the criterion we seek. And this criterion involves the exercise of control. Automatism, no matter how complex or how nicely adaptive, may be unconscious; but controlled action indicates conscious choice.

Whatever the physiological conditions of the process may be, it seems clear that consciousness, as choosing and controlling, stands in a sense outside that upon which it exercises control through its power of choice. And, thus, on passing from the merely organic to the conscious-organic phase of evolution, we have to consider the development of an *imperium in imperio*. In close touch and intimate relation with the merely organic and automatic system is a controlling system, the functional activity of which is accompanied by consciousness. How the physical processes and the conscious states are associated need not concern us here. This is a philosophical problem which lies beyond our present scope. The point on which we have here to fix our attention is that the organic mechanism, somehow associated with choice and control, is dependent on, and yet, in some degree, independent of, the merely organic system concerned in automatic response. Just as the cerebral hemispheres are dependent on the nervous system as a whole, and yet, as Prof. Michael Foster has said, seem to stand apart from the rest of the brain, playing down upon the lower brain centres and those of the spinal cord through the pyramidal tract or its equivalent; so does conscious choice and control stand apart from the involuntary and automatic activities; so is it independent of them in the sense that its sphere is not necessarily restricted to that of merely organic ends. It is, of course, a limited independence. From the organism the controlling system receives its support; and to the organism it affords, in return, effective guidance in the business of organic life; but these conditions being fulfilled, it is for the rest free to develop on its own lines. The body places itself under the control of the cerebral hemispheres; so long as that control is exercised with efficiency they may utilize their surplus energy in any way consistent with the laws of their own development.

It was long, however, in the history of life on our earth, ere consciousness succeeded in creating for itself a suitable environment under which this surplus energy could run into lines of effective development—not indeed, as is probable, until the human phase of development was reached. Between the first beginnings of choice and control, and this later phase when mental predominates over organic development, lie the several stages of mental evolution in animals. What may be the limiting conditions of this portion of the ascending curve of evolution; how control had its early genesis; how the mental evolution of animals passed into the mental evolution distinctive of man, cannot now be discussed.* We must devote our attention to the relation which organic evolution bears to that mental evolution which is its accompaniment throughout the stages of animal development above indicated.

No one is likely to question the importance of conscious adjustment to environment in the evolution of the higher grades of animal life. It matters not whether the selectionists are right in contending that those individuals who vary in the direction of more adequate conscious development are selected and transmit their innate powers, or the transmissionists are right in contending that acquired powers of conscious adjustment are transmitted from parent to offspring; in either case conscious adjustment as a factor in organic evolution is of the utmost importance. The intelligent animal, the animal that can avoid danger, can secure prey, can win or enforce himself upon a mate; that is quick to see and hear, quick to select, quick to act; that hesitates not, blunders not, and does not flinch; this is the animal that survives and becomes the parent of a good stock. But in the animal world this conscious adjustment is wholly subservient to the needs of animal life. At this stage of evolution, mind or consciousness is an adjunct to organic development. Just in so far as it ministers to the progress of animal development will natural selection favour it, or will it in some way be rendered an effective factor in organic evolution. In the stress of the struggle for existence among animals consciousness has enough to do in fulfilling this its primary

* I have attempted to discuss the latter point in my "Introduction to Comparative Psychology."

function; more than this, it has neither the energy nor the opportunity for doing; and any organism in which it failed to do this would inevitably succumb and suffer the stern fate of elimination.

Thus in the many and various inter-relations and inter-dependencies of animals with reference to each other, and to their inorganic environment, the mental system of any individual must be of such a kind as to give opportunities for choice and control by which the needs of organic life may be met, and adjustments made in relation to these needs. For this experience affords the data. Experience brings the animal into more extended touch with its surroundings than is possible in the merely organic phase of life-progress. And if the expression of emotions has suggestive value, experience also brings the animal into wider touch with other animals. The horse reacts to the varying moods of its companions; the lonely chick restored to its fellows no longer utters its querulous note of complaint. All this has reference to the development of the more or less complex mental system of any animal; and so far we are regarding the mind of the creature as a whole, just as we regard its body as a whole.

There is, however, another aspect of organic evolution that must be clearly grasped and steadily borne in mind. As there is a delicate and intricate inter-dependence of organic forms, so that no individual is isolated, but must adjust itself to a complex environment of other individuals of its own kind, and of other species in varying degrees, so too within the organism every constituent particle or cell is in more or less close relationship with all the others that are incorporated in the same bodily system. Take, for example, a secreting cell in one of the glands, the products of which minister to digestion. It plays its part in the nourishment of the whole body. But

nerve-fibres convey to it the currents by which it is stimulated to functional activity: the nutritive processes to
which it contributes are necessary for its maintenance;
respiratory processes are essential for its continued vitality
and for the elaboration of its special secretion; for it the
heart beats and the blood circulates. All this is so familiar
and well recognized as to savour of the biological common-
place. It is a matter of common knowledge that the
individual cell is in nice adjustment to an environment
of the body of which it is a constituent unit, and that it
is only in virtue of this adjustment that its continued
existence is possible.

But when we come to the mental development that
is implied in and grows out of conscious adjustment, the
analogous facts, though equally important, are not so well
recognized. Just as there is an organization of the
material body into a unity of interdependent parts, so too
there is an organization of states of consciousness into a
body of experience. And just as the adjustment of the
parts to the whole in the material body is essential to the
continued existence of both, so too is the adjustment of the
parts to the whole in the body of experience essential to
that progressive unification without which mental development would be impossible. Conscious adjustment involves
choice; and this implies the selection of that which is
acceptable or pleasing, or in other words (and more generally), in harmonious adjustment to the conscious system;
and the rejection, so far as possible, of that which is distasteful, discordant, or incongruous. Just as every organ,
every tissue, every cell within the animal body, has to
make good its claim to continued existence at the bar of
the incorporated society of its biological peers; so does
every bit of experience stand its trial at the bar of consciousness; it has to make good its claim for repetition in

virtue of its being in harmonious accord with the mental system of the animal possessed of the power of conscious choice.

Attention must here again be drawn to the difference in method between the process of natural selection through elimination and the process of conscious choice. The former is characteristic of organic evolution as such; the latter is the distinctive feature of mental evolution. Let us take the former, natural selection, first. Given a number of individuals, differing in fitness to meet the conditions of their life, and subjected to the inevitable struggle for existence. There results a process of elimination. The first to go are the most unfit; then others in the order of their unfitness; until there results a survival of the fittest; and these alone contribute to the continuation of the race by the propagation of their kind. The elimination begins at the unfit end of the scale, and works its way upwards progressively, until a fit remainder survives. This is the natural selection of Darwin. It is a method by which, under the struggle for existence, there is an elimination of the unfit, with the consequent survival of the fittest. Conscious choice, on the other hand, the method of mental evolution as such, throughout its whole range deals with the given material in a different way. It works along the scale in the opposite direction. The first to be chosen is that which evokes most strongly and most harmoniously the selective consciousness in the mental system of the chooser. The fittest in this sense is the first to be selected, not the last to survive. Then the next in order of fitness is chosen; and so on, beginning at the fittest end of the scale and working its way downwards.

Now suppose that in either case there are one hundred variations; and suppose that natural selection, working up the scale, eliminates ninety-five, and leaves a survival residue of five. Suppose, further, that conscious choice, working down the scale, selects the five fit, neglecting the residue of ninety-five unfit. And suppose yet further, that the surviving five in the one case are similar in character to the selected five in the other case. Then it is clear that the ultimate products in the two cases are practically similar. But this similarity of products does not one whit alter the diverse nature of the processes by which the similar products are reached. And if in some cases the products of human choice seem to be similar to those which would, we think, be reached by progressive elimination, this does not justify the assertion that they are due, in any logical sense, to natural selection. A failure to grasp the distinction between the method of natural selection and the method of conscious choice, vitiates much that has been written on social evolution in man; * but of this I have nothing further to say at present. What I desire to make clear is that, with the advent of effective consciousness, not only a new factor, but a new method of evolutionary progress is introduced. If, for example, sexual selection by preferential mating be a factor in evolution, its method is that of conscious choice, and not of the progressive elimination of the unfit, even if the products be similar to those which a process of elimination would also give. And all conscious acquisition, based as it is on intelligent choice, is reached by a method different from that of natural selection. Hence transmissionists are right in contending that if the inheritance of acquired characters be accepted as an established fact, this factor in evolution is different in its essential nature, and in its method, from natural selection.

Granting that conscious choice is a factor in the

---

* It vitiates, for example, Mr. S. Alexander's otherwise very valuable contributions to the problem of moral evolution.

evolution of the individual; granting that its method is that of a real selection in virtue of a felt congruity with the mental nature of the individual that exercises its power of choice; we have next to note that the choice primarily and in the first instance depends on innate proclivities. In the growth of experience association plays an important part. It serves to link together the data given in experience. But the value of the data is independent of association. In the utilization of experience, choice and control come into operation. But the value of the data for consciousness is rather the condition, than the product, of choice. What shall be chosen and what rejected depends upon the nature of the individual consciousness. So far as the individual is concerned we must just accept the fact that it likes some things and dislikes others. As a matter of observation, it tends, on the whole, to like what is good for it and dislike what is bad for it. How these likes and dislikes have been ingrained in the individual nature, so as to constitute innate proclivities, is no doubt partially explained by the obvious fact that the animal which is led by its likes and dislikes to better organic adjustment to his normal surroundings will survive to procreate his kind; while the animal which is led thereby to maladjustment, will be hurried to his own destruction.* The latter will perish, and with him will go his fatal proclivities; while the survival of his more happily constituted neighbour will lead to the survival of that neighbour's more favourable likes and dislikes, which, by constant repetition of this process, will become hereditary and innate.

The direction in which the likes and dislikes tend to set in the course of mental evolution is thus determined

* It is probably to the comparative absence of natural selection among civilized races that the continuance of such types as the drunkard is due.

by the necessities of organic existence. A rigorous process of elimination, under natural selection, decides which shall survive. It is just because experience is a guide to practical life that it has been fostered and developed. But experience is a mental product. Only in so far as the events of practical life are symbolized in consciousness can they be effective for guidance and control. And here it is absolutely essential to grasp this truth; that *throughout its whole range, from the earliest glimmerings of sentience to the highest products of human idealism, the environment in mental development is itself of the psychical order.* If this truth be not grasped, all attempts at solving the problems of mental evolution are inevitably foredoomed to failure.

This is not likely to be gainsaid or misunderstood by those who are acquainted with the teachings of psychology. Others may be assured that there is nothing here that is in the least opposed to a full and free acceptance of the objective reality, as such, of the world in which the animal is developed. Stress is indeed laid on the fact that the world is objective *to and for conscious experience.* But this is precisely the view of common sense, when it is not spoilt by a little dose of ill-digested philosophy. If experience is itself a mental product, it is in terms of mental products and in these alone that it must be explained. Suppose, to illustrate the matter by a concrete example, a young bird seizes a bee and proceeds to swallow it, but is stung in the process; he thus practically learns the nature of a bit of the objective world in which he lives. But every step of the process is taken in the field of his conscious experience; and the whole drama of his life-experience is a drama in and for consciousness. For experience is, it must be repeated, a conscious process. And every bit of experience, no matter how trivial, no

T

matter how elaborate and far-reaching, exists as such for consciousness. It must be of the conscious order or it is not experience at all. And it is out of conscious experience that individual consciousness as a complete whole of related elements is developed. The related elements themselves therefore must be conscious elements, and can be nothing else. And if this truth be not grasped, I repeat, all attempts at solving the problems of mental evolution are inevitably foredoomed to failure.

Within the individual organism, then, there is developed during the progress of conscious organic evolution, an organ, the cortex of the brain, whose function it is, from the biological point of view, to subserve the purposes of conscious adjustment and adaptation; its functioning has a mental aspect, and its development is somehow linked and associated with the development of mind; and, so far as this mental development is concerned, every step and stage of the evolutionary process lies within the mental world of conscious experience. Thus, in the conscious animal we have a mental system in association with an organic system, an *imperium mentale in imperio corporale.* Two points have now to be noticed; first, that, so far as the race is concerned, continuity of mental development is conditioned by organic heredity; secondly, that in its initial stages and for a prolonged period, mental development is conditioned by organic development, of which it is an adjunct, and to which it is subservient. Concerning the first of these points, nothing further need now be said; but to the second particular attention must be directed.

The *raison d'être* of consciousness in its earliest beginnings is to enable the incipiently conscious organism to extend its adjustment to the environment further than is possible under merely organic conditions. Every step in its early development was strictly limited within the narrow lines of complete subservience to this end. Mind was evolved in closest touch and most vital linkage with organic development; but only in so far as it ministered to that organic development was it permitted to evolve at all. Whatever may be the efficient causes which are at work in organic evolution, they inexorably limit throughout animal life, individual and racial, the range of mental evolution. In so far as conscious adjustment aids in the struggle for existence; in so far as through it the animal is better able to escape danger, to secure a more favourable habitat, to gain a mate and beget progeny; the animal possessed of intelligence will escape elimination, transmit his power of conscious adjustment, and contribute to the propagation of his race. Without fully subscribing to the doctrine of the all-sufficiency of natural selection, we may yet say that natural selection will exercise a determining influence in deciding the course which conscious adjustment must take.

We may thus regard the drama of conscious organic evolution from two points of view; from that which has reference primarily to organic progress, and from that which has reference primarily to mental development. Let us take the organic point of view first. Before the introduction of consciousness as a factor in progress, organic evolution is dependent entirely upon the directly responsive adjustment of the plastic organism to the environmental influences. If consciousness accompanies this adjustment, it is merely as an adjunct without power of guiding. It is like the passenger on a ship that is aware of her evolutions, but is absolutely without control over them. So far, therefore, there is adjustment which is either unconscious or merely accompanied by consciousness as an adjunct—we have no means of determining which. But with the advent of effective consciousness there is developed in association with the organism a special organ, dependent on, but exercising control over, the rest, by which it is enabled to profit by experience. The happenings of the surrounding world are here symbol- ized, the symbols are linked by association, and the special organ exercises a guiding influence on the actions and activities of the animal, restraining or stimulating, in accordance with that conscious symbolism which we call experience. The better the conscious symbolism, the better will be the adjustment to the conditions of life. And the more effectually the organ, associated with this symbolism, is in touch with the executive machinery of the body, the more effectually will the animal profit by its controlling administration. For practical purposes it is developed; and by the test of practical success in the business of life it must stand or fall. Consciousness is no longer merely a passenger in the ship of life. We may rather liken it to the captain of a modern ironclad, who, seated in the conning tower, directs all the movements and all the actions of the ship under his command. He alone is in possession of the requisite data for working the vessel; he alone can control her every movement, make her guns speak and disengage her torpedoes; how she goes into and comes out of action is in his hands. As captain, he exists for his command; his experience has been developed for this end; by his efficiency he stands or falls, and so bound up is he in the life of his ship that together they succeed or fail. So is the conscious symbolism of the higher brain-centres bound up with the life of the body in such intimate association that together they succeed or fail. Thus we may regard the matter from the point of view of organic evolution under the guidance of consciousness.

Turning now to the point of view from which mental evolution assumes the predominant place, the analogy of the captain may be pressed a little further. The development of that experience on which his efficient control of the vessel depends lies wholly within the sphere of his consciousness. It is, of course, throughout symbolic of the occurrences in the outside world—or, to speak more accurately, it is symbolic of those occurrences which are also symbolized in *our* consciousness as external events. The point is, however, that, no matter how close the touch between the symbolism and that which it symbolizes, it is as symbolism that it is developed. Symbol becomes associated and correlated with symbol, and thus there is evolved a symbolic system. And the laws of this symbolism are the laws of mental evolution. In the animal world it is under these laws that the effective consciousness by which the activities are guided and controlled reaches systematic development; but it has to stand its trial at the bar of practical success. In the captain's mind there may be evolved a system of tactics of admirable consistency, without an incongruous element in the whole fabric. But will it work ? Will it stand the test of an engagement ? If so, it will survive, and captain and ship come out of action victorious and winners in the war-struggle. If not, it will be eliminated; captain and ship will go to the bottom together. So, too, in the animal there may be evolved a symbolic system of perfect self-consistency. But will it avail in the struggle for existence ? If so, the system and its possessor will survive to hand on the good seed; if not, animal and system suffer together the stern fate of elimination.

The nature of the relation of organic to mental evolution is one that we should endeavour to realize with the utmost clearness. In animal life the two are so closely

associated, the mental evolution is so completely subservient to organic needs, that the biologist is somewhat
apt to forget that, no matter how close this association
may be, mental development has its own laws, and
requires distinctive if not independent treatment. On
this, however, it is needless now further to insist. We
may conclude this chapter by indicating concisely the *rôle*
of consciousness in organic evolution.

In what was termed the merely organic phase of
evolution, we may note, as the result of heredity, two
products : first, congenital definiteness of structure or
responsive activity, subject, indeed, to variation, but otherwise relatively fixed and stereotyped ; and, secondly, that
innate plasticity which renders possible modifications of
structure or mode of growth; so that, in virtue of this
second product, the individual possesses the power of
adapting itself to the special conditions of its own particular environment. Such modification is, in this phase
of evolution, purely organic, and altogether independent of
consciousness, which, if present, affords no guidance in the
process ; as, for example, in the adaptive modifications of
plants.

The primary *rôle* of consciousness, as a factor in race-
progress, is to extend in a new way this individual
adaptability, so that by modifications of its modes of
responsive activity, as the outcome of conscious choice,
the organism may yet further accommodate itself to the
special conditions under which its life is passed. This it
does through the agency of a special organ of control
associated with the conscious symbolism of experience.
The guidance afforded by intelligence is an individual
matter, as is the experience on which it is based, and the
association which renders this experience possible ; and
the intelligent faculty in and through which behaviour can

be modified in adaptation to the special circumstances symbolized in experience is in our terminology innate. The special modes of response learnt through experience are acquired, and this acquisition is therefore a purely individual matter.

In the merely organic phase of evolution race-progress is due, either (1) to natural selection through the elimination of unfavourable variations; or (2) to the direct inheritance or transmission of the results of modification in certain adaptive directions; or (3) to an inherent tendency of variations to occur in such adaptive directions; or (4) to some combination of these factors.

In the conscious-organic phase of evolution, one or more of these factors may be operative, either (1) in augmenting the innate store of intelligent faculty, and thus increasing the possibilities of individual adaptation to varied conditions of life; or (2) in stereotyping particular adaptations; or (3) in both these ways.

Omitting further reference to the supposed inherent tendency of variations to occur in adaptive directions irrespective of either natural selection or individual use, it is clear that our conception of the *rôle* of consciousness in organic evolution is largely dependent on the answer which we give to the vexed question of the inheritance of acquired characters. To the consideration of this question we must next proceed.

CHAPTER XIII.

ARE ACQUIRED HABITS INHERITED?

ATTENTION has already, more than once, been drawn to the distinction between variations on the one hand and modifications on the other. Variations take their origin in the germinal substance from which the organism is developed, and are unquestionably hereditary. Modifications are acquired in the course of individual life, being impressed, not primarily, if at all, on the germinal substance, but on the bodily tissues which are developed from the germ. And whether they are hereditary or not is the question we have now to discuss in its relation to habit and instinct. If they are hereditary, their effects must be in some way transferred from the bodily tissues to the germinal substance, so as to become a source of variation; modification in a given manner in one generation giving rise to a variation of similar nature in the next generation.

Take a particular case. No one is likely to question the fact that the maternal instinct of hens is subject to variation. Some are good mothers, some bad; and it is customary to select the good mothers to rear stock, a procedure based on the belief—founded on practical experience—that such excellence is hereditary. It would be interesting—if not very profitable—to experiment in the opposite direction; to set the bad mothers' eggs under good brood-hens; and thus to determine how far hereditary influence outweighed the effects of the individual experience of a foster parent's care. We need more experimental evidence of this kind; in the mean time the occurrence of variations in the maternal instincts and their hereditary nature may be taken as generally accepted.

But when hens bring up broods of species different from their own there arise, not variations but modifications of this instinct. Romanes quotes two cases. The first * is from Jesse's "Gleanings." "A hen who had reared three broods of ducks in three successive years, became habituated to their taking to the water, and would fly to a large stone in the middle of the pond, and quietly and contentedly watch her brood as they swam about it. The fourth year she hatched her own eggs, and finding that her chickens did not take to the water as the ducklings had done, she flew to the stone in the pond, and called them to her with the utmost eagerness. This recollection of the habits of her former charge is not a little curious." The second example was furnished by a correspondent, Mrs. L. Macfarlane, of Glasgow. "In this case," she says, "a hen had also reared three successive broods of ducklings in successive years, and then hatched out a brood of nine chickens. The season being late, she was confined for some weeks till the chickens became strong enough to face the cold weather. Then, in the words of my correspondent, 'the first day she was let out she disappeared, and after a long search my sister found her beside a little stream which her successive broods of ducklings had been in the habit of frequenting. She had got four of her chickens into the stream, which was fortunately very shallow at the time. The other five were all standing on its margin, and she

* "Mental Evolution in Animals," p. 215.

was endeavouring by all sorts of coaxing hen language, and by pushing each chicken in turn with her bill, to get them into the water also.'" The abnormal behaviour of these hens may be contrasted with that of a hen which after successive broods of chicks, hatches out a brood of ducklings. When they, prompted by instinctive impulse, take to the water, her fussy excitement knows no bounds. Here is something contrary to all her previous experience. What exactly passes through her mind it is exceedingly difficult to surmise. The farmer's wife naïvely says that the hen fears they will drown. But what experience has the hen of drowning? To adopt such an interpretation is to credit her with powers of anticipating the results of experience, which it is hard to conceive that she possesses. It is more probable that her fussy behaviour is partly the result of her little ones going where she has an instinctive aversion to following them, and partly the result of a breach of normal association due to previous experience with chicks. I am told that a hen which has had broods of chicks is far more fussy on such an occasion than a hen dealing with her first brood, and therefore without individual experience. If this be so, it would seem to show that the acquired association is as important as the instinctive element.

Now, in the hen that brings up successive broods of ducklings, there is, in our terminology, a modification of instinctive behaviour. Is there any tendency for such a modification to become hereditary? Would the hens, hatched from her eggs, incubated and brought up by a foster parent, show a variation of instinct in a direction similar to the modification she had acquired? We do not know. Transmissionists would probably say that the modification acquired in the one lifetime would not be sufficient to produce an observable variation; but that where similar modifications are acquired in each of many successive generations the cumulative effect becomes at last observable in variation. Such cumulative effect is obviously impossible in the case of the hen and her ducklings. And the case itself, it must be remembered, is only adduced to illustrate the distinction between modification and variation, and to make clear by a concrete example the true nature of the question whether acquired modifications are hereditary. The transmissionist says that they are hereditary, though perhaps in too slight degree to be observable in the course of a single generation. Some regard the evidence of such transmission as insufficient, and others deny it altogether.

Let us note in passing the important *rôle* that, in any case, and quite apart from hereditary transmission, individual habit has to play. We start with an instinctive activity. But the instinctive activity is the congenital endowment of an organism which has also a certain range of intelligence; with the power of profiting by experience; with capacities for conscious adjustment to its environment; with the ability to acquire new modes of activity by modifying the old congenital types. The instinctive activity tends to meet the normal conditions of the particular species; and under such normal conditions individual habit endorses, through repetition, the instinctive activities, and tends to strengthen and firmly establish, as an individual possession, that which was congenitally given. Under abnormal conditions, however, intelligence tends to modify the congenital activity so as to enable it to meet the new requirements; and then habit, through constant repetition, tends to establish this modified type of activity as an individual possession. In either case, whether its tendency be conservative or adaptive, whether it confirms the old instinct, or confirms the new modification, whether it sets its seal on specific uniformity or leads to somewhat divergent individualism,—in either case the *rôle* of intelligence in the establishment of habits is an important one.

I must here again insist on the importance of ascertaining whether any habit has an instinctive foundation, by observing the young when placed under such conditions that imitation of the parents is impossible. There is a curious habit of the motmot (*Momotus*), the use of which is quite unknown. It tears off with its somewhat serrated bill the barbs of the middle pair of tail feathers, in such a way as to lay bare the shaft for an inch or so, and to make the feathers racquet-shaped. Mr. G. U. Cherrie* has shown that this procedure is probably instinctive ; for it was performed by the young birds (*Momotus lessoni*) which had been taken from the nest before the tail feathers had grown. Mr. Chapman kindly showed me young specimens in which these feathers, still immature, had not been thus trimmed. There appeared to be a slight line of weakness along the bases of the barbs where they would in due time have been torn away. He suggested the possibility that there was some slight obstruction here to the drawing of the feathers through the bill. Perhaps the line of weakness causes these barbs to catch in the serrations of the bill. Such catching would no doubt draw the bird's attention to the feathers in question, and lead to a frequent repetition of the habit. In the adult motmot the tail is kept in constant jerky motion as the bird utters a cooing note, and the peculiar trimming of the central feathers *may* have a sexual import. In any case, Mr. Cherrie's observation as to the treating of the feathers in this way, with little opportunity of imitation, is of interest ;

* *The Auk,* 9, p. 323.

though, if the trimming arise from some defect in the feathers, all that is necessarily inherited is such congenital deficiency.

It would seem, then, to revert to our main theme, that so far as the activities and behaviour of animals are concerned, evolution is tending to produce two things— congenital uniformity and innate plasticity; if we may use this latter term for susceptibility to modification by the intelligent utilization of experience. Both are due to heredity; but whereas the one, congenital uniformity, presents a certain amount of initial definiteness, the other, innate plasticity, is in its nature initially indefinite; whereas the former, the initial definiteness, has its origin in past uniformity of response; the latter, susceptibility to modification, allows of future variety of response; and whereas the definiteness is specific and racial, the plasticity allows of individualism. The two are to a certain extent antagonistic, and to a certain extent complementary. Evolution has to strike a balance between them; to hit the happy mean between a congenital uniformity which leaves no room for individual adaptation, and an innate plasticity that is devoid of sufficient stability.

To these two, however, a third must be added when the whole life of an organism is taken into consideration. Just as hereditary stability as it is seen in the uniform performance of definitely instinctive activities is in contrast with the individual plasticity shown in the phenomena of adaptation to new circumstances, so too is the relative plasticity of the young in contrast with the relative stability of the old. We have to take into account acquired stability due to habit as well as congenital stability due to heredity. The three factors are, therefore, (1) congenital stability, (2) youthful plasticity, and (3) acquired stability. Now, regarding, as seems not unreasonable, youthful plasticity as a mediating term between the two extremes of stability, congenital and acquired, there are, as current biological literature shows, two opposing views as to the relations which stability, acquired and congenital, bear to each other. According to the one view they are directly connected through heredity. The acquired stability of one generation becomes through inheritance the basis of the congenital stability of the rest. The adaptation rendered possible by youthful plasticity affords the basis of evolutionary progress, while the inheritance of the acquired stability gives the element of continuity in evolution. According to the opposing view, on the other hand, the two types of stability, congenital and acquired, are completely independent. Individual adaptation through youthful plasticity and habitual repetition, plays no part whatever in racial progress, and contributes nothing to congenital stability.

Both sides may invoke the aid of natural selection, but in very different degree. To the transmissionist it is merely an accessory aid, of value in keeping up a general standard of organic efficiency; to the selectionist it is vital to the very existence of specialized types of organic stability.

Let us translate this from the abstract into concrete terms. It is the habit of the house martin to build beneath the eaves. Forsaking its ancestral rocky haunts, it has been led to accommodate itself to and utilize the houses that man has built. This, we may fairly assume, was originally due to individual plasticity, the adaptation to new circumstances being the outcome of intelligence. But it has long since ceased to be an individual matter. It is characteristic of all house martins now; hence the name. That which was an acquired habit in certain house martins of the past has become, it is argued, through inheritance, a congenital instinct in the house martins of to-day. Natural selection has no doubt been keeping up the standard of organic efficiency and of average intelligence, the weakly and foolish having been weeded out ; but it has not been the efficient cause of the specialized instinct of building beneath the eaves. Such would be the view of those who accept the hereditary transmission of acquired habits.

Those who hold the other view would, I take it, begin by questioning, or at least demanding satisfactory proof of, the fact that the habit of building in this special manner and place is a truly congenital instinctive activity. They would remind us that the adaptive intelligence which enabled the house martins of the past to adopt this method of nidification is still operative. They would further urge that the nestlings are brought up under the eaves, and that there is ample opportunity for the formation of an association between nests and eaves. They would contend that there is nothing in the nest itself that cannot fairly be interpreted as the direct outcome of the conditions under which each particular nest is built, nothing, that is to say, for which any congenital variations of instinctive activities is required. Any congenital tendency (at present quite unproven) which there might be, they would attribute entirely to natural selection. In the open country, far from rocky fastnesses, those martins in which there was a congenital tendency to build beneath the eaves, would bring up their broods and transmit this tendency; those in which this tendency was absent would either go elsewhere or fail to bring up broods at all. This would be their second line of defence in case the habit be shown to have a truly instinctive basis.

So far it has been my aim merely to bring out the distinction between the rival theories of the manner in which the evolution of truly congenital instinctive activities has been effected; not to decide between them. The first is based on the hereditary transmission of acquired modifications of activity; the latter is based on congenital variations in definiteness. Both factors may be accepted, as they were, indeed, by Darwin and by Romanes; some instincts being regarded as due to the first, others as due to the second, and yet others as due to the combination of the two, being, in fact, as Romanes phrased it, of blended origin. The tendency of modern biological thought in Germany and in England, under the influence of Professor Weismann's writings, has been towards the latter view— that which denies the transmission of definiteness which is acquired. And whatever may be the result of our discussion of the matter, it cannot be denied that Professor Weismann's contention has done great service in forcing us to examine and test our facts with renewed and added care.

It is questionable whether there is much to be gained by considering at any length what may appear to be the general biological advantages of the one view or the other. The transmissionist, on the one hand, claims that his conception of organic nature has the advantage of relative simplicity; he contends that, so long as the conditions of life remain uniform, the resulting uniformity of habits will ensure as much congenital stability as can be of advantage to the race; while under changing conditions of life the breaking up of this stability through the transmitted effects of new habits is decidedly advantageous to the species, and must contribute not a little to racial progress. On the other hand, the non-transmissionist, after a reminder that transmission is not only not proven, but, if it exist, is difficult to explain on the basis of our present knowledge of the relation of the germinal cells to the other bodily tissues, argues that if the organic progress of the race through natural selection is a slow process, it is a very sure one. He contends that the organic stability wrought into the race by natural selection is more permanently valuable, less at the mercy of merely temporary changes of conditions, than that which is liable to frequent modification through transmission. And he further contends that in individual plasticity the organism possesses all that is required to enable it to meet such temporary changes of environment as are likely to occur. Thus both sides claim for their own views certain general organic advantages; and both are quite clear that had they the ordering of the organic world they would unhesitatingly carry out their own principles for the advantage of the organisms under their control!

Now all this is very interesting, and affords considerable scope for ingenuity. But it does not touch the question at issue; and this is—not which method is apparently the most advantageous, not which method we should have adopted, had the work of creation been entrusted to our care, but which has been adopted by nature. For let us suppose that the transmissionist is successful in showing that his method is for the greater advantage of the race, and is that which best furthers organic progress; and let us further suppose him to contend that even on the natural selection principles of his opponents this advantageous method would itself be established by the elimination of less advantageous methods. The non-transmissionist will reply, first, that natural selection can only lead to the survival of such variations as are within the range of organic possibility, and the transmission of characters acquired during individual life by, say, brain tissue to the germinal cells, seems to be, as he contends, an organic impossibility; and secondly, that the question is after all one of fact. Has natural selection, as a matter of observation,

U

led to the establishment of the transmission of acquired characters ? If so, produce unquestionable and unimpeachable evidence of the fact.

This, however, is just what it is exceedingly difficult to do. At first sight, for example, the nesting habit of the house martin would appear to afford satisfactory evidence of the conversion of an acquired habit into a congenital instinct. But quite possibly it is the result of intelligent adaptation through the influence of tradition. Our first difficulty, then, is to prove conclusively that a given mode of behaviour is truly congenital and instinctive, and not due to the play of animal tradition. One or two further cases which illustrate this difficulty may be given. Where telegraph wires have been led across Scottish moors, grouse have been killed in numbers by flying against them. But after a season or two the destruction has ceased. Have the young birds inherited the habit of so flying as to avoid the wires ; or has the habit been handed down by animal tradition ? The old birds are said to lead the flocks ; and if they have either themselves been hurt when they were young, or followed those who had so learnt to avoid the wires, they would have acquired caution, and thus lead their followers to be cautious. Hence a habit of caution would be handed on by tradition. The difficulty is represented in another form in the case of the duck (*Dendrocygna autumnalis*), which is found in the well-timbered region along the Rio Grande of Texas, at Lomita. Since the river furnishes no sort of food, being cold and muddy from the melting snows of the mountains whence it flows, the duck adapts itself to circumstances and feeds upon seeds and grain. It can alight on a stalk of growing corn with the ease of a blackbird, and is quite at home among the lofty trees where it makes its nest.* It would

* *Nature*, vol. xliv. p. 529.

be most interesting to know how far this complete modification of duck habits is now congenital and how far it is due to the individual plasticity which enables an organism to adapt itself to its special environment. The habits of the magpie in England have altered greatly. "It is no longer the merry, saucy hanger-on of the homestead, as it was to writers of former days, who were constantly alluding to its disposition, but is become the suspicious thief, shunning the gaze of men, and knowing that danger may lurk in every bush."* How far are the sly and thievish habits of the magpie in England now congenital; how far are they acquired under the influence of tradition?

Our second difficulty is to find cases in which all effects of selection are excluded. The habit from which a breed of dogs has received the name of pointers is, it would seem, truly congenital. Darwin states that he had himself "gone out with a young dog for the first time, and his innate tendency was shown in a ludicrous manner, for he pointed fixedly not only at the scent of game, but at sheep and large white stones; and when he found a lark's nest, we were actually compelled to carry him along." But there has been selection all along the line of pointer ancestry. As Darwin says,† "The young pointer often points without any instruction, imitation, or experience. . . . The most important distinction between pointing, &c., and a true instinct is that the former is less strictly inherited, and varies greatly in the degree of its inborn perfection." In other words, there is much congenital variation, and selection is still in progress. The congenital variations will be claimed by the non-transmissionist as evidence

* " Dictionary of Birds," p. 721.
† The quotation is from the uncondensed MS. of the " Origin of Species," Romanes' " Mental Evolution in Animals," pp. 236, 237.

in favour of his view; for were the acquired habit inherited in the degree claimed by the transmissionist, there should not be so much variation. But in any case it is obvious that such a habit as pointing cannot be adduced in evidence of transmission as against the hypothesis of selection, since selection is undoubtedly by no means excluded.

In face of these alternative difficulties, that on the one hand of proving the truly congenital nature of a habit affirmed to be the result of transmission, and that on the other hand of excluding the influence of all forms of selection, it is by no means easy at present to decide, by direct appeal to observed fact, between the rival hypotheses. Perhaps one of the strongest cases, if trustworthy, in favour of the occasional transmission of an acquired habit is that of begging. Mr. Hurt describes in *Nature* * how a skye terrier was taught with difficulty to beg. "One of his daughters, who has never seen her father, is in the constant habit of sitting up, although she has never been taught to do so, and has not seen others sit up." And Mr. Lawson Tait informed Romanes that " he had a cat which was taught to beg for food like a terrier, so that she developed the habit of assuming this posture—so very unusual in a cat—whenever she desired to be fed. All her kittens adopted the same habit under circumstances which precluded the possibility of imitation, for they were given away to friends very early in life, and greatly surprised their new owners when, several weeks afterwards, they began spontaneously to beg." "Very early in life" is somewhat indefinite; and one may ask whether all possibility of imitation was actually precluded. One peculiarity about such cases is their sporadic and occasional character. Of the thousands of individual dogs

* Aug. 1st, 1872; quoted in " Mental Evolution in Animals," p. 195.

which are taught to beg, how few would seem to transmit the acquired habit to their offspring! Or, at any rate, how few are the recorded instances of such transmission! If the non-transmissionist has a difficulty in accounting for them—has presumably to fall back upon the suggestion that, if correctly observed and reported, they are rare congenital variations—the transmissionist is, it would seem, confronted by an equal difficulty in accounting for the non-transmission in the great majority of instances. In any case they seem but a slender basis on which to rest a far-reaching theory of organic development.

Romanes, in support of the proposition that acquired habits are inherited, gives, as an example, the fact that in Norway the ponies are used without bridles, and are trained to obey the voice. As a consequence, a race-peculiarity has been established; for Andrew Knight says, "the horse-breakers complain, and certainly with very good reason, that it is impossible to give them what is called a mouth. They are, nevertheless, exceedingly docile, and more than ordinarily obedient, when they understand the commands of their masters." But here the selective factor cannot be altogether excluded, though the transmissionist would no doubt contend that it must be quite subordinate. Apart from this case and that of begging, Romanes can only adduce the hereditary wildness or tameness of animals under changed conditions. But to this class of examples I am not disposed to attach much weight; for in the first place selection undoubtedly plays an important part; and in the second place, as already stated, my own observations show that even such shy birds as the moorhen, wild duck, plover, and partridge, when brought up by hand, are almost ridiculously tame. It has before been mentioned that, while a young moorhen was drinking, my fox terrier came up and lapped the water, but received such a vigorous peck on his nose, followed by a second which narrowly missed his eye, that he beat a hasty retreat. I am not aware of any well-substantiated evidence which has been published since Romanes wrote,* and am forced to conclude that though it must not be summarily set aside, that which we at present have is surprisingly small in amount, and peculiar in distribution, if transmission be the predominant factor in organic evolution. There is, however, a growing conviction that to solve some of its most pressing problems biologists must pass from the observational to the experimental stage. Perhaps experiment will show, more conclusively than has yet been shown, that transmission is a fact, and will afford the means of estimating its strength in the evolution of the world of living things.

There is, however, another, though less direct means of approaching the problem. Let us fix our attention on any two individuals of the same species: the one survives and mates; the other either dies or fails to mate. Now, the former survives in virtue of the possession of some excellence which the other does not possess. It is this excellence, of whatever kind it may be, that determines the survival on the one hand, or elimination on the other; and it obviously must reach a certain amount —termed by Romanes "selection-value"—in order to determine which individual will survive and which succumb. What the survival-value must be in any particular case we do not know—it varies no doubt with the severity of the struggle; but to say, as some do, that an infinitesimal advantage suffices to differentiate the one from the other, appears to be an assumption based rather on logical than biological grounds.

Now, natural selectionists fall into two wings. Those

* The evidence adduced by Prof. Eimer fails to carry conviction.

on the more extreme wing contend that every character
of each organism owes its existence *directly* to natural
selection, and that there is no character in any organism
which is not founded on utility.   The influence of natural
selection is, they say, so penetrating and all-pervading,
that nothing useless, nothing without selection value, can
escape elimination.   The utmost modification of this view
which they will accept, is that involved in the principle of
correlation.   Every character is, they contend, either itself
of direct use, or definitely correlated with some other
character which is useful.   Correlation, like Mesopotamia,
is a blessed word, and full of comfort and solace in the
midst of difficulties.   Thus modified, the views of the more
extreme wing approach those of the other section of
natural selectionists, who hold that while steady and
continuous elimination has led to the survival of those
individuals which are best adapted to the conditions of
their environment, it is not necessary that all the
characters of these individuals should be of utility or
definitely correlated with useful characters.   There may
thus be congenital traits which are not themselves useful,
but are merely incidental; characterizing to some degree
a group of organisms, but without direct bearing on the
struggle for existence, not themselves, that is to say, of
selection value.   It is clear that if we extend the meaning
of the term "correlation" to the whole of that nexus by
which a number of congenital traits are linked together
in the same organism, these are correlated with useful
characters.   This seems, however, a little like begging the
question at issue.   We may have a number of congenital
traits coexisting in the same organism; but if, when a
series of generations are carefully observed, these traits
are found to vary independently, they can scarcely be said
to be correlated, unless we use this term in a sense so

vague as to rob it of all valid biological significance. By correlated variations should surely be meant those which have been shown to occur in some direct or inverse ratio to each other. When the correlation of any two variations has thus been definitely established, a study of either of them will enable us to infer the condition of the other. This is how Darwin used the term : * and we should aim rather at increased than at diminished exactness.

Bearing all this in mind, it is worth while to consider how far truly instinctive activities may be fairly considered to be (*a*) of direct utilitarian value ; (*b*) correlated in the narrower sense with useful characters; or (*c*) merely incidental, without traceable relationship to other useful characters, though involved in the congenital nexus.

There can be little question that a large number of instinctive activities in birds fall under the first class, and are of direct and obvious utilitarian value. The instinctive activities connected with pecking and feeding; of locomotion, whether of running, swimming, or flying; the sexual instincts and that of nidification, those associated with incubation and the rearing of young; all these, and they form perhaps the most remarkable and stable of instinctive activities, are of decisive use, and are readily explicable as the direct outcome of natural selection. To the same class belong, it would appear, the protective instincts of hiding, crouching, or shamming dead; the aggressive activities such as the hissing of geese or ostriches, and the scolding of young moorhens and other birds; perhaps the scratching of the ground by fowls and their allies; the secondary sexual activities, dancing, display, singing, together with those associated with recognition marks, such as the flirting of the tail of moorhens,

* "Animals and Plants under Domestication," second edition, vol. ii. p. 311.

and, as Mr. Warde Fowler suggests, of wagtails, and a great number of peculiarities in behaviour, and perhaps differentiæ in the mode of flight among birds that flock together.   It will be seen how many instinctive activities may not unreasonably be claimed by the non-transmissionist as directly due to natural selection.

Among instincts, there are few examples of the second class which includes those due to definite correlation. Perhaps we might place among them the development of the cuckoo instinct, as definitely correlated with variations in laying, possibly due to the effects of polyandry.

A small percentage of activities remains—or rather perhaps they should be termed instinctive traits—which are performed with congenital definiteness, but which do not appear to fall very readily under either of these heads. They must, therefore, either find their explanation in the transmission of acquired habit, or must be regarded as incidental characters associated with the essential activities of the organism in what has been termed the congenital nexus.   It may indeed be contended that the moorhen's water-bath, or the chick's sand-bath, and the preening of the feathers and down by young birds are of utilitarian import, since they keep the organism in health, and serve to remove parasites; though whether they can fairly be regarded as of selection-value, deciding between survival or elimination, is open to question.   Let us for the moment grant this much to the natural-selectionist. There remains the fact that these operations are performed with delicate but quite recognizable shades of distinction by the young birds, in each of which the distinctive traits are congenitally true to those of their kind.   Chicks, ducklings, moorhens, all perform their toilet in their own way.   To one who carefully watches from day to day the habits of young birds, there are many minute characteristics, difficult to describe severally, but none the less distinctive when taken together and collectively, and serving to distinguish kind from kind. One can hardly suppose that the special behaviour of the pheasant, the characteristic demeanour of the duckling, the high-stepping walk of the downy plover, the pretty little ways of moorhen chicks, and the familiar traits of domestic chickens, all of which are truly congenital in their definiteness, have been of selection-value, and have saved the ancestors of these several groups from elimination. Nor can it be said that they have any traceable relation with other activities or characters of essential utility to the species. Whence, then, comes their definiteness? How have they arisen? Are they evidences of that transmission of acquired habits for which one school of biologists are in search? On this view it is difficult to see how they have come to be so definite. One can understand how habits which are intelligently adaptive may pass by transmission into definite instincts, even if one feels bound to demand adequate proof of such transmission. But these traits do not bear the marks of such intelligent adaptation. Just as the delicate shades of distinction in behaviour and demeanour do not appear to be of selection value, or to have reached definiteness through the elimination of all those that failed to behave in just this way, so too do they seem too trivial to be worthy of intelligent choice from among the numberless possibilities of individual demeanour and behaviour. It would seem more reasonable to suppose that they are incidental characters, wrought into the congenital nexus, and thus though not directly, still indirectly, due to natural selection. Even so, however, their definiteness is somewhat difficult to explain. If one says that a duckling behaves just in this particular way because it is a duckling, and that a moorhen has just these special traits because it is a moorhen, one seems on natural-selection principles to lay one's self open to the question:—But what about the constant and inherent tendency to variation upon which Darwin laid such stress? The transmissionist finds a source of adaptive variations in the acquired and transmitted modifications of individual life. But the non-transmissionist has to be content with inherent germinal variations, without which progress would be impossible. By natural selection these germinal variations are guided into definite lines. But in these incidental traits, the variations being indefinite, and the guidance of elimination being *ex hypothesi* absent, whence comes their continued definiteness?

Perhaps we may be permitted to ask the counter-question, Whence comes any tendency to a definite departure in any particular direction? Since these variations are *ex hypothesi* small in amount and indefinite in direction, they will, through interbreeding, neutralize each other, so that the stability is, so to speak, the net result of the tendency to depart therefrom *in all possible directions*, none of which is of selection value, and therefore no one of which is emphasized and rendered a line of definite departure. In a word, panmixia, or indiscriminate non-selective mating, secures an average mean of relative stability. It is best, however, honestly to confess that we do not yet know everything about organic nature.

Furthermore, we have seen—to consider the matter from a slightly different standpoint—that experience in one of its aspects is apparently not inherited. Association links have to be forged by the individual. At sight of the conspicuously marked cinnabar caterpillar there is no inherited suggestion of its nasty taste. That is the outcome of individual experience. Objects of all kinds, if they be of suitable size and at suitable distance, are indifferently pecked at; their value as food has to be individually learnt. It may be, however, that the transmission of association links is an organic impossibility, and is not to be expected on any theory.

On the other hand, particular stimuli do unquestionably give rise congenitally to particular and hereditary responses. The transmissionist contends that this is due to the repetition of the activity, in response to the given stimulus, and the transmission of the acquired habit. The natural-selectionist regards the congenital connection between stimulus and response as the result of the gradual elimination of those in whom this connection was not adequately established. What is needed in order to distinguish between the rival hypotheses is some really crucial case. If we could in some way exclude natural selection in some instances, and allow it to act in others, we should obtain such crucial cases. And if the habit were equally transmitted, whether natural selection be present or absent, that would present an exceedingly strong point for the transmissionist.

The nearest approach to such a crucial case which my own observations have afforded me, is that of the reaction of young birds to water. As I have already stated, there does not seem to be any instinctive reaction to the sight of still water, even on the part of ducklings. But so soon as the bill incidentally touches the water, the appropriate drinking response is at once called forth. It may be said that most young birds probably drink first by pecking at dew-drops or rain-drops on the vegetation. Still, ducks, chickens, and other birds have surely had much experience for many generations of drinking from the water of pools and ponds. Now, why does not a chick or duckling respond instinctively to the sight of something so essential to its existence as water? I have very little doubt that under natural conditions the mother bird teaches them to drink, her actions giving ample opportunity for imitation. But what does this imply? It implies that the presence of the mother, as a source of instruction and a model for imitation, *shields her young from the incidence of natural selection.* To put the matter figuratively, natural selection would fain get at the young to exercise its eliminative influence, to remove those that failed to respond instinctively, and to permit the survival of those in whom the appropriate response was congenital. But the mother is there to teach them all; elimination by natural selection is excluded. And we find that the habit of drinking in response to the sight of water, though birds have done so for untold generations, has not become instinctive and congenital.

Now, there is an old adage that whereas one man may lead a horse to the water, a dozen cannot make him drink. So with the hen and her chicks. Though the mother can lead her young to peck at the water, she cannot suggest the appropriate drinking response. She cannot teach them those special movements of beak, mouth, and gullet, which are essential for drinking. In this matter she does not shield them from the incidence of natural selection. Those which, on pecking the water, failed to respond to the stimulus by the complex behaviour involved in drinking, would die of thirst and be eliminated. Those in which there was a congenital variation in the direction of thus responding would survive, and their congenital response would, in successive generations, become more and more completely organized as an instinctive response—or a congenital reflex, if that expression be preferred.

Thus it would seem that when natural selection is

excluded, the habit has not become congenitally linked
with a visual stimulus; where natural selection is in
operation, the habit has become congenitally linked with
a touch or taste stimulus.

Allusion has already been made to the fact that the
young jungle pheasants of Assam, when left motherless,
die of starvation, if their attention be not attracted to
grains of food; and the same is said to be true of incubated
ostriches. Here, too, the normal action of the mother
shields the young from the incidence of natural selection.
But young megapodes are not fostered by the parent;
they are not shielded from the incidence of natural selection.
In these birds we might, on selectionist principles, expect
to find a more definitely congenital response to the sight
of certain appropriate kinds of food. "I have several
times," says Dr. D. C. Worcester, in a letter to me,
"observed young megapodes feeding quite by themselves
in the woods, and, upon shooting them, have found them
to agree perfectly in size and plumage with specimens
caught in the mounds where they are hatched. It is my
opinion that they have to shift for themselves from the
day of their birth, as I have never yet seen old birds anywhere near the young ones that I have come across." It
would be of great interest to ascertain whether these young
megapodes show an instinctive response to their appropriate
food that in other birds is absent or less marked. But
though the fact of their finding their own food without
guidance from the mother bird, may lead one to surmise
that this will be found to be the case, we must remember
that they may be guided, like hand-reared chicks, by the
results of experience after trying the various objects that
are presented to their choice.

It would seem then that, though the evidence is by no
means all that could be desired, what there is suggests that

if natural selection be excluded, instinctive definiteness of response has not been developed. Are there any cases of the converse kind, where that kind of influence on which transmissionists rely is necessarily excluded? Among birds to which our attention has been chiefly confined I know of no such cases. But there is the oft-quoted instance of the instincts of neuter hymenoptera. The matter has been so fully discussed that only a few words on the subject are here needful.

In the case of the hive-bee, of the eggs laid by the queen-mother those which she does not fertilize from the store of spermatozoa received from the male during the nuptial flight, develop into drones. The others, which she does so fertilize, are developed either into fertile queen-mothers, or into the sexually imperfect females known as neuters; and which they develop into is entirely dependent on the food they are supplied with in the larval condition. Fed on a specially rich nutritious pap they become fertile queens: otherwise, under ordinary conditions of nutrition, they become infertile neuters. This is one of those many cases, where the conditions of early life determine which of two or more definite forms an organism shall assume. And, in the bee, different instincts and innate powers are correlated with the queen and neuter types respectively.

Notwithstanding all the admirable work of many careful observers, we are scarcely in a position to say how much of the behaviour of the nurse or worker bee is due to a congenital instinctive tendency, and how much to the influence of tradition through imitation. We may, however, accept provisionally the generally received opinion that there are special instinctive endowments in these infertile workers. But they are inherited through parents, in neither of which are these special instincts developed. If transmissionists contend that these instincts were established as habits in ancestral insects before the present divergence into queens and neuters as established, they must admit that, in this case, their doctrine that disuse influences the germ is inapplicable. For disuse of these special instincts has prevailed in the germ-bearing individuals for we know not how many generations. And if they admit that their doctrine of the effects of disuse is here inapplicable, they so far weaken its claim for consideration in other instances.

Leaving now the special case of the hymenopterous insects, there is one general argument against the selectionist interpretation which is not infrequently urged, but which I do not regard as by any means fatal. It is sometimes said by transmissionists that, if we consider one of the more complex congenital activities, such as the diving of the young moorhen when the puppy frightened him, the accuracy and delicacy of the orderly sequence of activities is such as to be beyond the scope of mere natural selection. It is in the highest degree improbable, they say, that natural selection could produce so complex a mode of behaviour. I would meet such an argument by directing attention to the cases of the Yucca moth and the Sitaris given in the first chapter. Here there are extraordinarily complex trains of activities. But they are, and can be, performed only once in a lifetime. And I fail to see how such instincts can possibly be accounted for as the results of transmitted habit individually acquired. There is no opportunity for that repetition which is essential to acquired skill. We must, presumably, regard every step of the long and complex process as affording the appropriate stimulus for the performance of the next succeeding step. At all events, if natural selection have produced the instinctive behaviour of the Yucca moth and the Sitaris, what becomes of the inherent improbability of the moorhen's dive?

If pressed to summarize my own opinion on this vexed question, I should say, first, that there is but little satisfactory and convincing evidence in favour of transmission, but that variation does seem in some cases to have followed the lines of adaptive modification, so as to suggest some sort of connection between them; secondly, that there are many instincts, relatively definite and stable, which may fairly be regarded as directly due to natural selection, though here again, if we could accept the view that adaptive modification marked out the lines in which congenital variation should run, our conception of the process of their evolution would be so far simplified; thirdly, that there are some peculiar traits, also seemingly definite and stable, which can only be attributed to the indirect effects of natural selection on the supposition that they form part of the congenital nexus, and that they have no intrinsic tendency to variation in any particular direction; and fourthly, that, in the present state of our knowledge, it is best to accept provisionally the view that they are thus indirectly due to natural selection.

There can be no question, however, that when we consider such instincts as those connected with nidification, incubation, and maternity, together with those associated with courtship, if indeed they be truly instinctive; when we see how individual effort runs in the same lines as congenital co-ordination, as in the perfected flight of birds, or the diving of water-fowl; when we regard dispassionately such a performance as that of the lapwing or duck that decoys an intruder from her nest or young;—we feel that though the evidence for the transmission of acquired habit is insufficient, yet some connection between variation

X

and modification is suggested by the facts. I propose in the next chapter to approach the subject from a new standpoint, and to sketch in outline an hypothesis according to which acquired modification may pave the way for congenital variation without any direct transmission as such.

CHAPTER XIV.

MODIFICATION AND VARIATION.

Up to a time still comparatively recent, the transmission to offspring, in greater or less degree, of those modifications of habit or structure which the parents had acquired in the course of their individual lifetime, was generally accepted. Lamarck is regarded as the intellectual father of these—the transmissionists. In his "Histoire Naturelle" he said, "the development of organs and their power of action are continually determined by the use of these organs." This is known as his third law. In the fourth he insisted on the hereditary nature of the effects of use; "all that has been acquired, begun, or changed," he said, "in the structure of individuals during the course of their life, is preserved in reproduction and transmitted to the new individuals which spring from those which have experienced the changes."

Darwin accepted such transmission as subordinate to natural selection, and attempted to account for it by his theory of pangenesis. According to that hypothesis all the component cells of an organism throw off minute gemmules, and these and their like, collecting in the reproductive cells, are the parental germs from which all the cells of the offspring of that organism are developed. This theory, here given in briefest outline, came in for its full share of criticism. The problems of heredity were recognized as being of supreme biological importance and

were warmly discussed. Meanwhile, a different view of
the relation between the organism and its reproductive
cells came into prominence. With it the names of Francis
Galton in England and August Weismann in Germany are
inseparably connected. Of late years it has gained the
approval of many, though by no means all, of our fore-
most biologists. This view, again in briefest possible
outline, is as follows: the fertilized egg of any many-
celled organism gives origin to all the cells of which that
organism is composed. In some of these, the reproductive
cells, germinal substance is set aside for the future continuance of the race; the rest give rise to all the other
cells of the body, those which constitute or give rise to
muscle, nerve, bone, glands and so forth. Thus there is
a division into germ-substance and body-substance. Germ
gives origin to germ, plus body; but the body takes no
share, according to Prof. Weismann, in giving origin to—
though it ministers to, protects, and may influence—the
germinal substance of the reproductive cells.

The logical development of this theory led Prof. Weismann to doubt the inheritance of characters acquired by
the bodily substance in the course of individual life, and to
examine anew the supposed evidence in its favour. If
brain-substance, for example, contributes nothing to the
reproductive cells, any modification it acquires during
individual life can only reach the germ through some indirect mode of influence. But does it? does any modification of the body-substance so affect the germ-substance
as to become hereditary? Prof. Weismann answers this
question by asserting that the evidence for the direct transmission of acquired characters is wholly insufficient, and
by contending that, until satisfactory evidence is forthcoming, transmission must not be accepted as a factor in
evolution.

How then is progress possible if none of the modifications which the body suffers is transmitted from parent to offspring? To this question the reply must be that though modification is, on this view, excluded from taking any direct share in race-progress, yet there is still variation. Modifications are those changes which are in some way wrought in the body structure; and variations, those differences which are of germinal origin. That variation of germinal origin is a fact in organic nature is admitted on all hands; and that some variations are adaptive is also unquestioned. Transmissionists contend that modification in a particular direction in one generation is, through transmission of the change in some, at present unexplained, way from the bodily tissues to the germinal cells, a source of similar variation in the next generation. Selectionists, on the other hand, exclude this source of variation, contending that the supposed evidence in its favour is insufficient or unsatisfactory. But their whole theory depends on the occurrence of variations, of which those that are in unfavourable directions are weeded out, while those that are useful and adaptive remain. How these variations originate in the germ need not here be discussed. Let us assume that variations of germinal origin in a great number of directions do as a matter of fact occur.

This then is how the matter stands. All acknowledge the existence of variations, and admit that their proximate source is in the fertilized ovum. All admit that the individual is through its innate plasticity in greater or less degree capable of adaptive modification. Transmissionists contend that the effects of modification are somehow transferred to the germinal substance, there to give origin to variations. Selectionists deny this transmission, and contend that adaptive variations are independent of adaptive modifications.

Now, what is natural selection, at any rate, as understood by Darwin? It is a process whereby, in the struggle for existence, individuals possessed of favourable and adaptive variations survive and hand on their good seed, while individuals possessed of unfavourable variations succumb, and are sooner or later eliminated, standing therefore a less chance of begetting offspring. But it is clear that, to make the difference between survival and elimination, the favourableness of the variation must reach a certain amount, varying with the keenness of the struggle. And one of the difficulties which critics of natural selection have felt is that the little more or the little less of variation must often be too small in amount to be of selection-value, so as to determine survival. This difficulty is admitted by Prof. Weismann as a real one. "The Lamarckians were right," he says, "when they maintained that the factor for which hitherto the name of natural selection had been exclusively reserved, viz. personal selection [*i.e.* the selection of individuals], was insufficient for the explanation of the phenomena." * And again,† "something is still wanting to the selection of Darwin and Wallace, which it is obligatory on us to discover, if we possibly can."

The additional factor which Dr. Weismann suggests is what he terms "germinal selection." This, briefly stated, is as follows: There is a competition for nutriment among those parts of the germ named determinants, from which the several organs or groups of organs are developed. In this competition the stronger determinants get the best of it, and are further developed at the expense of the weaker determinants, which are starved and tend to dwindle and eventually disappear. The suggestion is

* "Germinal Selection." *Monist*, Jan., 1896, p. 290.
† *Op. cit.*, p. 264.

interesting, but one well-nigh impossible to test by observation. If accepted as a factor, it would serve to account for the inordinate growth of certain structures, such as the exuberance of some secondary sexual characters, and for the existence of determinate variations, that is to say, variations along special or particular lines of adaptation.

Such determinate variations are, however, explicable on the theory of natural selection. Writing in 1892, I put the matter thus.* " Take the case of an organism which has in some way reached harmony with its environment. Slight variations occur in many directions, but these are bred out by intercrossing. It is as if a hundred pendulums were swinging just a little in many directions, but were at once damped down. Now, place such an organism in changed conditions. The swing of one or two of the pendulums is found advantageous ; the organisms in which these two pendulums are swinging are selected : they mate together, and in their offspring while these pendulums are by congenital inheritance kept a-swinging, the other ninety-eight pendulums are rapidly damped down as before.

" Let us suppose, then, that the variation in tooth structure, in a certain mechanically advantageous direction, be such a selected pendulum swing. That particular pendulum, swinging in that particular direction, will be the subject of selection. The other pendulums will still be damped down as before, and in that particular pendulum variations from the particular direction will be similarly damped down. It will wobble a little, but its wobbling will be as nothing compared with the swing that is fostered by selection. In this case, then, selection will choose between the little more complexity that is advantageous, and the little less complexity that is disadvantageous. The little

* *Natural Science,* vol. i. April, 1892, pp. 100, 101.

less complexity will be eliminated, the little more complexity will survive. The little less and the little more are, however, in the same line of developmental swing. Hence, the variations discoverable in fossil mammals in which tooth-development along special lines is in progress, will, on the hypothesis of selection, be plus and minus along a given line; in other words, the variations will be determinate, and in the direction of special adaptation."

Prof. Weismann adopts a similar position in his recent paper on Germinal Selection. He says,[*] "By the selection alone of the plus or minus variations of a character is the constant modification of that character in the plus or minus direction determined. . . . We may assert therefore, in general terms, that a definitely directed progressive variation of a given part is produced by continued selection in that definite direction. This is no hypothesis, but a direct inference from the facts, and may also be expressed as follows: By selection of the kind referred to, the germ is progressively modified in a manner corresponding with the production of a definitely directed progressive variation of the part."

In his Romanes Lecture, Prof. Weismann makes another suggestion which is valuable and may be further developed. He is there dealing with what he terms "intraselection"[†]—or that which gives to the individual its plasticity. One of the examples that he adduces is the structure of bone. "Hermann Meyer," he says,[‡] "seems to have been the first to call attention to the adaptiveness as regards minute structure in animal tissues, which is

---

[*] *Monist*, January, 1896, p. 268.

[†] Prof. Mark Baldwin's "organic selection" appears to be a new and not very satisfactory term for the same process.

[‡] Romanes Lecture on "The Effect of External Influences on Development" (1894), pp. 11, 12.

most strikingly exhibited in the structure of the spongy
substance of the long bones in the higher vertebrates.
This substance is arranged on a similar mechanical
principle to that of arched structures in general: it is
composed of numerous fine bony plates, so arranged as
to withstand the greatest amount of tension and pressure,
and to give the utmost firmness with a minimum expenditure of material. But the direction, position, and strength
of these bony plates are by no means congenital or determined in advance : they depend on circumstances. If the
bone is broken and heals out of the straight, the plates of
the spongy tissue become rearranged so as to lie in the new
direction of greatest tension and pressure : thus they can
adapt themselves to changed circumstances.''

Then, after referring to the explanation by Wilhelm
Roux, of the cause of these wonderfully fine adaptations
by applying the principle of selection to the parts of the
organism in which, it is assumed, there is a struggle for
existence among each other, Prof. Weismann proceeds
to show * ''that it is not the particular adaptive structures themselves that are transmitted, but only the quality
of the material from which intra-selection forms these
structures anew in each individual life. . . . It is not the
particular spongy plates which are transmitted, but a cell-
mass, that from the germ onwards so reacts to tension and
pressure that the spongy structure necessarily results.'' In
other words, it is not the more or less definite congenital
adaptation that is handed on through heredity, but an
innate plasticity which renders possible adaptive modification in the individual.

This innate plasticity is undoubtedly of great advantage in race progress. The adapted organism will
escape elimination in the life struggle ; and it matters not

* Romanes Lecture, p. 15.

whether the adaptation be reached through individual modification of the bodily tissues or through racial variation of germinal origin. So long as the adaptation is there—no matter how it originated—that is sufficient to secure survival. Professor Weismann applies this conception to one of those difficulties which have been urged by critics of natural selection. "Let us take," he says,* "the well-known instance of the gradual increase in development of the deer's antlers, in consequence of which the head, in the course of generations, has become more and more heavily loaded. The question has been asked as to how it is possible for the parts of the body which have to support and move this weight to vary simultaneously and harmoniously if there is no such thing as the transmission of the effects of use or disuse, and if the changes have resulted from processes of selection only. This is the question put by Herbert Spencer as to '*co-adaptation*,' and the answer is to be found in connection with the process of intra-selection. It is by no means necessary that all the parts concerned—skull, muscles, and ligaments of the neck, cervical vertebræ, bones of the fore limbs, etc.— should simultaneously adapt themselves *by variation of the germ* to the increase of the size of the antlers; for in each separate individual the necessary adaptation will be temporarily accomplished by intra-selection," that is, by individual modification due to the innate plasticity of the parts concerned. "The improvement of the parts in question," Professor Weismann urges, "when so acquired, will certainly not be transmitted, but yet the primary variation is not lost. Thus when an advantageous increase in the size of the antlers has taken place, it does not lead to the destruction of the animal in consequence of other parts being unable to suit themselves to it. All parts of

* Romanes Lecture, pp. 18, 19.

the organism are in a certain degree variable [*i.e.* modifiable], and capable of being determined by the strength and nature of the influences that affect them, and this capacity to respond conformably to functional stimulus must be regarded as the means which make possible the maintenance of a harmonious co-adaptation of parts in the course of the phyletic metamorphosis of a species. . . . As the primary variations in the phyletic metamorphosis occurred little by little, the secondary adaptations would as a rule be able to keep pace with them."

So far Professor Weismann. According to his conception variations of germinal origin occur from time to time. By its innate plasticity the several parts of an organism implicated by their association with the varying part are modified in individual life in such a way that their modifications co-operate with the germinal variation in producing an adaptation of double origin, partly congenital, partly acquired. The organism then waits, so to speak, for a further congenital variation, when a like process of adaptation again occurs; and thus race progress is effected by a series of successive variational steps, assisted by a series of co-operating individual modifications.

If now it could be shown that, although on selectionist principles there is no transmission of modifications due to individual plasticity, yet these modifications afford the conditions under which variations of like nature are afforded an opportunity of occurring and of making themselves felt in race progress, a farther step would be taken towards a reconciliation of opposing views. Such, it appears to me, may well be the case.*

* In an article entitled "A New Factor in Evolution," published in the *American Naturalist* for June and July, 1896, Prof. Mark Baldwin has given expression to views of like nature to those which are here developed. And Prof. Henry F. Osborn, in a paper read before the New York Academy of Sciences, propounded a somewhat similar theory, but with, he tells me, less stress upon the action of natural selection.

To explain the connection which may exist between modifications of the bodily tissues due to innate plasticity and variations of germinal origin in similar adaptive directions, we may revert to the pendulum analogy. Assuming that variations do tend to occur in a great number of divergent directions, we may liken each to a pendulum which tends to swing—nay, which is swinging through a small arc. The organism, so far as variation is concerned, is a complex aggregate of such pendulums. Suppose, then, that it has reached congenital harmony with its environment. The pendulums are all swinging through the small arcs implied by the slight variations which occur even among the offspring of the same parents. No pendulum can materially increase its swing; for since the organism has reached congenital harmony with its environment, any marked variation will be out of harmony, and the individual in which it occurs will be eliminated. Natural selection then will ensure the damping down of the swing of all the pendulums within comparatively narrow limits.

But now suppose that the environment somewhat rapidly changes. Congenital variations of germinal origin will not be equal to the occasion. The swing of the pendulums concerned cannot be rapidly augmented. Here individual plasticity steps in to save some members of the race from extinction. They adapt themselves to the changed conditions through a modification of the bodily tissues. If no members of the race have sufficient innate plasticity to effect this accommodation, that race will become extinct, as has indeed occurred again and again in the course of geological history. The rigid races have succumbed; the plastic races have survived. Let us grant then that certain organisms accommodate themselves to the new conditions by plastic modification of the bodily tissues,—say by the adaptive strengthening of some bony structure. What is the effect on congenital variations? Whereas all the other pendulums are still damped down by natural selection as before, the oscillation of the pendulum which represents a variation in this bony structure is no longer checked. It is free to swing as much as it can. Congenital variations in the same direction as the adaptive modification will be so much to the good of the individual concerned. They will constitute a congenital predisposition to that strengthening of the part which is essential for survival. Variations in the opposite direction tending to thwart the adaptive modification will be disadvantageous, and will be eliminated. Thus, if the conditions remain constant for many generations, congenital variation will gradually render hereditary the same strengthening of bone structure that was provisionally attained by plastic modification. The effects are precisely the same as they would be if the modification in question were directly transmitted in a slight but cumulatively increasing degree; they are reached, however, in a manner which involves no such transmission.

To take a particular case : Let us grant that in the evolution of the horse tribe it was advantageous to this line of vertebrate life that the middle digits of each foot should be largely developed, and the lateral digits reduced in size; and let us grant that this took its rise in adaptive modification through the increased use of the middle digit and the relative disuse of the lateral digits. Variations in these digits are no longer suppressed and eliminated. Any congenital predisposition to increased development of the mid-digit, and decreased size in the lateral digits, will tend to assist the adaptive modification and to supplement its deficiencies. Any congenital predisposition in the contrary direction will tend to thwart the adaptive modification and render it less efficient. The former will let adaptive modification start at a higher level, so to speak, and thus enable it to be carried a step further. The latter will force it to start at a lower level, and prevent its going so far. If natural selection take place at all, we may well believe that it would do so under such circumstances.* And it would work along the lines laid down for it in adaptive modification. Modification would lead ; variation follow in its wake. It is not surprising that for long we believed modification to be transmitted as hereditary variation. Such an interpretation of the facts is the simpler and more obvious. But simple and obvious interpretations are not always correct. And if, on closer examination in the light of fuller knowledge, they are found to present grave difficulties, a less simple and less obvious interpretation may claim our provisional acceptance.

In his recent paper on Germinal Selection, Prof. Weismann says : † "I am fain to relinquish myself to the hope that now after another explanation has been found, a reconciliation and unification of the hostile views is not so very distant, and that then we can continue our work together on the newly laid foundations." As one to whom Prof. Weismann alludes as having expressed the opinion that the Lamarckian principle must be admitted as a working hypothesis, I am now ready to relinquish myself also to the same hope. Germinal selection does not convince me, though it may be regarded as a suggestive hypothesis ; and, assuredly, I am not convinced by the argument that because in certain cases, such as the changes in the chitinous parts of the skeleton of insects and crustacea, and in the teeth of mammals, use and disuse can have played no part, therefore in no other

---

* Prof. Weismann's "germinal selection," if a *vera causa*, would be a co-operating factor, and assist in producing the requisite variations.

† *Monist, loc. cit.*, p. 290.

cases has use-inheritance prevailed. But it appears to me that, on the lines above sketched out, we may accept the facts adduced by the transmissionist, and at the same time interpret them on selectionist principles.

It may be well now briefly to summarize the line of argument in a series of numbered paragraphs.

1. In addition to what is congenitally definite in structure or mode of response, an organism inherits a certain amount of innate plasticity.

2. Natural selection secures

    (*a*) Such congenital definiteness as is advantageous.

    (*b*) Such innate plasticity as is advantageous.

3. Both *a* and *b* are commonly present ; but uniform conditions tend to emphasize the former ; variable conditions, the latter.

4. The organism is subject to

    (*a*) Variation, of germinal origin.

    (β) Modification, of environmental origin, affecting the soma or body tissues.

5. Transmissionists contend that acquired somatic modification in a given direction in one generation is transmitted to the reproductive cells to constitute a source of germinal variation in the same direction in the next generation.

6. It is here suggested that persistent modification through many generations, though not transmitted to the germ, nevertheless affords the opportunity for germinal variation of like nature.

7. Under constant conditions of life, though variations in many directions are occurring in the organisms which have reached harmonious adjustment to the environment, yet natural selection eliminates all those which are disadvantageous,. and thus represses all variations within narrow limits.

8. Suppose, however, that a group of plastic organisms is placed under new conditions.

9. Those whose innate plasticity is equal to the occasion are modified, and survive. Those whose plasticity is not equal to the occasion are eliminated.

10. Such modification takes place generation after generation, but, as such, is not inherited. There is no transmission of the effects of modification to the germinal substance.

11. But variations in the same direction as the modifications, are now no longer repressed and are allowed full scope.

12. Any congenital variations antagonistic in direction to these modifications will tend to thwart them and to render the organism in which they occur liable to elimination.

13. Any congenital variations similar in direction to these modifications will tend to support them and to favour the organism in which they occur.

14. Thus will arise a congenital predisposition to the modifications in question.

15. The longer this process continues, the more marked will be the predisposition, and the greater the tendency of the congenital variations to conform in all respects to the persistent plastic modifications; while

16. The plasticity still continuing, the modifications become yet further adaptive.

17. Thus plastic modification leads, and germinal variation follows: the one paves the way for the other.

18. Natural selection will tend to foster variability in given advantageous lines when once initiated; for (*a*) the constant elimination of variations leads to the survival of the relatively invariable; but (*b*) the perpetuation of variations in any given direction leads to the survival of

the variable in that direction. Lamarckian palæontologists are apt to overlook this fact that natural selection produces determinate variation.

19. The transmissionist fixing his attention first on the modification, and secondly on the fact that organic effects similar to those produced by the modification gradually become congenitally stereotyped, assumes that the modification *as such* is inherited.

20. It is here suggested that the modification *as such* is not inherited, but is the condition under which congenital variations are favoured and given time to get a hold on the organism, and are thus enabled by degrees to reach the fully adaptive level.

When we remember that plastic modification and germinal variation have been working together all along the line of organic evolution to reach the common goal of adaptation, it is difficult to believe that they have all along been wholly independent of each other. If the direct dependence advocated by the transmissionist be rejected, perhaps the indirect dependence here suggested may be found worth considering.

It only remains to say a few words concerning the bearing of the above discussion on our special subject, habit and instinct. Habits are of the nature of individual modifications rendered possible by intelligent adaptation to the conditions of life; instincts are due to congenital variations of germinal origin. But instinctive activities so often take the line which is marked out by adaptive habit, that it is not surprising to find many who believe that instinct is neither more nor less than inherited habit. Special modes of flight, special ways of bathing, peculiar methods of courtship, specific types of behaviour; these and many other activities may well be regarded as having their origin in habit, though they may now be more or less definitely instinctive. It would seem, however, that if natural selection be accepted as a potent factor in organic evolution, and unless good cases can be brought forward in which natural selection is necessarily excluded and yet habit has become instinctive, we may, in face of the biological difficulties which render direct transmission more and more hard to accept, adopt some such view as the foregoing, and, while still believing that there is some connection between habit and instinct, admit that the connection is indirect and permissive rather than direct and transmissive.

CHAPTER XV.

HEREDITY IN MAN.

An investigation which deals with habit and instinct is in large degree a study in heredity. It will be of interest to inquire whether the conclusions we have reached are of any assistance in interpreting the phenomena of human life; and whether what we may learn of heredity in man reflects any light on the problems of heredity in the animal world.

To this end it will be well to pass rapidly in review the more salient of our conclusions. Stated with the utmost brevity, they are as follows :—

1. The activities termed instinctive are characterized by relative definiteness of motor co-ordination, probably dependent on congenital structure in the lower brain and spinal centres. Under appropriate conditions a stimulus gives rise to adaptive behaviour without previous learning or experience.

2. The instinctive response is, as such, unconscious ; but the performance of the instinctive activity affords, through afferent channels, data to consciousness.

3. These data are linked by association with those supplied by the special senses.

4. In addition to the co-ordinated outgoing currents to the motor organs concerned in the instinctive response, there are co-ordinated outgoing currents to the viscera

—heart, blood-vessels, lungs and respiratory apparatus, digestive organs, glands, skin, and so forth.

5. From the organs thus innervated and called into activity, there proceed ingoing currents to the sensorium. These afford the primary data of the states of consciousness termed emotions. And these data are linked by association with those given by the special senses, and by motor responses. The emotions are instinctive in that the co-ordinated outgoing currents are of like nature with those concerned in instinctive response.

6. The data of consciousness are all of afferent origin, and any of them, whether sensory, motor, or visceral in origin, may be either pleasant or painful.

7. The power of association by which the data of consciousness are linked in experience—so that on the recurrence of certain data, a revival in memory of other associated data is rendered possible—is innate. Innate also are susceptibilities to pleasure and pain.

8. Accompanying the functional activity of the higher brain centres, called into play by incoming currents, is a control over the lower centres, exercised through augmentation or inhibition of their automatic action, in the light of experience. This again is innate.

9. Acquired activities are those the definiteness of which is reached by the exercise of control.

10. The term "congenital" is applied to inherited definiteness of response in instinctive behaviour, reflex action, or the distribution of innervating currents to the viscera; the term "innate," to inherited faculties, and susceptibilities to pleasure and pain. Instinctive definiteness is congenital and prior to experience. Acquired definiteness is due to experience, and is rendered possible by innate faculties and susceptibilities.

11. The frequent repetition of acquired activities gives

rise to the secondary automatism of habit, which is thus to be distinguished from the primary automatism of instinct.

12. Impulse is the tendency of the organism to carry out its instinctive or habitual activities under the appropriate internal conditions and external stimuli. The accompanying consciousness is due to afferent currents.

13. Imitative behaviour may be either (1) instinctive, when the stimulus afforded by the results of the activities of another gives rise to a congenital response of like nature; or (2) intelligent, where there is conscious selection of the activities or their results. The latter is dependent upon an innate susceptibility to pleasure when the results reached by the imitating individual resemble the copy.

14. Intelligence involves true selection or choice. And the method of mental evolution, by the exercise of choice, is to be clearly distinguished from the method of organic evolution, by natural selection.

15. Similar activities may be—(1) acquired *de novo* by the individuals of successive generations through the similar exercise of intelligent choice; (2) handed on by tradition through the instinctive or conscious imitation by the young of their elders; or (3) transmitted as congenital instinctive behaviour.

16. It is a matter of importance, but of no little difficulty, to determine whether the similar activities of individuals in successive generations are acquired *de novo*, are handed on by tradition, or are directly due to hereditary transmission.

17. There is no conclusive evidence that the secondary automatism of habit is transmitted by heredity, so as to give rise to the primary automatism of instinct.

18. At the same time there are cases in which

behaviour, generally believed to be instinctive—such as that of birds "feigning wounded"—appears to run curiously parallel with that due to intelligent acquisition.

19. Though there may be no direct transmission of acquired characters, yet acquired modifications of structure may permit congenital variations of a similar kind; other variations being suppressed by natural selection.

20. The balance of evidence appears to favour the view that instinctive behaviour is the result of natural selection working on variations of germinal origin without the direct transmission of acquired modifications of structure.

Such in outline are the conclusions we have reached. There is, however, one more aspect of the problems of heredity and acquisition to which attention must be directed before passing from the life of animals to the life of man. There are two important processes which fall under the head of acquisition. We acquire experience, and we acquire skill. The first involves the correlation of incoming data from the special senses, from the motor organs, and from the viscera. The second implies the more or less accurate co-ordination of outgoing impulses to the viscera and to the motor organs, both those concerned in ministering to sensation and those concerned in general activity. If, then, the term "experience" be applied to the correlation of incoming data from whatever source, it would appear that such experience is wholly a matter of acquisition. To illustrate once more by a very simple case, if nasty taste or the power of stinging be associated with colour or form in a caterpillar or insect, there appears to be no inherited transmission of such an association in experience; no inherited suggestion of the taste on sight of the colour or form. The associative foundations of suggestion have to be laid in individual experience, and are solely a matter of acquisition. Heredity seems to have nothing to do with them save to supply the requisite faculty. On the other hand, the co-ordination of outgoing impulses may be and often is congenitally definite. But it may be, and often is, the result of individual acquisition. Whereas, therefore, experience is in all cases acquired; motor co-ordination is in some cases congenital, and in other cases acquired. If this conclusion stand the test of further investigation and critical study, it will afford an important line of demarcation. We may expect to find further and fuller evidence of inherited co-ordinations of a markedly definite kind; but we must not expect to find any evidence of inherited knowledge. Co-ordination may be in a surprisingly definite manner instinctive; but knowledge, and that correlated experience which is its precursor, though founded on innate faculty, owes all its definiteness and exactitude to individual experience.

We are now in a position to consider the relation of the hereditary to the acquired in man. The first fact —one of a broad and general nature—that strikes us is how far what is innate is, in the hereditary endowment of man, in excess of what is instinctive. No one is likely to deny the assertion that man inherits an innate power of acquisition and application, which enables him to cope with an environment of extraordinary complexity, and of a peculiarly specialized nature. But of definite instinctive performance he inherits perhaps a smaller share than any other organism. If, then, the question be asked, whether man has a large or a small endowment of instinct, the answer will depend upon the precise definition of 'instinct.' If we take congenital definiteness as characteristic of instinct, we shall agree with Darwin * that "the fewness and the comparative simplicity of the instincts of the higher animals are remarkable as compared with those of the

* "Descent of Man," vol. i. p. 101.

lower animals ; " and with Romanes,* that "instinct plays a larger part in the psychology of many animals than it does in the psychology of man." If, on the other hand, a broader definition of instinct be accepted, so as to include what is innate, in the sense before defined, we shall agree with Prof. Wundt † that human life is "permeated through and through with instinctive action, determined in part, however, by intelligence and volition ; " and shall not profoundly disagree with Prof. Wm. James,‡ who says that "man possesses all the impulses that they (the lower creatures) have, and a great many more besides." The higher animals have, he continues, a number of impulses, such as greediness and suspicion, curiosity and timidity, all of them "congenital, blind at first, and productive of motor reactions of a rigorously determinate sort. Each of them, then, is an instinct, as instincts are commonly defined. But they contradict each other—'experience' in each particular opportunity of application usually deciding the issue. The animal that exhibits them loses the 'instinctive' demeanour, and appears to lead a life of hesitation and choice, an intellectual life ; not, however, because he has no instincts—rather because he has so many that they block each other's path." This theory of the equilibration of instinctive tendencies is, no doubt, ingenious. But there is an old adage—*de non apparentibus et non existentibus eadem est ratio.* And in any case, according to the method of interpretation we have adopted, activities, congenitally definite, must be objectively manifested, as such, if they are to make good their claim to the instinctive class.

What, then, in the narrower acceptation of the term,

---

* " Mental Evolution in Man," p. 8.
† " Lectures on Human and Animal Psychology," p. 397.
‡ " Principles of Psychology," vol. ii. pp. 392, 393.

are the instinctive activities of man? They appear to be for the most part certain performances, some of them rising little if at all above the level of reflex actions, which are the heritage of our animal nature. Sucking and taking the breast, hanging to one's fingers or to a stick, as Dr. Louis Robinson * has well shown, certain methods of progression on all fours, according to Mr. S. S. Buckman,† co-ordinated leg movements for walking, an early and probably instinctive differential response in arm and hand movements according as an object is within or beyond their reach, and a tendency to use the right hand where strong effort is required, as Prof. Mark Baldwin ‡ has shown (the latter, so far as we know, a distinctively human trait); these and the sexual instincts, together with the coarser emotions and their more or less definite expression, well nigh exhaust the list. And there is little in them to throw any light upon these problems of instinct which it is our business to discuss; little to help us in deciding between the rival claims of a purely Darwinian and an exclusively Lamarckian theory of origin.

The faculty of speech has been suggested as likely to afford evidence of a decisive sort; but as matters stand there is not much to be gained from it when it is cross-examined as a witness. Prof. Weismann indeed brought forward the absence of any instinctive result of the habit of speech as an argument against the transmission of acquired characters. "Not even are our children," he said, "able to talk of their own accord; yet not only have their parents, but more than that, an infinitely long

* *Nineteenth Century*, November, 1891.

† *Nature*, November 8, 1894, vol. li. p. 31. Cf. *Nineteenth Century*, for November, 1894.

‡ "Mental Development in the Child and the Race," pp. 54 and 64.

line of ancestors have never ceased to drill their brains
and to perfect their organs of speech. From this alone we
may be disposed to doubt whether acquired capabilities in
the true sense can ever be transmitted." Romanes,[*] in
reply to this, brought forward a general argument, drawn
from the complexity of language and the connection of
speech with man's intellectual powers, and the consequent
improbability that definite use of words should become
hereditary. He then asked whether "it is not the case
that the particular feature common to all languages—the
combination of vowel and consonant sounds which go to
constitute what we know as articulate syllables—as a
matter of fact *are* instinctive? Long before a young child
is able to understand the meanings of any words, it begins
to babble articulate syllables; and I do not know," he
adds, "that a more striking fact can be adduced at the
present stage of the Weismann controversy than is this
fact which he has thus himself unconsciously suggested,
namely, that the young of the only talking animal should
be alone in presenting the instinct of articulation." This
argument was met, in the discussion at the Newcastle
meeting of the British Association (1889), by the counter-
argument that since language has made man what he is,
articulation would be under the sway of natural selection.
Only those who possessed a congenital power of articulation could possibly be evolved into a race of speakers.
Romanes uses this as an illustration of what he terms
the elusiveness of Prof. Weismann's theory. First, the
absence of any instinctive result of the long use of speech
is adduced as evidence that acquired characters are not
transmitted; and then, when it is shown that the only
element in articulate speech which we could reasonably
expect to be transmitted *is* actually so transmitted, the

[*] "Darwin and after Darwin," vol. ii. pp. 335–336.

reply is that obviously this is a congenital character on which natural selection would take effect. But if the selectionists have thus changed their ground and taken up new lines of defence, this does not concern us here. The question is, whether their new line of defence is valid and tenable or not. It appears to me, that if natural selection took any share in the development of man from some lower form of life, the argument is valid. A power of articulation is a *sine quâ non* if a race of speakers is to be evolved; and unless natural selection be ruled out altogether, the congenital nature of this power, and some instinctive manifestation of it, is just what may be fairly expected on Darwinian grounds. On the other hand, if use-inheritance be operative, this again is, as Romanes says, just what may be expected on Lamarckian grounds. In fine, here, as in so many cases, we have nothing which can conclusively decide between the rival hypotheses. What we have is the sort of thing that may be due to one or other or both, if both be established as *veræ causæ*.

Dr. Arbuthnot Lane * has expressed his belief that certain occupations, such as shoe-making and coal-heaving, produce recognizable effects upon the skeleton and other parts, and that these effects are inherited, being more marked in the third generation than they were in the first. And Sir Wm. Turner informed Prof. Herdman that in his opinion, the peculiar habits of a tribe, such as tree-climbing among the Australians and the inhabitants of the interior of New Guinea, not only affect each generation individually, but have an intensified action through the influence of heredity. The inference may be drawn that with acquired structure acquired habits would be transmitted. But of this there is, so far as I know, but little

* " Journal of Anatomy and Physiology," vol. xxii. p. 215.

direct evidence; and the structural question * does not call for discussion here.

It would seem, then, that of acquired habit passing into congenital instinct of demonstrable definiteness, there is but little, if any, reliable evidence of a crucial kind. We must therefore turn to the other aspect of heredity —that which has reference to innate power or faculty— and must ask whether there is any such marked increase of inborn capacity as may reasonably be attributed to direct transmission of acquired increments of faculty.

It must here be remembered that innate capacity affords to the individual what is at first a relatively unspecialized power of dealing with the particular conditions of individual life as they are presented to experience. The amount and quality of this innate capacity unquestionably varies in different individuals. Its specialization and the particular mode of its application are determined by the conditions of individual development, and the environment to which there is need of adaptation. This serves to distinguish innate capacity, the definite application of which is acquired in the course of individual life, from the congenitally determined adaptiveness of instinctive behaviour. The distinction was illustrated in our introductory chapter by an analogy drawn from the familiar facts of the inheritance of wealth. That which is instinctive was likened to the inheritance of specific drafts for particular and relatively definite purposes in the conduct of life, over the initial application of which the individual is given no control; innate capacity to the inheritance of a legacy which may be drawn upon for any purpose as need arises.

* Dr. Gustav Retzius has shown ("Biologishe Untersuchungen," neue Folge, vii. 1895) that the modifications of structure due to civilized habit (*e.g.* the use of chairs) are not inherited, the fœtus retaining the ancestral condition. His arguments for transmission of habit appear to take little account of the effects of tradition.

If the need become habitual, the animal may, so to speak, instruct his banker to set aside a specific sum to meet this need as often as it arises. But this arrangement is a purely individual matter, and no wise dictated by the terms of the bequest. The human infant inherits a certain number of specific drafts; but the bulk of his inheritance is an invaluable legacy of innate capacity, the specific application of which is in his own hands, under the conditions of his social environment, and under the guidance of his parents and guardians. What we must consider, then, is whether there is any such marked increase of innate capacity as may fairly be ascribed to the direct transmission of acquired increments of faculty, and whether the innate susceptibilities are specialized through the effects of such transmission. The adequate discussion of these questions would require a separate treatise; all that can here be attempted is an outline of what would seem to be the more salient features in a field of inquiry which the multiplicity of details renders extremely complicated.

In considering these questions, we must take up the thread of the discussion which occupied most of the chapter on the Relation of Organic to Mental Evolution. The conclusions there reached were, it will be remembered, as follows. Mental evolution, as such, is dependent upon individual choice; throughout animal life it is subservient to organic needs, and is conditioned and controlled by natural selection; continuity of mental development in the race is rendered possible by organic heredity; and progress in mental development is predominantly due to the combined effects of heredity and natural selection acting upon organisms possessed of mental powers.

We must be particular to note the *subservient position which mental evolution holds in the life of animals.* What then is its position in the life of civilized man ? Let us put the case in sharp antithesis to the conclusions of the preceding paragraph. While mental evolution as such is still dependent upon individual choice, it is no longer wholly subservient to organic needs ; nor is it, save to a limited extent, conditioned and controlled by natural selection. Mind to some extent escapes from its organic thraldom, and is free to develop, still in accordance with the natural laws of its own proper being, but in relation to a new environment. And though continuity of mental development in the race is still rendered possible by organic heredity, mental progress is mainly due, not to inherited increments of mental faculty, but to the handing on of the results of human achievement by a vast extension of that which we have seen to be a factor in animal life, namely tradition.

We must first endeavour to make good the position that mental evolution in civilized man is no longer wholly subservient to organic needs, and that it is no longer, save to a limited extent, conditioned and controlled by natural selection. The first point is so obvious and so generally recognized as to stand in no need of detailed demonstration. Among civilized races, at any rate, mental evolution has far outstripped what is required to maintain bare organic existence. Among lower races and savage tribes this is not so markedly the case, and among them natural selection is still no doubt a factor, though perhaps even with them a diminishing factor, in progress. But it would seem that, when we have to deal with civilized mankind, natural selection is no longer a factor of predominant importance. The microbe is indeed still at work eliminating the weakly, notwithstanding all that medical skill can do; the drunkard and the sensualist are still working out their own physical damnation, the unchecked result of which would be the elimination of drunkenness and sensuality * ; society is at war with the criminal, and doing its best, so far as the sometimes short-sighted leniency of public opinion will permit, to eliminate him. But, when all is said and done, natural selection plays but a subordinate part in the life of civilized mankind. The method of conscious choice has in large degree superseded that of natural selection.

Now we must use the phrase "natural selection" in its biological acceptation, and not, as is so often done in discussions on social evolution, in a vague general and half metaphorical sense, through neglecting the difference between natural selection through the elimination of failures, and choice through the play of intelligence.† By

* I leave this passage as it stood in the MS. of my Lowell Lectures. Dr. G. A. Reid has since published a work on "The Present Evolution of Man," in which the point is worked out with great care and skill. He contends that drunkenness and the excessive opium habit tends to disappear in communities wherein the free use of these drugs has led to the elimination of those who abused them to a fatally deleterious extent.

† As before noted, Mr. S. Alexander, in his interesting contributions in the domain of ethics, fails to distinguish between natural selection and conscious choice. "The war of natural selection," he says, "is carried on in human affairs not against weaker or incompatible individuals, but against their ideals or modes of life. It does not suffer any mode of life to prevail or persist but one which is compatible with social welfare." "Persuasion and education, in fact, *without destruction*, replace here the process of propagation of its own species and destruction of the rival ones, by which in the natural world species become numerically strong and persistent." And again, "Persuasion corresponds to the extermination of the rivals." But, as Mr. Alexander himself indicates, persuasion is the condition, not to natural selection through elimination, but to conscious choice. We endeavour by persuasion to induce others to choose the ideals which have been the objects of our own choice. This is *not* natural selection; and the loose application of this term to the process can result only in a confusion of ideas. (See "Moral Order and Progress," and an article on "Natural Selection in Morals" in the *International Journal of Ethics*, vol. ii. (1882), pp. 409, 439.) It is instructive to compare Professor Huxley's treatment of ethical and social problems with that of Mr. Alexander. No one can read the ninth volume of Huxley's "Collected Essays,"—that on "Evolution and Ethics"—without seeing that he clearly perceived the distinction between the method of natural selection and that of conscious choice which supersedes it in

natural selection was meant by Darwin, and should be meant by us, a process whereby in the struggle for existence certain individuals are either killed, or, what is really the essential point, prevented from begetting offspring. Such a process, I take it, plays but a small and insignificant part in social progress, among ourselves, for example. No doubt there is an apparently large body of unskilled workers who are ousted in the keen competition of the labour market. But are they in any appreciable degree eliminated either by death or by exclusion from all share in the procreation of their race ? They may be excluded from the labour market, and thus leave others more fitted than themselves to survive as efficient workers. In that sense, no doubt natural selection is operative in all ranks of human society. But, from the biological point of view, the *rôle* of natural selection may be condensed, with almost brutal plainness, into a few words: *To breed or not to breed; that is the question.* In this sense, and this sense only, is natural selection efficient in race-progress. And it is in this sense that the term is used when I express the conviction that in race-progress among civilized nations natural selection holds an altogether subordinate position. If those who endeavour to apply biological conceptions to social phenomena would only remember that the essence of natural selection is the exclusion of the weakly, the inefficient, and the anywise unfit, from transmitting their

social evolution. The criticisms called forth by his Romanes Lecture and the reiterated assertions that he had abandoned the naturalistic interpretation of ethical phenomena, together with the defence of his position in the prolegomena prefixed to this ninth volume, all serve to indicate how essential it is that the method of conscious choice should be clearly distinguished from that of natural selection. What we strive to effect in the social evolution which embodies the results of human choice, is often very different from that which natural selection alone would produce. Our ideals are the products of a mental evolution which has escaped from the bondage of natural selection.

inefficiency, and the consequent hereditary increment of efficiency in those who remain to contribute as parents to the continuation of the race, much confusion of thought would be avoided. In this sense I contend that natural selection is not an important factor in human progress among the civilized races of to-day.

What does take place is a good deal of selective arrangement of the individuals constantly coming to maturity. But, as I have elsewhere contended,* it is obvious that such selection, without the removal or exclusion of the non-selected, does nothing to alter the general level of faculty, in the race of Englishmen for example. Nay, more, if the elimination of the unintellectual may be excluded, and if they steadily increase by natural generation more rapidly than the intellectual, the general level of faculty must, on purely natural selection principles, be steadily *falling*. Be this as it may, such selection, *without elimination*, as occurs is merely a classification of the individuals in order of merit. It arranges the individuals in classes, but does nothing more. Let me exemplify by an analogous case. Fifty boys who have been admitted to a public school, await examination in a class-room. They are at present unclassified, but there is a mean of ability among the whole fifty. A week afterwards they are distributed in different forms. Some are chosen for a higher form, others have to take lower places. But though selection has classified the material, it has not altered the mean of ability among the fifty boys. This can only be done by rejecting a certain number altogether, or excluding them from the school. Then the mean ability *of those that remain* will of course be raised. Selection, without elimination, involves no racial progress.

* "Animal Life and Intelligence," p. 499, from which some of the material of this paragraph has been extracted.

Emigration may perhaps be adduced as affording
evidence of the operation of natural selection among mankind. But though it must, beyond question, affect the distribution of human individuals, it is not clear in what
manner it gives opportunity for that elimination which is
essential to natural selection. The effects of emigration
are indeed worthy of a fuller and more careful discussion than they have yet received. From the older
centres of European civilization, there has proceeded for
some centuries a stream of emigrants to distant countries.
What have been the effects on the old centres and on the
new? They have no doubt varied as the facilities of tran-
sport increased. There have proceeded to the new centres
a few of our best and some of our worst. In earlier times
the more adventurous and energetic left our shores; now
perhaps there is a preponderance of our failures, or more
accurately, of those who do not find suitable opportunities
in our social system. Since the rate of propagation, in
at any rate some of the new centres, has been more
rapid than that in the old centres, the mean level in all
the centres, taken collectively, has been proportionally
altered. The subject is too large a one to be discussed
incidentally. But it would seem that the alteration is due
rather to changes of distribution than to natural selection
properly so called.

Does sexual selection, by preferential mating, have a
far-reaching influence? There can be no doubt that, whatever be the case among animals, there is preferential
mating among mankind. In marriage, at its best and
highest, the man selects his ideal woman, her in whom
beauty and grace, physical, moral, and intellectual, are
embodied; and the woman selects her ideal man, conspicuous among all others for strength in mind and body,
character and conduct. Herein lies the value, from the

evolution point of view, of our marriage system. The more enduring the marriage bond, the more careful will the contracting parties be to select wisely and well, looking not merely to immediate satisfaction of natural impulse, but to life-long association. But granting all this, we must remember that marriage, as a practical fact, is not always contracted on these grounds. There are many disturbing causes which mar the good effects of the system. Moreover, from the point of view of the community as a whole, the question is: Who are excluded, by such selection, from participating in the duties of parenthood? One has met so many charming and intellectual old maids and confirmed bachelors, and though for obvious reasons it must not be breathed aloud that one has met, still one has at any rate heard of so many fathers and mothers who are neither charming nor intellectual, that one questions whether the average ability of married folk is much in excess of that of those who die unmated. If so, sexual selection does not have any marked effect on the mean level of faculty in our community; and this factor, like that of emigration, may be left on one side.

If then in the relative absence of natural selection the mean efficiency of civilized man is not, from this cause, undergoing progressive development, wherein lie the possibilities of race progress? The first and most obvious answer is: By the hereditary transmission of acquired increments of faculty. There are some who have contended that if there be no inheritance of acquired characters, the past history of our race is inexplicable, and for the future there can be no hope. But when they are pressed for definite and conclusive evidence of such transmission it is not forthcoming in any measure proportional to the confidence of their assertions. Nay, more; the question may be raised whether the supposed

increment of human faculty in successive generations is
an established fact. As we shall presently see, there
are careful thinkers who are not prepared to admit it as a
fact at all. But if these be right in denying the fact, the
consideration of the Lamarckian answer is unnecessary,
and we must seek another solution of the problem.
This is that evolution *has been transferred from the
organism to his environment.* There must be increment
somewhere, otherwise evolution is impossible. In social
evolution on this view, the increment is by storage in
the social environment to which each new generation
adapts itself, with no increased native power of adaptation. In the written record, in social traditions, in the
manifold inventions which make scientific and industrial
progress possible, in the products of art, and the recorded
examples of noble lives, we have an environment which
is at the same time the product of mental evolution,
and affords the condition of the development of each
individual mind to-day. No one is likely to question
the fact that this environment is undergoing steady and
progressive evolution. It is not perhaps so obvious that
this transference of evolution from the individual to the
environment may leave the *faculty* of the race at a
standstill, while the *achievements* of the race are pro·
gressing by leaps and bounds. This is no new doctrine.
Buckle, in his "History of Civilization," wrote as follows : *
" Whatever, therefore, the moral and intellectual progress
of men may be, it resolves itself not into the progress of
natural capacity, but into a progress, if I may say so, of
opportunity; that is, an improvement in the circumstances
under which that capacity after birth comes into play.
Here then is the gist of the whole matter. The progress

---

* " History of Civilization," vol. i. (1858), p. 178. Quoted in Dr. Reid's
" Present Evolution of Man," p. 179.

is one not of internal power, but of external advantage. The child born in a civilized land is not likely as such to be superior to one born among barbarians; and the difference which ensues between the acts of the two children will be caused, so far as we know, solely by the pressure of external circumstances; by which I mean the surrounding opinions, knowledge, associations, in a word, the entire mental atmosphere in which the two children are respectively nurtured." No doubt the case is here overstated. It would probably be more correct to say that the differences in natural capacity between the civilized and barbarian infant are due to natural selection; the rest being due to "the mental atmosphere." And since, on our view, natural selection is a constantly diminishing factor in the evolution of civilized man, it follows that the innate differences are of constantly diminishing value.

Huxley,[*] writing in 1863, says of man that "he alone possesses the marvellous endowment of intelligible and rational speech, whereby, in the secular period of his existence, he has slowly accumulated and organized the experience which is almost wholly lost with the cessation of every individual life in other animals." Further quotations to a like effect might easily be collected. Prof. Weismann [†] himself clearly saw the bearing of these facts on the Lamarckian controversy, and in one of his most luminous essays clearly indicates how man, "availing himself of tradition is able to seize upon the acquirements of his ancestors at the point where they left them." The matter was at about the same time very ably dealt with by Prof. Ritchie in his "Darwinism and Politics,"

[*] "Man's Place in Nature." See "Collected Essays," vol. vii. pp. 155, 156.
[†] "Thoughts upon the Musical Sense in Animals and Man" (1889), Essays, vol. ii. pp. 50, 51.

where he contends that language renders possible the handing on of experience irrespective of transmission by heredity. " Might we not," he asks,* " define civilization in general as the sum of the contrivances which enable human beings to advance independently of heredity ? "

According to this conception of human progress, then, organic heredity keeps up a mean level—possibly even permits only a diminishing average—of mental capacity, with which succeeding generations have to deal with an ever-evolving environment of mental products. And this mean level, or even diminishing average, of mental capacity, together with the wide variation around the mean, is due to the comparative absence of natural selection.

It is clear that, in this handing on of experience irrespective of transmission by heredity, there is an enormous extension of that tradition which we have already seen to be a factor, though only a subordinate one, in the life of animals. But the question for special consideration now is whether, in view of these facts, there is any increment of human faculty in civilized races on which to base an argument for hereditary transmission. Writing in 1890,† I expressed myself somewhat guardedly on the subject. With regard to the diffusion of knowledge, I suggested that this, though it brings more grist to the intellectual mill, may have no effect in raising the mean

* "Darwinism and Politics," 3rd edition, p. 101. In the same essay, is an able criticism of Mr. Wallace's contention that the large brains of savages are inexplicable on the theory of natural selection. The large brain was required to deal with a complex environment; the somewhat larger brains of civilized folk with an environment of a different order of complexity; and it is this environment, rather than brain-power, which is now undergoing development in civilized society. Mr. Ritchie unfortunately does not avoid the error of identifying to some extent the effects of conscious choice with those of natural selection. See p. 106.

† "Animal Life and Intelligence," pp. 500, 501.

standard of excellence in the mill itself. There is more
to grind; but this does not necessarily improve the grind-
ing apparatus. If, however, it does improve the mill, this
tells so far in favour of the Lamarckian and against the
neo-Darwinian hypothesis. Or to vary the analogy, the
diffusion and storage of knowledge while it increases the
stock of available food, does not necessarily bring with
it any additional power of digesting the food. But if
it does improve the faculty of assimilation, this may be
through inherited increments of digestive power. It may,
however, be contended that there is no conclusive proof
that the mean intellectual level of Englishmen to-day is
any higher than in the days of the Tudors. If so, of course
the argument for transmission falls to the ground. Having
no desire to dogmatize on the subject, I merely set down
the reasons which led me to entertain a general belief
that the intellectual progress of Englishmen during, say,
the past three hundred years has been in part due to the
inheritance of individually acquired faculty.

I must confess that this general belief has since then
been weakened rather than strengthened. Those who are
far better fitted to form an opinion in this matter seem to
regard the supposed raising of the mean standard of faculty
as, to say the least of it, exceedingly doubtful. Mr. Kidd,
in his "Social Evolution," has collected some of the evidence
and quotes this statement of Mr. Gladstone's in an inter-
view with Mr. Stead * : "I sometimes say, that I do not
see that progress in the development of the brain-power
which we ought to expect. . . . Development, no doubt, is
a slow process, but I do not see it at all. I do not think
we are stronger but weaker than men of the Middle Ages.
I would take it as low down as the men of the sixteenth
century. The men of the sixteenth century were strong

* *Review of Reviews*, April, 1892. Quoted in "Social Evolution," p. 256

men, stronger in brain power than our men." Mr. Kidd himself writes as follows * : "Not only is it probable that the average intellectual development of the races which are winning in the struggle for existence to-day is below that of some of the peoples which have long ago disappeared from the rivalry of life, but there seems every reason to suppose that the average intellectual development of successive generations amongst ourselves does not show any tendency to rise above that of the generations immediately preceding them." And he quotes with evident approval this passage from an article of Mr. Bellamy's † : "All that man produces to-day more than did his cave-dwelling ancestors, he produces by virtue of the accumulated achievements, inventions, and improvements of the intervening generations, together with the social and industrial machinery which is their legacy." Mr. Kidd's conclusion is that social evolution is not primarily intellectual. But surely the main inference to be drawn from all this, supposing it to be true, is, not that social evolution is not primarily intellectual, but rather that intellectual evolution, whether of primary or secondary value, is no longer by increment of human faculty, but by summation and storage in the environment it creates.

So far as intellectual evolution is concerned, Mr. Kidd's contention is that natural selection affects it, if at all, only in a secondary and subsidiary way. In this we may agree with him. But no further. For he contends that natural selection does affect man as a moral agent. "Natural selection seems," he says,‡ "to be

* "Social Evolution," p. 255.
† *Contemporary Review*, January, 1890. Quoted in "Social Evolution," p. 267.
‡ "Social Evolution," p. 286.

steadily evolving in the race that type of character upon which these [altruistic] forces act most readily and efficiently; that is to say, it is evolving religious character in the first instance, and intellectual character only as a secondary product in association with it. The race would, in fact, appear to be growing more and more religious, the winning sections being those in which, *cæteris paribus*, this type of character is most fully developed." I cannot agree with this, for it is difficult to see in what way elimination is at work so as to produce any such result. All the arguments Mr. Kidd uses to show that the average intellectual development of successive generations amongst ourselves does not show any tendency to rise above that of the generations immediately preceding them, apply also with equal force to the average moral and religious development. The power of conscience and what we may term, somewhat loosely perhaps, the religious impulse, do not, I imagine, stand at a higher average level to-day than at the time of the Reformation. But I do believe, and trust, that the moral and religious environment has undergone evolution, and that the individual conscience and religious impulse have to-day freer play than under the narrower and more cramping conditions of the past.

It would seem, in fine, that if mental evolution in man be manifested rather in the progressive advance of human achievement than in progressive increment of human faculty; if the developmental process have been transferred from the individuals to their environment; if it be rather the intellectual and moral edifice that is undergoing evolution, than the human builders that contribute in each generation a few more stones to take a permanent place in its fabric; if there be thus no conclusive evidence that faculty is improving, but rather the opposite; if all this be so, then it would seem that the ground is cut away from under the feet of those who regard mental evolution in man as due to inherited increments of individually acquired faculty. Nay, more; if the average level be not rising, some explanation must be demanded from transmissionists of this fact. For surely if there be transmission of individually acquired increment, the average level of faculty ought to be steadily rising.

The conclusions reached, then, in this chapter are somewhat as follows. There is little or no evidence of individually acquired habits in man becoming instinctive through heredity. Natural selection becomes more and more subordinate in the social evolution of civilized mankind; and it would seem probable that with this waning of the influence of natural selection there has been a diminution also of human faculty. Hence there is little or no evidence of the hereditary transmission of increments of faculty due to continued and persistent use. A discussion of heredity in man thus confirms the inference drawn from the study of habit and instinct in some of the lower animals.

INDEX.

LONDON: PRINTED BY WILLIAM CLOWES AND SONS, LIMITED,
STAMFORD STREET AND CHARING CROSS.

Printed in the United States
101566LV00005B/67/A